DECENTRALIZATION, FORESTS AND RURAL COMMUNITIES

Decentralization, Forests and Rural Communities
Policy Outcomes in South and Southeast Asia

Editors

EDWARD L. WEBB
GANESH P. SHIVAKOTI

⑤SAGE Los Angeles • London • New Delhi • Singapore
www.sagepublications.com

First published in 2008 by

 SAGE Publications India Pvt Ltd
B1/I-1 Mohan Cooperative Industrial Area
Mathura Road, New Delhi 110 044, India
www.sagepub.in

SAGE Publications Inc
2455 Teller Road
Thousand Oaks, California 91320, USA

SAGE Publications Ltd
1 Oliver's Yard, 55 City Road
London EC1Y 1SP, United Kingdom

SAGE Publications Asia-Pacific Pte Ltd
33 Pekin Street
#02-01 Far East Square
Singapore 048763

Published by Vivek Mehra for SAGE Publications India Pvt Ltd, typeset in 10/12 pt Sanskrit-Palatino by Star Compugraphics Private Limited, Delhi and printed at Chaman Enterprises, New Delhi.

Library of Congress Cataloging-in-Publication Data

Decentralization, forests and rural communities policy outcomes in South and Southeast Asia / editors Edward L. Webb and Ganesh P. Shivakoti.
   p. cm.
   Includes bibliographical references and Index.
1. Forest policy—Asia—Case studies. 2. Forest management—Asia—Case studies. 3. Decentralization in management—Asia—Case studies. I. Webb, Edward L., 1967– II. Shivakoti, Ganesh.

SD641.D43   333.750954—dc22   2007   2006033870

ISBN: 978-0-7619-3548-3 (HB)   978-81-7829-707-1 (India-HB)

The SAGE Team: Sugata Ghosh, Maneet Singh and Rajib Chatterjee

Dedicated to our parents

Beatrice L. Webb and the late Clifton R. Webb, Jr.,
for providing opportunity and unconditional support.

The late Mrs. Januka Shivakoti and the late Mr. Nanda Shivakoti,
who valued education and rural environment the most.

CONTENTS

LIST OF TABLES

LIST OF FIGURES

LIST OF MAPS

FOREWORD

'Centralize!' 'Decentralize!' 'No, centralize. We need more control!',
'We must decentralize! Centralizing is not working.' Organizations
and agencies around the world have gone through reversing this
pendulum swing time and again, in an effort to improve management or to make their programs more effective and efficient. But
they find it difficult to truly know which aspects to control at which
level. So when they arrive at one or the other pole, problems and
unintended consequences become evident and they swing back.

The same is true for the way governments and agencies handle
forest and tree resources. Many countries in the past, and even
today, have nationalized ownership and management of forestland
or even of specific tree species. They often do this with the expectation that they will have more control, increased revenue and in
some cases longer term sustainability. But there is a multitude of
examples of centralizing not reaching these goals and the resource
finally becoming so degraded that it is no longer of much interest
to the central authority.

After centralization of forest management largely fails, some
at the center see decentralization as an inexpensive way to rehabilitate degraded forests, to shift blame when forests are not well
managed, or to rid the center of the burden of providing income
to local governments. Often local people experience 'partial' or
'incomplete' decentralization, when they are given responsibility,
while authority or benefits remain in the hands of agencies, local
officials or local elites. Forest-dependent people then, may find
themselves in the same poverty level as when forest management
became centralized. At that time they lost access to a resource upon
which their livelihoods depended.

As this book suggests, many Asian and other countries are now
swinging toward decentralization of forest management as a tool
to reach current national and international goals. Many people
have come to believe decentralization, done effectively, could empower local people and form a step towards democracy and transparency, as well as improve local livelihoods. In relation to forestry,
legitimate questions arise: 'How can we turn forest management

over to local people in a way to encourage sustainable use?' 'How can we judge the effect of markets for forest products on a sustainable basis and for benefits going to the poor?' 'What role should central authority play?'

If a policy or activity is changed, without the right baseline information there is no way to predict or monitor both intended and unintended consequences. Many policy makers have been demanding better tools to use in planning, monitoring and evaluating forestry activities. They have requested tools that describe the biophysical resource and the social and economic impact on the local people and that clarify information on local institutions.

Unfortunately, although there has sometimes been data on the condition of forest resources and sometimes even socio-economic or household studies, the research is usually *ad hoc*, incomplete and lacks integration. Forest and human interaction is complex and only carefully crafted research protocols can allow study of change, comparisons over time and space, and begin to illuminate outcomes. Without such integration, comparable data and analysis, there can be no understanding of the larger issues or the beginning of general concepts that offer predictions. Policy makers faced with degrading forests have often been left with inadequate advice and with the temptation to fall back on the 'knee jerk' reaction of blaming local people and making rules to keep them out—centralizing even though they may know that this seldom solves the problem.

This exciting book is the first major collection of its kind from the Asian region. It illustrates how much clarity the approach these researchers took can offer to understanding complex and important questions. The Institutional Analysis and Development Framework (IAD) gave authors an approach to analyzing their case studies. The research protocols from International Forestry Resources and Institutions (IFRI) were designed specifically to address the above mentioned issues. IFRI, described more comprehensively in several chapters of the book, was developed with serious input from an experienced multidisciplinary team and fine-tuned through field trials, all under the careful and expert guidance of Dr Elinor Ostrom. An international network of research centers and researchers is now adding to a global data bank, not only from Asia but also from Africa, Latin America and elsewhere. It is hoped that soon there will be enough information and analysis that the data these methods and protocols provide will reach a tipping point. Fewer evaluations will then identify the problem of failed or disappointing forestry activities on lack of adequate and timely information. Thereafter, policies will be tailored to reach positive outcomes in support of local, national and international goals.

I, for one, wish to congratulate the editors and authors of this important, informative and useful book and the step it has taken to add to our understanding of policy outcomes in South and Southeast Asia, related to decentralization, forests and rural communities.

Marilyn W. Hoskins

PREFACE

It is a great joy to read this volume. Though it is composed of eight case studies on what is and what has happened in six Asian countries regarding community-based ecosystem management activities, its reach is both larger and more important than its authors might imagine. The studies reported here run hidden under the international media hype so excited by the glitz about the rising Asian tiger economies. You do not read on the pages of *The New York Times* or *The Economist* or *The Guardian* much about the explorations in self-government, entrepreneurship and controlled development being done in thousands of forest communities and villages throughout South and Southeast Asia. Yet, it is these very places that often survive and even thrive when the center implodes. It is self-governance but without the guns and violence when imposed by outsiders. Rather, it is tentative trials of hope and failures and success—all driven by the patience of learning processes tied to natural resources and with a revival of a heritage going back many generations.

Further, it represents the Asian thrust of a worldwide trend, indeed, a most revolutionary trend whether in the north of Scotland or small towns along the British Columbia coast, or in the inner city of Baltimore, USA, or among native peoples in Panama or in small villages near Chainpur in Western Nepal. A paper in Arborvitae (White *et al.*, 2004) reports that 'community-owned forests now account for 22 percent of all forest lands ... the forest area owned by communities doubled between 1985 and 2000 and looks set to double again by 2015 ... [communities invest] more than either their own governments or external donors, making them the largest investors in forests.' Though the IUCN (International Union for Conservation of Nature and Natural Resources) report is just considering developing regions, Mark Poffenberger's survey of community-based management systems demonstrates that such 'decentralization' is global from rural to urban, from rich to poor, from high mountains to low land arid zones. And many of the lessons learned have been tried, tested and demonstrated in rural areas of Asia.

All of these chapters go quietly about their scientific business. No whistles. No bells. No shouting in the streets. Yet, each chapter reflects the care and attention to reliability and validity of data along with the care and consideration of local people long taught and demonstrated by Elinor Ostrom. Indeed, this entire book could be considered a celebration and confirmation of the wisdom she has shared with her students, colleagues and interested outsiders at the Indiana University workshop in Political Theory and Policy Analysis.

For Professor Ostrom and her colleagues it is careful social science in application to deep concerns about people and their environments. Here, in each chapter, we are given some part of the exploration and the answers to the question, 'what have been the outcomes of these recent forestry decentralization solutions, both practically and theoretically, to the forest-accessing communities upon which these policies have been imposed?' Another way to put it might be what works, what does not, and how come in the realm of downloading responsibility for natural resource systems to participatory community institutions. Forestry is as much about community governance institutions as it is about the physics and chemistry and soils of forest ecosystems. Dr Ostrom has made this revolutionary change in the social silvics of our time. Both our social science and our practice of forestry are the better for such a new vision. The evidence is clear in these 11 chapters. Welcome to the new future, dear reader.

William R. Burch, Jnr
Hixon Professor of Natural Resource Management
Yale School of Forestry and Environmental Studies
USA

Reference

White, Andy, Khare, Arvin, and Molnar, Augusta. (2004). 'Who Owns, Who Conserves and Why it Matters'. *Arborvitae*, September, 8–12.

ACKNOWLEDGMENTS

In May 2002, the biennual meeting of the International Forestry Resources and Institutions (IFRI) global research group was held in Nairobi, Kenya. It was our first meeting since 2000, the year of the release of *People and Forests: Communities, Institutions, and Governance* (The MIT Press), the first research-based volume by the IFRI group since its establishment in the 1990s. At the time of the 2002 Kenya meeting, the Asian IFRI collaborating research centers were in the midst of several studies scattered across Bhutan, India, Nepal and Thailand. During the meeting we discussed the possibility of preparing an edited volume that focused on the decentralization policy changes occurring in South and Southeast Asia and the potential impact on rural, forest-accessing communities. A brief side meeting among the potential authors confirmed our desire to publish such a volume. Over the next three years we compiled the case studies, adding new ones from Indonesia and Vietnam only in late 2005 as data became available.

Since 1999, the editors have received support from a variety of sources. First and foremost was the Workshop in Political Theory and Policy Analysis, co-directed by Professor Elinor Ostrom at Indiana University. The financial and professional support that we have received from the Workshop since 1999 has been enormous and allowed us to initiate IFRI-based research, contribute to the global network, and ultimately to put together this volume. The John D. and Catherine T. MacArthur Foundation provided funding to the Workshop, which subsequently partially or fully funded much of the research in this volume. The MacArthur Foundation's Program in Conservation and Sustainable Development also has directly supported AIT's research in central Vietnam since 2003. The Jakarta office of the Ford Foundation supported the collaboration and research between Andalas University, West Sumatra and AIT since 2003.

The Asian Institute of Technology provided generous professional support to the authors. The administration, particularly Professor Mario Tabucanon (Provost) and Professor Chongrak Polprasert (Dean), remained flexible and supportive of the authors during times of field work, crisis and writing.

1 | FOREST POLICY AS A CHANGING CONTEXT IN ASIA

EDWARD L. WEBB

South and Southeast Asia are undergoing a remarkable period of transition. Over the last several decades, the region has received enormous inputs in the form of foreign investment as well as development aid across a wide array of societal sectors. The region is growing rapidly in many respects and as a result it is expected to 'return to the center of the world economy' (Radelet and Sachs, 1997).

Investments geared towards economic development have made significant strides over the last few decades. In the countries of India, Indonesia, Nepal, Thailand and Vietnam, for example, the per capita GDP increased during the period 1990–2003, while the percentage of the population considered 'undernourished' declined (data from United Nations Economic and Social Commission for Asia and the Pacific and United Nations Statistics Division for the Millennium Development Goals). Vietnam appears to have been particularly successful in both of these developments. A substantial amount of information is available, which, taken together, points towards rapid development, increased wealth and improvements in people's lives throughout Asia.

Given the statistics showing increased incomes and reductions in poverty indicators throughout South and Southeast Asia, it is tempting to deduce that soon these Asian societies will lower their dependence on natural resources such as forests. However, the majority of capital accumulation occurs in urban areas (United Nations, 2001), which is why rural people will enjoy significantly less economic improvement than the urban populations. Moreover, the rural populations of most countries in Asia are not expected to decrease through 2030, although the percentage of total inhabitants living in rural areas may decline (Table 1.1). As a result, for the

TABLE 1.1
Population Statistics for Six South and Southeast Asian Countries

(Numbers in Thousands)

	Total Population			Rural (%)			Total Rural Population		
	1970	2005	2030	1970	2005	2030	1970	2005	2030
Bhutan*	1,048	2,163	3,460	97	91	80	1,016	1,966	2,765
India	554,911	1,103,371	1,449,078	80	71	59	445,039	786,704	849,160
Indonesia	119,936	222,781	270,844	83	52	32	99,427	116,069	87,483
Nepal	12,155	27,133	41,424	96	84	71	11,681	22,846	29,245
Thailand	36,257	64,233	73,827	79	68	53	28,679	43,357	39,128
Vietnam	42,898	84,238	108,128	82	73	57	35,048	61,746	61,417
Total	**767,205**	**1,503,919**	**1,946,761**	**81**	**69**	**55**	**620,889**	**1,032,688**	**1,069,197**

Source: Data and population models from United Nations Population Division (2005).

Note: *The UN population statistic for Bhutan does not tally with the official statistics of the Bhutanese government. Nevertheless, these values are used only to demonstrate the relative changes in total and rural population numbers.

foreseeable future, the needs of rural societies for natural resources—particularly forest products—is expected to remain high and in India it will almost assuredly increase dramatically. It is, therefore, not justifiable to expect that simply because Asian societies are 'developing' or becoming wealthier, pressures on forests should decrease.

Rural societies are, and will remain, closely linked with the natural resource base, particularly forests. For example, the total consumption of fuelwood throughout Asia is expected to continue to increase (Lefevre *et al.*, 1997). Although investments in private and plantation fuelwood are increasing, a substantial proportion of total fuelwood comes from natural forests (ibid.). Other natural resources as well are extracted from forests by rural communities. Non-timber forest products, wildlife, timber and the vegetation itself that is cut and burned for temporary swidden agriculture are all forest-based products and contribute significantly to the livelihoods of rural societies throughout Asia. Even if one takes a conservative estimate that only 25 percent of the rural population is actually dependent directly on forests, it is still more than 250 million people requiring access to and rights for forest use and management. The precise number of people directly dependent on forest resources is actually not a relevant number; the reality is that a vast number of people rely on forests and require them for their livelihoods, either directly or indirectly.

Whereas the forest is seen as a fundamental component of life for millions of rural inhabitants, governments have generally viewed forests as sources of income. The timber industry has been a strong contributor to the national coffers and has supported the direct development of urban areas of most South and Southeast Asian nations. The trend continues to this day. Conflicts have arisen and continue between local people and the state over the rights to manage and utilize forest resources. The rights of local people over forests are often claimed for customary and historical reasons, whereas the rights of national governments are claimed through policies and imposed upon society at large. These policies have been in the form of centralization: the passing of legislation whereby the central government claims the ultimate rights over forests and the land on which forest resides. Indeed, within the last century all countries in South and Southeast Asia have centralized authority over forest resources.

In recent decades, however, the tradition of centralized bureaucracies that control community-accessed forest resources seems to have been broken and we may be entering a new era of decentralized governance over forests. Governments, for reasons that are discussed at length in Chapter 2 of this book, have been shifting the power and authority to make decisions about how forests are managed to lower levels of government and in some cases to local people themselves. This turnaround in policy appeals to those who believe that people should have control over their own affairs.

But decentralization also brings up new concerns. Can governments simply decentralize authority over forests away from the center, or are there certain elements necessary to achieve the sustainable management and conservation of forests in a decentralized world? What have been the responses of local governments and local communities to forest policy decentralization? Indeed, the contextual situations including people, ecosystems and governments are diverse throughout Asia, and therefore the incentive structures to participate in the decentralized forest management process are equally diverse.

This book is about the impact of decentralization of authority over forests to rural communities and lower echelons of governance. A case study approach is adopted to investigate how decentralization is affecting local stakeholders and their management of forest resources. Through this approach, we arrive at the conclusion that the diversity of contextual situations requires a similarly diverse set of institutional solutions. Those solutions must be crafted at the local level. In other words, *flexible* decentralization appears to provide the greatest opportunity for sustainable management of forests by local communities and local governments.

The case studies included in this volume are drawn from Bhutan, India, Indonesia, Nepal, Thailand and Vietnam. These countries were not chosen randomly. Their selection was guided by the opportunities and limitations of the Editors and their collaborative network. The Asian research centers of the International Forestry Resources and Institutions (IFRI) research network (described at http://www.indiana.edu/~ifri) was first established in Nepal, and subsequently in India and Thailand. Hence, these countries are naturally included in our case studies. The greater number of chapters on Nepal does not mean that greater value or emphasis is placed on Nepal. Rather, it is a function of the fact that the IFRI collaborative research group began in Nepal and therefore our research group has a larger sub-network in that country. The Bhutan, Indonesia, Nepal (Chapter 6), Thailand and Vietnam case studies represent collaborations with doctoral students from these countries at the Asian Institute of Technology who chose to use the IFRI protocol for their research. Indeed, it would be fascinating to increase the scope of our research to other countries throughout the Asian region, but funding limitations always exist.

Before describing the conceptual framework and organization of the book, let us first take a look at the processes of centralization and decentralization in the countries discussed in this volume. This will provide an appropriate and necessary perspective with which to propose the conceptual framework and the case studies contained in the rest of the book.

CENTRALIZATION OF AUTHORITY OVER FORESTS

Governments Claiming Control

The centralization of political authority over natural resources is a theme repeated across every country in South and Southeast Asia. Centralization of power has usually been preceded by the implementation of a central administration by an external colonial power, or by the rise of a modern bureaucracy from within the country itself. When a colonial power eventually relinquished power, this was usually followed by continuation of that centralized mechanism by the new government even after attaining independence.

For each of the countries treated by this volume, Bhutan, India, Indonesia, Nepal, Thailand and Vietnam, we can identify a specific policy through which the state affirmed its eminent domain over forests, thus centralizing power. In Bhutan, it was *Thrimzhung Chenmo* (Supreme Law of Bhutan) of 1959, drafted by the new National Assembly that was established in 1953, followed by the Forest Act of 1969. In India, the 1878 Indian Forest Act succeeded in centralizing power over forests and classifying forests as either reserved, protected or communal/village. However, the provision for villages was essentially non-existent. Moreover, the Act provided for eminent domain of the state over all forests, even private forests, when 'public welfare' was an issue. In Indonesia, under the Basic Forestry Law No. 67 of 1967, the central government claimed control over the forests and issued concession permits for logging. This was followed in 1979 with the Village Administration Law, under which the desa system of Java was universally imposed across the country. In Nepal, the 1957 Private Forests Act, drafted by the new government after the overthrow of the Rana regime, nationalized all forests and placed any non-titled land under the purview of the central government. In Thailand, the 1913 Forest Protection Act was the formal policy that allowed the government to claim ownership of all teak forests, established a concession system and began collecting royalties on timber extraction by the private companies holding the concessions. In 1941, this was extended to all forests claimed to be under the Royal Forest Department (RFD) management, that is, about 40 percent of the total land area of Thailand. In Vietnam, the nationalization of the forests in the areas covered in Chapter 10 of this volume took place in 1975 with the reunification of the country, the implementation of the commune system and the management of all forests by the State Forest Enterprises (SFEs).

Preceding all of these policies were highly varied and important political histories, ranging from the relatively peaceful rise of a new government to successful liberation from a colonizing power to military coups. Indeed, it is a remarkable feature of human societies that national governments, almost without exception, succeeded in gaining control over the vast resources ostensibly belonging to 'the people', regardless of the history prior to the emergence of the state. What is equally remarkable, however, is that almost without exception the centralization of authority over forests has been a colossal failure.

The Failure of Centralization

The immediate or short-term impact of centralization policies was that traditional forest users were labeled as illegal and their activities were deemed contrary to the objectives of state management, regardless of the state's objective. For example, in India and Thailand the centralization of the forest management was for the extraction of timber and therefore local use of forests was a threat to the future income of the administration. In contrast, the main objective of state-run forest management in Bhutan was conservation and local practices of live tree cutting for timber, subsistence wildlife hunting and other extraction was contrary to the maintenance of forest cover and biodiversity. In Vietnam, local users could no longer cut trees because those trees were under the legal authority of the SFEs. In some cases, the criminalization of forest activities by local communities, not surprisingly, resulted in increased conflict between the state agencies and the people dependent on forest resources. Major conflicts have arisen in India, Nepal and Thailand over the policing of forests by the state, which have further galvanized resistance against the state in rural areas.

Two long-term outcomes of centralization of forest resources were (*a*) loss of incentive for long-term community management and (*b*) unregulated encroachment on state forests. Centralization, by legally stripping away access, use and management rights from communities, concurrently removed incentives for those communities to maintain locally-crafted institutions in places where they existed. This has been widely discussed in the literature, particularly in the context of Nepal (Hobley, 1985; Messerschmidt, 1993). However, there is some disagreement over whether this outcome was as widespread as some authors proposed, or whether communities did in many cases make attempts to maintain traditional arrangements and institutions despite the loss of *de jure* usufruct rights (Gilmour and Fisher, 1991). Indeed, local communities in India have a long history of grassroots environmentalism and there is evidence to suggest that although the legal framework shifted *de jure* rights to the state agencies, communities continued to practice *de facto* systems and even resisted government-supported management and extraction activities (Banerjee, 1997).

Notwithstanding the arguments suggesting that some communities could continue to practice local forms of management, it is clear that in all the countries we are discussing, there were widespread changes in the way local communities practiced forest management after centralization policies were enacted. Government forests may have become open access resources that were subsequently encroached upon or accessed by multiple stakeholders who had no legal capacity (or in some cases, the desire) to protect the resource or promote good local governance. Research has suggested that government-controlled forests in Nepal may be unsustainably utilized by communities for fuelwood, fodder and timber when there is no local control or protection of the resource. In Thailand, forests gazetted as 'reserve forest' were made open access by the fact that protection by the state was nearly absent and that the Land Code of 1954 allowed conversion of degraded forest—such as logged teak forest—to agricultural land. In Vietnam, the traditional institutional arrangements that had shaped forest use, protection and management by indigenous inhabitants prior to 1975, were made legally irrelevant overnight and in some cases have degraded to the point where they are almost extinct (Thang, 2004).

Finally, the centralization of authority over forests was not successful at its purported goal of conserving forests and maintaining forest cover. Statistics bear this out: in India, Nepal and Thailand, forest cover has measurably declined after centralization. Thailand's forest cover, for instance, was estimated to be approximately 50–55 percent in 1960, and by the year 2000, natural forest cover was about 23 percent, with plantations comprising an additional 6 percent (FAO, 2005). Perhaps only in central Vietnam and Bhutan have there been relatively low levels of forest loss since centralization. For example, recent data suggest that since 1975, forests in Thua Thien Hue and Quan Nam provinces have been stable in terms of overall forest coverage (Koy *et al.*, 2006; Thiha, 2006). In Bhutan, the forest cover estimate of 72 percent in the 1980s declined to nearly 65 percent (Penjore and Rapten, 2004) and may be further declining (Rai, 2005); however, this is far better than most other countries in the region.

Nevertheless, it may not be fair to say that forest centralization policies are categorically the cause of forest loss. Indeed, an assortment of underlying factors conspired against the ultimate success of centralized management and there are variable factors both within and across countries. However, it may be concluded that centralization policies have generally not prevented forest loss. It may be argued that in many instances, centralization facilitated new degradation events or even accelerated existing trends. There is widespread agreement that total centralization of forest management is not a sustainable solution for the majority of community-accessed forests in Asia.

FOREST DECENTRALIZATION AND THE
DRIVE TOWARDS COMMUNITY PARTICIPATION

In recent years, important steps have been taken by governments either to reduce their claims over forests or to increase the rights of local users over forests. Usually, these developments are under the umbrella of decentralization, which is defined by Agrawal and Ostrom (Chapter 2) as 'a political process in which governments or other political coalitions use institutional change to redistribute power away from the center in a territorial–administrative hierarchy.' In other words, decentralization means that the central government relinquishes the authority to make decisions about individual actions over natural resources. However, as discussed by Agrawal and Ostrom, recognizing policy failure and relinquishing authority and power is contrary to the nature of a centralized government. Nevertheless, the efforts by citizens, foresighted bureaucrats and international aid agencies to change the system have made significant inroads to bring about new changes that decentralize particular aspects of forest management.

In India, for example, both the British administration and the government of independent India attempted to gain ever increasing control over the forests of India. However, when faced with vociferous opposition and protest at the local level, the government was 'capable of retreating and sharing benefits with new claimants' (Agrawal and Ostrom, 2001). Local opposition was an important driving force in shaping the National Commission on Agriculture's social forestry program, initiated in 1976. The social forestry program provided a framework for more significant forest legislation in India over the past century. Local user's rights were recognized with the 1988 forest policy stating that forests were no longer solely for revenue generation. In 1990, the government drafted a resolution 'specifically asking the state governments to involve local communities and voluntary agencies in the protection and management of degraded forest lands' (Saigal, 2000).

The contemporary Joint Forest Management (JFM) policy was drafted in 1990 because policy makers acknowledged the existence of community-based activities that appeared to be working to maintain forest cover (Jeffery and Sundar, 1999), and also that there was a high incentive for those communities to participate if they could share in the economic benefits. The drafting of JFM policy was seen as the culmination of efforts by many stakeholders struggling to gain control over forests.

JFM works on the premise that local communities will collaborate in conservation if they have exclusionary rights over traditional forest lands and receive benefits of the forest products. The forest department will provide exclusive rights over forests, as well as a share of the income from forest products (with the state receiving the remaining share of income from commercially extracted products), to forest protection committees. As described by Sarin (1996) and Ghate and Mehra (Chapter 4), forest protection committees can be formed through the initiation of communities themselves, through the local offices of the forest department, or in collaboration with non-governmental organizations (NGOs). A major question that remains is whether those initiatives share similar outcomes in terms of sustainability. This is the main question explored by Ghate and Mehra.

The Nepal government's solution to failed centralization has been to initiate aggressive programs to return the management and use rights of forests to local users who held those rights in the first place. These programs are the community forestry and the leasehold forestry programs, the former being the most prioritized program of the Ministry of Forests.

With the realization that forest cover was declining, combined with strong grassroots movements to provide more forest-related rights to communities, the Nepal government drafted a forestry plan in 1976. This plan led to subsequent attempts at decentralizing forest management, first by empowering panchayats to manage barren and degraded lands, and later by specifically recognizing the role of communities in forest management. This was followed by the Forestry Master Plan of 1989, which made community forestry the most prioritized sector of the Ministry of Forests. It allowed the establishment of forest user groups (FUGs) to which authority over operational management, use and protection of designated forest tracts would be given. In addition, the Plan clearly stated that all accessible forests should be handed over to communities who were willing and able to manage them. Thus, while leaving open an obvious loophole with regard to what constituted an 'accessible forest', the legislators made substantial effort to devolve authority to local users.

An important revision to the Master Plan in 1993 broke down forests into five sub-categories: community forests, leasehold forests, government-managed forests, religious forests and protected forests. Each of these forest types had an associated policy dictating operation and management over the resource. Gautam and Shivakoti (Chapter 6) provide a succinct history as the framework for their discussion of the community forestry program's impact on forests of the Middle Hills of Nepal. As briefly described by Karmacharya and associates in Chapter 7, the leasehold forestry program began in 1989 and focuses on the economically most marginalized households in villages. This is in contrast to the community forestry program, which is open to all members of the community who hold a legitimate claim to usufruct rights over the forest in question.

As explained by Yonariza and Shivakoti in Chapter 5, the Indonesian New Order regime that was established in the late 1960s and collapsed in the late 1990s was largely unsuccessful in maintaining forest cover. The post-Suharto period has been marked with major decentralization legislation that extended immediately to forests. The principal laws paving the way for decentralization were Law 22/1999, which transferred 'authority over all sectors of government except those considered strategic ... to regions' (Resosusdarmo, 2004), and government regulation (*Peraturan Pemerintah Republik Indonesia*) No. 25, Year 2000, whereby local governments were allowed to manage their natural resources. Forestry and agriculture, not being strategic sectors, therefore, immediately fell under the purview of regional—usually district—governments. Forestry activities include afforestation, soil conservation, private forestry, forestry extension, management of protected forests, and purview over non-timber forest products, hunting and forest protection (Wardojo and Masripatin, 2002).

Local people's participation was part and parcel of several policies, such as the Forestry Act 41/1999, which allows individuals and cooperatives to receive a permit for private forestry enterprise and also recognizes land tenure and local user rights. Community forestry is also possible under the umbrella of Ministry of Forest Decree No. 31/Kpts-II/2000, although its implementation has been slow (ibid.). In contrast, large-scale timber estates continue to be under the purview of the central government, and the attempts of the government to establish sustainable plantations through industrial wood supply have focused on the establishment of plantations on traditional swidden land (Jong, 1997).

In Thailand, despite the seemingly entrenched view of the state against rural community forest utilization and management, there is decentralized forest management to some extent and it has a growing constituency of supporters both within and outside government. Interestingly, factions within the RFD have been quite progressive in considering people as a possible partner in conservation and forest management. In 1986, the RFD established a community forestry office, with the task of assisting communities in acquiring and registering qualifying forests as community forests under their control. The forests available for community forestry must reside outside protected areas or protected watersheds, which include national parks, wildlife sanctuaries, headwaters and critical watersheds. These last two designated areas are the source of major conflict in Thailand. Whereas there are more than 9,000 community forests in Thailand (Asia Forest Network, 2006),[1] many forests that rural people access are situated in the mountainous regions of northern and western Thailand, that is, in protected watersheds. Hence, many of those forests do not qualify for community forestry status and are under state control.

In the 1990s, a Community Forestry (CF) Bill was drafted with the support of the RFD, academics and NGOs,[2] and over the course of the subsequent decade was submitted, debated and voted on in the Parliament. This bill would have provided a formal setting for the establishment of community forests across all of Thailand, and would have given legal use rights to pre-established communities in protected forests. Although the bill was passed in the House, it was rejected in the Senate in 2002.

After the defeat of the CF Bill, the RFD underwent a major internal shift. Between 2002 and 2003, the RFD was split into two independently-operating agencies under the new Ministry of Natural Resources: the RFD and the Department of National Parks, Wildlife and Plant Conservation (DNP). The DNP maintained jurisdiction over national parks and wildlife sanctuaries, and the RFD maintained jurisdiction over all state-claimed forest lands outside protected areas. The RFD therefore remains the implementing agency for community forestry via the CF office. Despite its support of community forestry, it is unable to designate protected watersheds (Class 1 and Class 2) as community forests. On the other hand, the mandate of the DNP, to maintain 'pristine' protected areas, appears to be continuing the fences-and-enforcement approach to protected area management.

Kijtewachakul and associates, in Chapter 9, provide an excellent contemporary example of the intersection between the RFD, which aims to conserve forests outside of protected areas, and local people who have practiced forest management that is, according to the RFD, contrary to conservation. This is most notably swidden agriculture. The centralized management system of Thailand struggles with the need to conserve forests, and the most familiar mechanism for this is to remove people from the forest. However, as Kijtewachakul and associates show, local mechanisms of management can be successfully used in maintaining forest diversity (see also Kabir and Webb, 2006).

Decentralization in Vietnam began in December 1986, when the nation launched the *doi moi*, a policy of economic renovation to promote economic growth through capitalism. Although the initial impacts of *doi moi* were in the agriculture sector, it had major implications for the forestry sector. The essence of the new 'open market' system is that individuals can pursue entrepreneurial activities leading to individual economic success. Both the national and local governments have been releasing forest lands to private interests, including enterprises, households and communities. The government of Vietnam is facilitating the drive towards a free market society; natural resource management decentralization is part of that strategy.

Several contemporary policy developments in Vietnam have accelerated the process of decentralization and handing over of forests to non-state entities (Sam and Trung, 2001). In 1991, the Forestry Protection and Development Act classified forests as protection forest (critical watersheds), special use forest (including formally protected areas such as national parks) or production forest (unprotected forest for timber production). Moreover, it specified that production forest could be allocated to state enterprises, households and corporations. Allocation is the process

whereby legal use rights over a particular piece of forest or degraded land (for forestry purposes) is provided to the recipient
(enterprise, household or corporation) for 50 years. The rights and
duties of the recipient are given in a Land Allocation Certificate,
commonly referred to as the Red Book.

Decree 327/CT dated November 19, 1992 established a forest
protection and re-greening program for 1992–98. Moreover, the
policy also intended to eliminate rotational agriculture systems
(swidden or 'slash and burn' practices), which were viewed as
destructive to forests and low in productivity. This decree is the
foundation for current activities designed to eliminate swidden
agriculture in central Vietnam. Program 661 (for the period 1998–
2010), formulated under Decision No. 661/QD/TTg (1998) of the
Prime Minister, continued program 327, aimed at gaining forest
cover by developing 5 million hectares of plantations. This '5 million hectare' program was incorporated into the household allocation program, the contemporary policy of which is Prime
Minister Decision No. 178/2001/QD-TTg. A recent amendment
of Decision 178 now allows natural forest to be allocated to groups
of households, that is, communities. As a result, a framework for
community-based forest conservation is in place for long-term
management of forests by communities.

Dung and Webb (Chapter 10), however, reflect on the argument
of Agrawal and Ostrom (Chapter 2) that incentives must be in place
for decentralization—as in the Vietnamese case, forest allocation—
to be realized. The question posed by Dung and Webb is: what
are the incentives for the state agencies to participate in forest allocation, and what are the incentives for local people to participate
in those programs? The path of decentralization of authority over
forests appears to be rather clear for the next several decades, because households and communities gain control over the resource
(within national policy limits, of course) for 50 years according to
the land holding certificate. Incentives must be sufficient for all
actors involved in the forest allocation process, so it can proceed
effectively and remain sustainable over the coming decades.

Bhutan may be an outlier when comparing its decentralization
efforts with those of the other countries in Asia. In fact, it appears
that decentralization has not really taken off there. Several reasons may account for this, the foremost being that, according to

Webb and Dorji, some of the most unappealing features of the centralized policies may not be readily enforced. As a result, there has been less overt conflict between local people and the state over the vast resources remaining in the country, when compared with India, Nepal or Thailand. Moreover, given the relatively pristine condition of the forests and lack of research in the country, the evidence of failed centralization would not be readily apparent in the condition of forests.

Although the 1959 *Thrimzhung Chenmo* and the 1969 Forest Act centralized the country's forests, the Bhutanese government has claimed to be responsive to the needs of local communities. Legislation has been enacted that recognizes traditional management systems over locally-accessed forests, while nevertheless maintaining eminent domain over all forests. The Land Act of 1979 specifically recognizes communally-managed leaflitter forests (*sokshings*), grazing lands and private forests. Both social forestry and community forestry have been defined by the Forest and Nature Conservation Act of Bhutan (1996),[3] however those activities are well-controlled by the central government and do not represent a clear move towards decentralization. Nevertheless, this process is expected to ultimately lead to further developments of community-based forest management and perhaps control over the resource (Penjore and Rapten, 2004).

In fact, it has been argued that although centralization in Bhutan did indeed abolish total usufruct rights of communities to forests, this was part of a long-term strategy whereby the central government would gain complete control over the forests, and then slowly and methodically relinquish certain rights over certain forests to users for long-term sustainable forest management (ibid.). However, whether the government actually gained complete control over the forest with its centralization policy is not clear.

THE CENTRAL QUESTION AND
CONCEPTUAL FRAMEWORK OF THIS BOOK

What have been the outcomes of these recent forestry decentralization solutions, both practically and theoretically, to the forest-accessing communities upon which these policies have been imposed? This is the main driving question of this book. Practically, we need to understand whether the current solutions being promoted within Asia are leading towards 'success' or 'failure' within their relevant contexts. Theoretically, we need to understand how communities respond to those solutions envisioned by policy makers. Both the theoretical and practical implications of such investigation are profound. By comparing the responses of communities to the changing policies of their respective governments, we can begin to ask questions about both the policy and community features that may facilitate community adaptation, and those that may hinder the adaptation of communities to new policies.

However, from the review of forestry policies across Asia, we can conclude that the present day diversity of actors, governance structures and ecosystems across Asia is impressive. Simply cataloguing the contemporary relationships among these three components across South and Southeast Asia would be a daunting task indeed. Moreover, those relationships have not been stable over time. Entire governance structures—local and national—and their associated rules have evolved, gone extinct or been reborn. Rural societies have undergone demographic changes, thus altering the human landscape and the local institutional arrangements. Unsustainable management of ecosystems has resulted in the widespread degradation of a large portion of South and Southeast Asian forests. Indeed, the dynamism across Asia seems to preclude synthetic study.

How then can we begin to understand the processes occurring between people and forests under changing governance regimes? It seems clear that with the diversity of situations described earlier, a case study approach is necessary to draw general conclusions about what policy solutions are available, which ones work, and under what circumstances. Due to the enormous diversity of contexts in Asia, if we are interested in making Asia-relevant syntheses and cross-national recommendations, we must sample the diversity of policies and the diversity of responses by communities accessing diverse ecosystems. Admittedly, there may be no possibility to sample the entire diversity of all three of these dimensions (governance/policy × community × ecosystem), just as there is no way to sample across all possible settings to undertake robust statistical analysis of the contextual factors leading to, for instance, the evolution and maintenance of forest-related institutions (Agrawal, 2003).

This diversity leads us to two methodological challenges facing our research. First, we need a way to conceptualize the situations across South and Southeast Asia where diverse communities, diverse ecosystems, and diverse governance systems reside. Second, we need to be able to research those systems in a way that allows us to make regional comparisons that lead to novel conclusions about forest decentralization policy, communities, and forests.

First, having a clear conceptual framework is essential. The Institutional Analysis and Development (IAD) Framework (Oakerson, 1992; Ostrom *et al.*, 1994) provides an appropriate conceptual lens through which we can begin to tackle the question of community responses to policy development. The IAD Framework recognizes sets of actors engaged in an action arena, within which decisions are made about forest use and management. The action arena is a physically-bounded system (e.g., a place and time) that exists and is modified by three essential contextual components: resources, communities, and rules. The characteristics of those three components, along with the physical setting of the action are what 'surrounds' the actors making the natural resource decision.

A decision within the action arena will lead to a certain outcome. But prior to committing to a particular decision, actors certainly weigh the possible outcomes of the possible array of decisions available to them. This introduces the concept of *incentives*: rational actors will choose a particular decision based on the most attractive incentive available. Incentives can be viewed as the ratio benefits (potential or perceived) over costs (potential or perceived). Analyses of incentives within the IAD framework can occur at any level of society.

For example, in Chapter 2, Agrawal and Ostrom address the broader issue of the incentives to engage in the decentralization process and consider why governments are undertaking the costly process of decentralization. Their analysis reveals that decentralization occurs when the benefits accruing to governments and those within the government outweigh the costs. Such incentives, according to Agrawal and Ostrom, include increased access to the resources or power over the resources, reduced costs, deflection of blame or increased power over social affairs.

An example from the case studies in this volume comes from the chapter by Dung and Webb (Chapter 10). They analyze who the actors are in the action arena of forest allocation. The actors are the SFEs that relinquish the forest previously under their control, the Forest Protection Department and the local people. What are the incentives to each of these actors to engage in this process? Is there a sufficient incentive for the SFEs to allocate forest and lose potential future timber benefits, or is it more rational to not allocate in due course and risk reprimand from upper echelons of government? Do the potential benefits of non-compliance outweigh the potential costs of non-compliance? Using the IAD Framework, Dung and Webb analyze the actors within this action arena, the contextual modifiers, and the incentives leading to decisions regarding participation in the forest allocation process.

Second, we need a methodology that allows us to collect data in a way that permits robust comparisons across the Asian region. Careful sampling and data collection can lead to important conclusions across varying contexts. However, there is a general paucity of research that is directly comparable across sites, most commonly due to methodological differences. The need for a research framework leading to such important comparisons was the driving force motivating a group of researchers to develop the IFRI research program in the early 1990s (Ostrom and Wertime, 2000). This research protocol has been described in detail in other publications, and the global IFRI research group published an earlier book on the institutional regimes of communities managing forests (Gibson *et al.*, 2000). The present volume is the second book that has emerged from the IFRI network.

ORGANIZATION OF THE VOLUME

This volume contains eight case studies that investigate the outcomes associated with the forest policy developments in Bhutan,

India, Indonesia, Nepal, Thailand and Vietnam. It is an attempt to address the empirical question of how communities are responding to recent policy developments under the umbrella of decentralization. The majority of the chapters written here have their conceptual roots in the IAD Framework and most of the case study researchers in this book have used the IFRI research protocol to collect data at each study site. What is interesting is that the questions posed by each author relate either directly with the theme of adaptation to policy, or have collected data using ancillary information that, when combined with the core IFRI data set, can be used to address the question of adaptation to policy. The diverse array of analytical tools used in the case studies presented here attests to the flexibility of IFRI itself, as well as to its complementarity with other data collection protocols and analytical tools.

The book is loosely organized into three sections: an introduction, the case studies, and a synthesis. The present chapter and Chapter 2 introduce the reader to the policy context, in both a practical sense (history, Chapter 1) and theoretical sense (incentives for decentralization, Chapter 2). As noted earlier, Agrawal and Ostrom tackle head-on the question of why countries are embarking on the process of decentralization, and whether the rhetoric is met with actual decentralization of authority.

Chapters 3–10 present case studies from six countries in South and Southeast Asia, where the IFRI protocol, along with ancillary data collection methods were used to evaluate the responses of communities to the recent trend of decentralization of authority over forests to the sub-national level (or even the local level).

Chapter 11 by Shivakoti and Ostrom synthesizes the research and draws conclusions and lessons from the case studies in the context of the IAD framework and the theory of decentralization presented in Chapter 2. They find that because there is a remarkable diversity of challenges, structural variables, support structures and outcomes across these case studies, the solutions for sustainable decentralized forest management will be as diverse as the contexts themselves. Flexibility of policy and the willingness of governments to allow local actors to experiment, test and explore new potential solutions is absolutely essential for long-term success. Rigid governmental structures that do not fully decentralize the authority, and inherently the opportunity, to craft local solutions are destined to be less successful than those allowing—and supporting—local creativity and local institutions to thrive.

Map 1.1
Map of Asia Indicating the Study Sites

Study Sites
1: Twelve districts, Bhutan
2: Gadchiroli District, Maharashtra State, India
3: Barisan I Nature Reserve, West Sumatra, Indonesia
4: Kabhrepalanchok District, Nepal
5: Kabhrepalanchok and Sindhupalchok Districts, Nepal
6: Chitwan District, Nepal
7: Thawangpa District, Nan Province, Thailand
8: Nam Dong District, Thua Thien Hue Province, Vietnam

Notes

1. These include forests registered with the RFD community forestry office as well as those in the process of being registered.
2. This is not to say that there was complete consensus among those groups about the CF Bill. In fact, there was disagreement among many non-government sectors about the content of the CF Bill. In general, however, the majority of

non-political stakeholders appeared to support the final version put before the Parliament.

3. 'Social Forestry' means planting of trees and/or other forest crops on private registered lands, within the 25-acre land ceiling, such as *kamzhing, tseree* and *pangzhing* lands, and registered under the social forestry rules. 'Community Forestry' means any area of Government Reserved Forest designated for management by a local community in accordance with the Rules issued under this Act.

REFERENCES

Agrawal, A. (2003). 'Sustainable Governance of Common-pool Resources: Context, Methods and Politics'. *Annual Review of Anthropology, 32*, 243–262.

Agrawal, A. and Ostrom, E. (2001). 'Collective Action, Property Rights and Decentralization in Resource Use in India and Nepal'. *Politics & Society, 29*(4), 485–514.

Asia Forest Network. (2006). *Community Forest Management in Thailand.* http://www.asiaforestnetwork.org/tha.htm. Accessed April 28, 2006.

Banerjee, A.K. (1997). 'Decentralization and Devolution of Forest Management in Asia and the Pacific'. Working Paper APFSOS/WP/21. Bangkok: Food and Agriculture Organization of the United Nations.

FAO. (2005). *Global Forest Resources Assessment 2005 (Thailand).* Available online at www.fao.org/forestry/site/32094/en/tha. Accessed January 16, 2006.

Gibson, C.C., McKean, M.A., and Ostrom, E. (eds). (2000). *People and Forests: Communities, Institutions and Governance.* Cambridge, MA: The MIT Press.

Gilmour, D.A. and Fisher, R.J. (1991). *Villagers, Forests and Foresters.* Kathmandu: Sahayogi Press.

Hobley, M. (1985). 'Common Property does not Cause Deforestation'. *Journal of Forestry, 83*, 663–664.

Jeffery, R. and Sundar, N. (eds). (1999). *A New Moral Economy for India's Forests? Discources of Community and Participation.* New Delhi: Sage Publications.

Jong, W. de. (1997). 'Developing Swidden Agriculture and the Threat of Biodiversity Loss'. *Agriculture, Ecosystems and Environment, 62*, 187–197.

Kabir, Md. E. and Webb, E.L. (2006). 'Saving a Forest: The Composition and Structure of a Deciduous Forest under Community Management in Northeast Thailand'. *Natural History Bulletin of the Siam Society, 54*(2): 63–84.

Koy, K., Horning, N., and Laverty M. (2006). 'Monitoring Land Cover Change in Vietnam's Central Truong Son'. Paper presented at the conference on Participatory Forest Conservation in Central Vietnam: Implementing and Monitoring Strategies, January 9–11. Hue City: Hue University of Agriculture and Forestry.

Lefevre, T., Todoc, J.L., and Timilsina, G.R. (1997). *The Role of Wood Energy in Asia.* Publication FOPW/97/2 Food and Agriculture Organization of the United Nations, Forestry Department. Accessed online at http://www.fao.org/docrep/w7519e/w7519e00.htm.

Messerschmidt, D.A. (1993). 'Linking Indigenous Knowledge to Create Co-management in Community Forest Development Policy'. In K. Warner and H. Wood (eds), *Policy and Legislation in Community Forestry*. Proceedings of a workshop held in Bangkok, January 27–29. Bangkok: Regional Community Forestry Training Center.

Oakerson, R. (1992). 'Analyzing the Commons: A Framework'. In D.W. Bromley *et al*. (eds), *Making the Commons Work: Theory, Practice and Policy* (pp. 41–59). San Francisco: ICS Press.

Ostrom, E., Gardner, R., and Walker, J. (1994). *Rules, Games, & Common-Pool Resources*. Ann Arbor: The University of Michigan Press.

Ostrom, E. and Wertime, M.B. (2000). 'International Forestry Resources and Institutions Research Strategy'. In C.C. Gibson, M.A. McKean, and E. Ostrom (eds), *People and Forests: Communities, Institutions and Governance* (pp. 232–286). Cambridge, MA: The MIT Press.

Penjore, D. and Rapten, P. (2004). 'Trends of Forestry Policy Concerning Local Participation in Bhutan'. In K. Harada and M. Nanang (eds), *Policy Trend Report 2004* (pp. 21–27). Kanagawa: Institute for Global Environmental Strategies.

Radelet, S. and Sachs, J. (1997). 'Reemerging Asia'. *Foreign Affairs, 76*(6), 44–59.

Rai, B. (2005). 'Bhutan's Forests: The Real Picture'. *Kuensel* Online, October 22. www.kuenselonline.com. Accessed October 22, 2005.

Resosusdarmo, I.A.P. (2004). 'Closer to People and Trees: Will Decentralization Work for the People and the Forests of Indonesia?'. *European Journal of Development Research, 16*, 110–132.

Saigal, S. (2000). 'Beyond Experimentation: Emerging Issues in the Institutionalization of Joint Forest Management in India'. *Environmental Management, 26*(3), 269–281.

Sam, D.D. and Trung, L.Q. (2001). 'Forest Policy Trends in Vietnam'. *Policy Trend Report 2001*, 69–73. Kanagawa, Japan: The Institute for Global Environmental Strategies.

Sarin, M. (1996). 'From Conflict to Collaboration: Institutional Issues in Community Management'. In M. Poffenberger and B. McGean (eds), *Village Voices, Forest Choices* (pp. 165–209). New Dehli: Oxford University Press.

Sumarlan, Y. (2004). 'How Participatory is Thailand's Forestry Policy?' In K. Harada and M. Nanang (eds), *Policy Trend Report 2004*, 45–59. The Institute for Global Environmental Strategies.

Thang, T.N. (2004). *Forest Use Pattern and Forest Dependency in Nam Dong District, Thua Thien Hue Province, Vietnam*. MSc dissertation, Asian Institute of Technology, Bangkok.

Thiha. (2006). 'Monitoring Land Cover Change using RS/GIS: Historical Land Cover Dynamics and Its Determinants in Nam Dong District, Thua Thien Hue Province, Central Vietnam'. Paper presented at the conference on Participatory Forest Con-servation in Central Vietnam: Implementing and Monitoring Strategies, January 9–11. Hue City: Hue University of Agriculture and Forestry.

United Nations. (2001). *Reducing Disparities: Balanced Development of Urban and Rural Areas and Regions within the Countries of Asia and the Pacific*. Publication ST/ESCAP/2110. New York: UN.

United Nations Population Division. (2005). 'World Population Prospects: The 2004 Revision Population Database'. Available online at http://esa.un.org/unpp/. Accessed January 14, 2006.

Wardojo, W. and Masripatin N. (2002). 'Trends in Indonesian Forest Policy'. *Policy Trend Report 2002*, 77–87. The Institute for Global Environmental Strategies.

2 | Decentralization and Community-Based Forestry: Learning from Experience

ARUN AGRAWAL and ELINOR OSTROM

The Re-emergence of Decentralization for Forest Governance

Adaptation of local institutions in the context of natural resource use has been intimately shaped by government policies. Even when a specific policy addresses problems that are not directly related to forests, the problem may still have significant impact on forests and institutions governing them. Subsidies to promote irrigation, enhance agriculture, and promote exports can all have adverse impacts on forests. Depending on how policies articulate with existing socioeconomic forces and institutions, they can produce quite unintended effects. In this chapter, however, we focus on recent decentralization reforms that are reshaping local forest use and governance quite intentionally.

After decades of policies favoring centralization in much of the world, decentralization has become potentially the most significant and certainly the most distinctive and visible shift in national environmental policies since the late 1980s. Governments in much of the so-called developing world, including most Asian countries, claim to have undertaken institutional reforms that are changing the face of resource governance. The authors in this volume focus on experiences of decentralization in both South and Southeast Asia to examine how forest governance has been changing in the region. Our investigations in India, Bhutan, Nepal, Thailand, Indonesia, and Vietnam are in particular concerned with how relationships between central governments, local community institutions, and resource users have changed, and how these changes have influenced resource governance more generally.

Until the mid-1970s, governments in the countries under investigation had for the most part continued colonial policies over natural resources. They had extended and attempted to monopolize formal control over forests, water, pastures, and wildlife. The justification for centralized control was found in arguments dating back to the colonial period: local populations had neither the capacity nor the knowledge to exercise systematic control to protect valuable resources threatened by overuse, market pressures, and users' ignorance.

Post-colonial policies to centralize control over natural resources, however, seldom proved fully successful. Typically, they were spottily enforced; but equally often, many who were in charge of enforcement proved only too susceptible to bribery and corruption. In many cases, forests were mined heavily to generate revenues for the state. But even when formal laws aimed at strict restrictions, they generated perverse effects. By excluding local users, they enfeebled local arrangements to manage and govern. They produced incentives for guards to intimidate local users and in consequence, many rural residents dependent on resources became enemies of resource-related policies. Also, widespread corruption meant widespread deforestation. Rarely, if ever, were central governments able to provide the kind of protection and stewardship that they loudly professed as their goal.[1]

In contrast, governments have recently come to recognize a role for a broader range of actors in environmental governance. As central government actors create the policy space in which local resource claimants can formally be involved in resource governance, a variety of organizations at multiple scales are also beginning to get involved in the process of institutional change and resource management. Such organizations range from local bureaucracies and private associations to international and national non-governmental organizations.

Four important factors appear to be behind the recent changes. First, many national governments in the developing world face a fiscal crunch and they need to reduce costs and become more efficient. Second, decentralization is an obvious and convenient mechanism to transfer costs to others. Third, international donors are making significant funds available to support new mechanisms of cooperation and governance that convert local actors into partners. Finally, many national governments have begun to accept the view that protecting resources does not necessarily require exclusively private property arrangements, or government ownership and management.[2] Decentralization policies have the potential to be effective mechanisms to extend the reach of national governments. In diverse combinations, these factors have prompted the widespread recourse to decentralization as a policy choice.

Recent efforts at governmental decentralization are not radically new: the movement between centralization and decentralization has occurred before. Two relevant comparative experiences of decentralization occurred during the colonial period and in its immediate aftermath under the names of indirect rule and community development. However, current initiatives are qualitatively different in some ways. They affect a vast array of activities. Among them are general administrative procedures, provision of services, development and poverty alleviation programs, and environmental governance. They are part of a wider move away from big government and the distrust of state-centric solutions. In addition, the recent decentralization initiatives conceive of individual citizens as being responsible for their own actions rather than as persons who need to be developed or made modern. The greater attention to the creation of responsible citizens makes ongoing reforms different both in content and character.

Decentralized strategies of governance are appealing on many grounds. They embody the hope that citizens can have a greater voice in their own governance, but their results and effects remain uncertain. Indeed, in some cases, present-day reforms are already attracting many criticisms. Allegations that new reforms are limited, ineffective, or inequitable are already being made in relation to new initiatives whether it be community forestry in Nepal and Thailand, joint forest management in India, changing forestry laws in Indonesia, or community-based forest management in the Philippines.[3]

To assess the nature of decentralization processes, we ask three difficult questions: (1) How exactly are we to understand decentralization? (2) Rhetoric aside, to what extent have governments institutionalized the decentralization of environmental governance? (3) Is decentralization having a positive impact on the efficiency, equity, and long-term sustainability of natural resources? The third question is what many policy analysts consider 'the bottom line'.

It is also the most difficult to answer owing to the limited time that has passed since reforms were adopted and the problems involved in disentangling the specific effects of policy shifts.

In answering these questions it is necessary to avoid, and if possible undermine, a new set of orthodoxies that are assuming the status of conventional wisdom. Decentralization and the related phenomenon of community-based forest management are not the panacea to cure governance problems (Ostrom, 2005). Nor is local indigenous knowledge invariably superior to other forms of knowledge. And even if the participation of local communities can often help address problems of conservation, they cannot be taken as the repositories of a conservationist ethic. Actors at multiple scales, knowledge of different types, and a diversity of governance arrangements are typically necessary for successful and equitable resource management outcomes.

THE ROLE OF COLLECTIVE ACTION AND PROPERTY RIGHTS IN DECENTRALIZATION

At its most basic, decentralization aims to achieve one of the central aspirations of a just political governance and democratization process: the desire that humans should have a say in their own affairs. This way of thinking about decentralization identifies its relationship to democracy—surely a primary reason that decentralization policies have been in favor. A focus on ethical and normative aspects, however, can obscure the political roots of decentralization policies. A different way to understand decentralization would be to highlight it as a political process in which governments or other political coalitions use institutional change to redistribute power away from the center in a territorial–administrative hierarchy. Decentralization thus becomes the intentional act of a coalition of agents to redefine existing political relationships so that some local actors are involved more actively in decision-making processes.

A political–institutional understanding of decentralization shifts attention towards the specific actors involved in the process, their motivations and incentives in pursuing decentralization, and the way new powers are exercised as a result of decentralization reforms. It also prompts questions about how the potentially divergent interests of many actors might coalesce to produce common grounds for collective action. And since the target of environmental policy decentralization is the reconfiguration of institutional arrangements around valuable natural assets, it also becomes necessary to explain the changes in property rights that result from decentralization.

A focus on the combinations of diverse political actors, their powers, and the limits on their powers helps to move away from understandings of decentralization that are simple exercises in nomination. Terms such as delegation, deconcentration, dispersion, devolution, denationalization, and privatization depend on arbitrarily treating some element(s) of a decentralization program as the most critical area of coverage, functional focus, types of powers, identity of beneficiaries, or mechanisms of decentralization.[4] In choosing one such term as the main analytical innovation in thinking about decentralization, one eschews a common underlying analytical framework in favor of taxonomy.[5]

A different problem characterizes analyses of decentralization that view it as a combination of governmental activities in different spheres. Manor (1999: 7) argues, 'If it is to have significant promise, decentralization must entail a mixture of all three types: democratic, fiscal, and administrative.' Binswanger (1999: 2), in almost exactly the same terms, asserts, 'The three main elements of decentralization—political, fiscal, and administrative—should be implemented together.'[6] In both these cases, however, decentralization itself remains an aggregate, underanalyzed phenomenon. In contrast, our analysis directs attention toward the constituent elements of decentralization: actors and changes in their rights and powers.[7]

Collective Action in Decentralization and Community-Based Forest Management

Three sets of actors are most commonly involved in collective action aimed at environmental policy decentralization: central government politicians and bureaucrats; international donors, bilateral agencies, and multilateral institutions; and local communities and their leaders whom decentralization processes seek to invest with more power. These actors have different incentives and interests related to decentralization.

Central governments are best viewed as congeries of decision makers who may often have conflicting objectives rather than as monoliths with a unified rationality and common agenda. Instead of presuming that 'the' government decides on a decentralization policy after an integrated calculation of overall benefits and costs, one needs to examine the incentives of diverse actors in the process. Decentralization is likely to be initiated when central government actors compete for power among themselves and find in decentralization a mechanism to enhance their access to resources and power in relation to other political actors. When a central political actor, or a coalition of such actors, finds that decentralization may make it possible to reduce costs (and/or improve revenues), deflect blame, or extend the government's reach further into social processes, decentralization becomes likely. Actors from outside the central government can create pressures for change. As long as a central state is present, however, at least the acquiescence and usually the support of a political faction, ministry, or department is necessary to initiate decentralization reforms. In this sense, policy choices about decentralization are no different from policy choices in other domains. They are institutional choices about gaining relative political advantage.

The interests of central government actors who favor decentralization can overlap with those of international agencies and local leaders. International actors such as bilateral agencies (Danish International Development Agency [DANIDA], Canadian International Development Agency [CIDA], Swiss Agency for Development and Cooperation [SDC], United States Agency for International Development [USAID], or Norwegian Agency for Development Cooperation [NORAD]), non-governmental organizations (Ford Foundation, World Wildlife Fund, International Union for the Conservation of Nature and Natural Resources [IUCN], Consultative Group on International Agricultural Research [CGIAR] research centers, Conservation International), and multilateral institutions (World Bank, Global Environment Facility [GEF], and agencies of the United Nations system) often provide funds and expertise to assist decentralization reforms. Access to such resources can become the incentive to launch a decentralization program. Some donors may view decentralization as a means to accomplish other outcomes. Some bilateral donors give funds to developing countries but also encourage preferential treatment to companies located in their home countries (Gibson *et al.*, 2005). Others may see in it an instrument to leverage the funds they disburse more efficiently.

The involvement of local actors is often crucial to successful decentralization and an increased role for local forestry groups. Effective lobbying groups that local actors create by networking and/or social mobilization can decisively affect the implementation of decentralization policies. Local actors may or may not be interested in the ultimate objectives of decentralized policies: protection of forests, wildlife, or other resources. They are likely, however, to want greater access to the resources and decision-making powers that decentralization policies promise. Their interest in new sources of revenues and greater control over resources, and the decision-making responsibilities they come to gain in the wake of decentralization reforms make them the third important actor in environmental decentralization. Local forest users, farmers, and pastoralists may also learn of successful efforts to enhance their capabilities and achievements and push for programs.

Each of these actors brings different strengths to make decentralization programs a reality and a success. Central government actors have the power to launch decentralization programs as formal-legal initiatives. They do not have the capacity, however, to ensure significant participation from local actors. International actors and donors can provide monetary and financial incentives to prompt central governments into creating decentralization programs. They cannot monitor whether decentralization leads to actual and substantial devolution of power. The continued involvement of local actors at many levels is critical to making decentralization meaningful. By themselves, however, local actors are too weak to create sufficient pressures on a central government to undertake a decentralization program. Further, without strong support and persistent demands from local actors, opponents of decentralization can ensure that actual changes are limited.

This complex mosaic of interests and capabilities means that if only one of these actors is in favor of decentralization, little substantive institutional change is likely to occur. Differing levels of commitment and actions by these three sets of actors generate diverse types of collective action in favor of decentralization reforms (Andersson, 2002, 2004). The trick for advocates of decentralization is to align the interests of powerful decision makers who make policy choices, with organization and mobilization of local actors who can create additional pressures in favor of reforms. With such an alignment, thoroughgoing decentralization of powers and rights becomes possible.

Decentralizing Property Rights over Environmental Resources

The nature of environmental policy decentralization is usefully analyzed using property rights theory. Successful decentralization creates new opportunities as central governments delegate rights and powers. Local actors can gain control and decision-making powers in three arenas as a result of effective decentralization: use, management, and ownership.[8] These rights can be understood as being located at distinct levels of analysis. The exercise of use or withdrawal rights corresponds to an operational level of analysis (Ostrom *et al.*, 1994). Management and ownership rights, however, require that right holders operate at a collective-choice level of analysis that impacts future operational decisions. Further, for local actors to possess collective-choice making capabilities, some rules at a constitutional level (set locally or by a national government) must give them this authority. The analytical distinction between operational, collective-choice, and constitutional-choice arenas should not create the impression that these correspond to three different hierarchical levels of authority in a political or legislative system. What is crucial to understand is that for any resource, some operational rules affect day-to-day use and consumption; others at a collective-choice level structure the creation of operational-level rules; and still others at a higher constitutional level affect who can make collective choices and what procedures they must follow.[9]

In a highly centralized regime, almost all authority for making constitutional, collective choice, and operational-level rules is concentrated in a national government. Centralized control typically signifies strict regulations that prohibit use of protected wildlife and forests, or alternatively, allow a central government to allocate concessions to commercial firms to harvest resources to generate financial income to the government and its agents. Nor does centralized control leave much leeway for local actors to decide how to protect or manage resources. And when environmental resources are under a centralized regime, local populations and their representatives possess scant or no ownership rights. Decentralization initiatives promise to relax central control in each of these three spheres of activities.

One can disaggregate the three spheres of activities further. Consider use. Relaxation of controls over use can allow local communities and their leaders greater play in three ways: greater access to forest resources, higher levels of use and consumption, and more powers to monitor whether others are consuming harvesting forest products illegally. Note that greater freedom to access, use, and monitor is quite different from the power to make decisions about *how* goods and resources should be accessed, used, or monitored; in other words, how resources should be managed. The powers to make such collective-choice decisions are often retained by central governments who find it more convenient to set liberal policies regarding use but maintain overall control over management. Granting communities rights to harvest specific quantities of timber or firewood but preventing them from exercising rights to alienate or transfer forests is a frequent pattern in decentralization policies. Greater freedoms to access and consume a resource are among the advantages that local actors gain in exchange for higher expected efforts to monitor and protect.

Greater managerial discretion over forest resources can also be gained in three significant ways. Local actors can win powers to decide how resources should be protected and used, how compliance with decisions about protecting and using resources should be monitored and rule-breakers sanctioned, and over the adjudication of disputes. Possession of these three specific managerial powers is indicative of substantial autonomy and decentralization reforms creating such autonomy go a long way towards meaningful decentralization of powers to local actors.

Effective alienation rights confer on their holder(s) the ability to allocate benefits from and transfer control over a resource. Central governments assert alienation rights over resources because market failures are rife where public goods or common-pool resources are concerned. Governments also assert claims over forests and wildlife resources because of their commercial value. Sharing or transferring alienation rights implies the greatest relinquishing of control because those who possess such rights can sell use rights or dispose of resources. With decentralization of ownership, lower-level decision makers can dispose of resources by selling use rights or the resource itself in potentially irreversible ways. For this reason, one might expect decentralization of ownership to be rare.

Our examination of property rights should not be taken to mean that only a full set, including use, management and alienation rights, permits effective exploitation of resources. Studies of forest user groups, irrigation systems and pastoral groups show that even the rights to use and manage resources can help local actors develop boundary rules to exclude non-contributors, establish authority rules to allocate withdrawal rights, devise methods for monitoring conformance and use sanctions against those who do not conform to rules (see Blomquist, 1992; Schlager, 1994; Tang, 1994; Lam, 1998; Shivakoti and Ostrom, 2002).

The outcomes associated with the decentralization of different levels of property rights depend in significant measure upon the certainty of users about their rights—whatever they are—and the nature of governance arrangements to protect their rights.

ARE GOVERNMENTS DECENTRALIZING FORESTRY-RELATED DECISION-MAKING POWERS?

Many governments claim that they are decentralizing substantial decision-making authority to local actors. Similarly, in the past decade many scholars have identified it as a pervasive feature of environmental policy.[10] But it is also true that governments often 'perform acts of decentralization as theater pieces,' aimed at satisfying international donors and non-governmental organizations (Agrawal and Ribot, 1999). We use three studies that base their conclusions on a large number of cases to identify some of the general patterns in ongoing decentralization policies. The findings from these three large-N studies provide a background against which developments in the specific cases studied in this book can be assessed. The first of these studies is a meta analysis of 52 cases of forest policy decentralization in Asia, Africa, and Latin America. The second study (National Research Council [NRC], 2002; Dietz *et al.*, 2003) examines the effects of diverse property rights arrangements on resource-related outcomes. The final study concerns a large number of cases studied by colleagues networked with the International Forestry Resources and Institutions (IFRI) research program, and draws on evidence from around the world (Gibson *et al.*, 2005).

Our analysis of 52 cases of forest policy decentralization in as many countries in Asia, Africa, and Latin America reveals substantial variation in the type of property rights that are decentralized, the nature of powers that local actors come to exercise, and the degree to which reforms are institutionalized (Agrawal, 2004). Our meta-analytic study is a work in progress and the following analysis is based on findings from case studies of decentralization initiatives in which local authorities have come to exercise some control over resources upon which they depend. The studies were carried out by different authors, often belonging to different perspectives. We garnered these studies from published documents as well as the available gray literature from many international donor, conservation and research organizations. To examine these different studies in a consistent fashion, we analyzed the findings reported in them by using a research instrument with 38 questions that probed the available information on the extent of autonomy of local resource management institutions and the degree to which the autonomy of institutional arrangements went together with the involvement of different actors in the pursuit of decentralization reforms. Our conclusions can be seen as suggestive and require additional systematic work.

Our analysis of the 52 cases suggests that decision makers at the local level gain their positions of authority through processes ranging from inheritance, to direct appointment, to competitive elections. Their new powers can be investigated along the three dimensions discussed earlier: user activities (access, use, and monitoring), managerial control through rule making and enforcement (to determine access and use patterns, to guide monitoring and sanctioning, and undertake adjudication), and alienation (allocation of benefit streams and transfer of the resource itself).

At an aggregate level, our meta-analysis confirms what one might suspect about decentralization of environmental policy. Governments are loath to relinquish control over natural resources when it comes to alienation rights. If the ability to allocate benefits from forests and transfer alienation rights to the resource itself is a hallmark of effective use of resources, local actors gained such rights in any significant measure in less than 10 percent of our cases. In 49 out of the 52 cases (94 percent), central governments did not grant local actors—individually or collectively—any significant ability to allocate or transfer alienation rights to forests.

Significant rights to reallocate benefits from forests were also devolved only in less than a third of the cases.

In general, it seems that use, management, and ownership form an ordered set of increasingly meaningful decision-making powers over resources. As one proceeds from the ability to access and use a resource to the power to alienate it to others—it becomes less likely that local actors will gain the ability to make decisions. Where use of resources is concerned, decentralization reforms confer at least some rights on local decision makers to harvest benefits from environmental resources. In our cases, local actors came to exercise use rights in 50–60 percent of the cases.

When it comes to managerial control, the story is somewhat different. Central governments tend to permit local actors the powers to determine *how* resources are to be accessed and used, but the limits of reforms are visible when it comes to sanctioning and dispute adjudication. In less than a tenth of the cases did local decision makers come to exercise any significant powers to sanction rule breakers or adjudicate disputes.

We find it reasonable to infer that the current round of decentralization of environmental resources has mainly provided to local actors significant capacities to use and access resources. But the ability to use and access resources or to monitor them typically occurs in accordance with rules crafted by central government bureaucracies. Indeed, the ability to use resources comes at the cost of having to monitor the use of resources and report rule violations. In this sense, decentralization of environmental decision making is as much about conferring benefits on local users as it is about asking them to assume a higher proportion of costs involved in managing resources. In several important cases, local actors have gained the powers to decide and enforce how resources should be used, accessed and monitored. And, of course, there are also a few isolated cases in which local actors have begun to exercise even more comprehensive decision-making powers. But overall it is fair to state that factions opposing decentralization seem to be relatively successful in preventing meaningful reforms from occurring in a majority of the analyzed cases.

Our meta-analysis also suggests that although governments claim to be sharing powers with local partners, the actual experience of decentralization is more bounded than what the rhetoric in its defense might lead one to expect. There are also significant variations in the powers that governments decentralize. To explain these variations, it is useful to focus upon how support by different political actors—central government politicians and bureaucrats, international donors, agencies and institutions, and local communities and decision makers—affects the extent of decentralization.

There are relatively few instances—only about a fifth of the cases—in which any of these three actors initiates decentralization reforms by itself. This is not too difficult to explain. International donors and local actors do not have enough clout to launch formal decentralization policies; central government actors may not have sufficient incentives. Because of the lack of overlap between incentives and capacities of any single actor, more than 80 percent of the cases are ones where decentralization occurs because of the support of more than one set of actors. In addition, some central government support seems critical to launch a decentralization reform. Of the 52 cases of varying levels of decentralization, 44 (just over 80 percent) witnessed some support by central government officials and/or politicians.

We also find that local actors play a specialized and critical role in ensuring that decentralization programs are meaningful. By themselves, local actors are never able to force the initiation of reforms. But their involvement does relate positively with higher levels of decentralization of powers of use, management and ownership. Whether central government actors and international agencies and institutions act unilaterally or in concert, the results of decentralization initiatives are weak in terms of powers that get transferred to local levels. In cases where local actors actively seek forms of decentralization, however, the powers that central governments transfer are more comprehensive.

The fact that local actors are unable to bring about decentralization on their own is easily explained by their weakness in bending central government actors to their will and their limited access to international actors. Once some central government actors are willing to initiate a decentralization reform, the involvement of local actors ensures better representation of local interests. Donors and international NGOs have relatively limited capacity to monitor and track whether actual changes conform to professed policy. Their involvement is therefore mainly relevant for the initiation of decentralization policies rather than to ensure comprehensive reforms.

CRAFTING ADAPTIVE FORMS OF GOVERNANCE

Although some scholars strongly believe in the efficacy of one and only one kind of forest governance, our own work leads us to view the general ownership or governance arrangement as only one factor leading to successful, long-term, sustainable natural resources. In a recent study by the NRC (2002), scholars found government, private and common-property regimes capable of managing common-pool resources successfully over time. Instead of a particular form of governance, five general requirements of successful, adaptive forms of governance were identified (see Dietz *et al.*, 2003). These are:

1. *Providing trustworthy information* about the resource itself (stocks, flows and internal processes). Also needed is reliable information about human–environment interactions affecting resource systems. Systems characterized by substantial decentralization of some aspects of governance may enhance the congruence of information made available to those making decisions at the appropriate scale of the relevant environmental events (of course, there is no guarantee that information will be aggregated at the appropriate scale in a decentralized system—a problem likely to be especially intractable in situations where there are high levels of externalities related to resource governance—as, for example, is likely to be the case for wildlife or other mobile resources). On the other hand, highly aggregated information may overlook or average out local variations that could be extremely important in identifying levels at which a resource system can tolerate harvesting of products or benefits.

2. *Dealing with conflict.* Differences in power and interests among the parties involved in making choices affecting a resource can generally create substantial disturbances for any ongoing system. The people using a resource do bring diverse perspectives, interests and fundamental philosophies to problems of environmental governance and finding peaceful ways of dealing with conflicts, if escalation to the point of dysfunction can be avoided and can spark learning and change. Simply

delegating authority to national ministries does not always resolve conflicts satisfactorily, so some of the stimuli for developing forms of community governance of forest resources stems from the effort to experiment with various governance approaches to complement managerial ones.

3. *Providing infrastructure.* Infrastructure, including technology, affects how fast a forest resource can be exploited (e.g., use of power saws), the extent to which waste can be reduced in resource use (e.g., various hi-tech recycling processes) and the degree to which resource conditions and the behavior of human users can be effectively monitored (e.g., cellular phones and remote sensing). Indeed, the choice regarding the appropriate institutional arrangement to use in a particular setting depends in part on infrastructure. Effective communication and transportation technologies are also of immense importance. Institutional infrastructure is also important, including research, social capital, and institutions, to coordinate between local and larger levels of governance.

4. *Mechanisms to be prepared for change.* No matter what kind of governance institutions are in place, some mechanisms must be designed to allow for adaptation because some current understanding is likely to be wrong, the required scale of organization can shift and biophysical and social systems change. Any system of fixed rules is likely to fail. Systems that guard against the low probability and high consequence possibilities and allow for change may be suboptimal in the short run but prove wiser in the long run.

5. *Inducing rule compliance.* To govern resources effectively requires—at a minimum—that most of the rules related to resource use are followed, with reasonable standards for tolerating modest violations. Field research has found that it is generally most effective to impose modest sanctions on first offenders and gradually increase the severity of sanctions for those who do not learn from their first or second encounter (Ostrom, 1990; NRC, 2002). Whether enforcement mechanisms are formal or informal, those who impose them must be seen as effective and legitimate by resource users or resistance and evasion will overwhelm the commons governance strategy (Dietz *et al.*, 2003).

The requirement of inducing rule compliance appears from some of our own research to be close to a necessary (but not sufficient) condition for achieving sustainable forests over time (Agrawal and Yadama, 1997; Gibson *et al.*, 2005; Hayes and Ostrom, 2005). Gibson *et al.* (2005) drew on data collected by a network of scholars associated with the IFRI research program for a large number of local forest resources in Africa, Asia and the Western Hemisphere (see Gibson *et al.*, 2000; Poteete and Ostrom, 2004, 2005). In the analysis reported in Gibson *et al.* (2005), the unit of analysis is a user group. In the IFRI research protocol, a user group is a group of people who harvest from, use, or maintain a forest, and who share the same rights and duties to products from a forest whether or not they are formally organized. For this analysis, we used only data collected at the time of the first site visit. These first research visits were to forests located in 12 countries (Bolivia, Brazil, Ecuador, Guatemala, Honduras, Kenya, India, Mexico, Nepal, Tanzania, Uganda and the United States).

For each of the forests included, we identified one or more user group per forest. The 178 resultant user groups utilize 220 forests and vary substantially in their level of activities, organization and age. Some user groups were officially recognized by national governments as part of a decentralized effort to encourage community forest governments, and some user groups shared similar rights but did meet regularly to undertake joint activities.[11] For this preliminary test, we chose four explanatory variables: (*a*) the regularity with which individuals in a user group monitor or sanction others' rule conformance, (*b*) the group's social capital, (*c*) the group's dependence on forest resources and (*d*) whether the group was formally organized or not.

The first variable—rule enforcement—is measured by a scale based on information about how frequently the user group undertakes monitoring and sanctioning efforts: never, occasionally, seasonally or year-round. For this analysis, we recoded never or sporadic as 'sporadic' and seasonally or year-round as 'regular'. We measured social capital by combining a number of variables regarding the cooperative activities (e.g., cooperative harvesting, cooperative processing, cooperative marketing or sales, and financial contracts) that individuals from a user group undertake in the forest. We especially focus on cooperative activities so as to distinguish them from forms of collective work that are impelled by top-down controls over group action. We calculated dependence by adding the percentage of needs that individuals in a user group claim are met by a forest for their food, biomass, timber and firewood provided by the forest and then dichotomized at the mean. The measure of a user group's formal organization derives from whether or not they have created a formal organization that has meetings and officials.

The dependent variable in this study was forest conditions computed from the assessment made by members of the user group at the time of the study. Forest users were asked to rate their forest as: very abundant, somewhat abundant, about normal for this area, somewhat sparse, very sparse. The resulting score has been dichotomized. Since the forests studied are located in a wide diversity of forest zones, we cannot utilize the extensive forest mensuration data collected as part of every IFRI study. (A low number of trees or basal area may represent a forest in excellent condition in one ecological zone and in poor condition in another zone.) Varughese and Ostrom (2001) and Agrawal and Chhatre (2006) provide a reassuring initial test of the accuracy of user's assessments.

The statistical results reported in Gibson *et al.* (2005) revealed that regular monitoring improves the conditions of forests, *regardless* of levels of social capital, formal organization, or forest dependence. Given the high level of faith by some scholars in the effectiveness of local groups regardless of how well they are organized, some will find it surprising that we did not discover that formally-organized forestry user groups were more likely to have better forest conditions (only 71 out of 150 of the formally organized forest groups [47 percent] had better forest conditions). Even for groups that are not formally organized, better forests are associated with higher levels of rule enforcement. We did not find a significant relationship between forest outcomes, rule enforcement, and groups that are formally organized, although the relationship is in the hypothesized direction. For levels of social capital and dependence on the forest, we found very strong statistical evidence that regular rule enforcement is the strongest explanatory variable affecting forest conditions.

How Communities Adapt to Decentralization Policies

Efforts by central governments to change the formal rules through which to incorporate communities and their representatives in the governance of forests are creating outcomes that involve mutual accommodations both by communities and government agencies. It may be fair to say that decentralization reforms related to forests aim to create many new centers of local decision-making authority that would have a direct relationship with government agencies at the central level. The creation of these new centers of decision-making authority, or the allocation of new powers of decision making to existing local bodies, has both intended and unintended effects.

Three intended characteristics of relationships between central and local government decision makers are worth mentioning: standardization, formalization and harmonization of state-local relationships. Local decision-making bodies tend to have broadly similar powers over resources rather than large variations in their capacity to manage or gain benefits from the forests in question. This effort to bestow broadly similar authority on local bodies helps central governments manage the process of decentralization more easily. Two, the powers and responsibilities of local decision makers in relation to central authorities tend to be formally articulated— either through legislation or executive orders. Formal and written statements are a means through which to ensure that local decision makers clearly understand the scope of what they can do and they can be held accountable by central officials and in some cases also by their local constituents. Finally, central government agents attempt to create greater harmony between the goals and interests of local decision makers and their own goals and interests, often through a variety of incentives that structure the kind of benefits local users gain from forests in exchange for undertaking to protect vegetation from overuse and overexploitation. The production of greater harmony and common interests is essential to reduce the costs of enforcement for which many decentralization programs are designed to begin with.

But decentralization processes also produce unintended effects. Two of these concern the possibility of elite capture and local mobilization. The rules embodied in formal legislation or executive orders to devolve decision-making powers tend to be enforced by some collection of agents at the local level. These decision makers, depending on the extent to which their authority is based upon new forms of selection and representation, can be instrumental either in exacerbating existing political inequalities within localities, or create avenues through which to challenge existing elite over time. Quite often, decentralization programs are criticized on the grounds that their design fails to incorporate safeguards against elite capture—indeed, some observers may even go so far as to claim that the frequency with which local elite are able to capture new decision-making arrangements may be a result of the unwillingness of central government actors to confront local power structures through the reforms they are introducing. A second unintended consequence, observed perhaps less frequently, is the possibility that new decision-making bodies come together in confederal structures to wield the power of numbers through their organization and influence the nature of legislation that governs the activities of their members. The Federation of Community Forest Users of Nepal (FECOFUN), which aims to articulate the problems and demands of community groups in Nepal, is one example of such an unintended outcome. Similar structures and networks of community federations can also be cited at the global level.

Conclusion

The most important lesson from empirical research on decentralization policies is that any analysis of decentralization policies requires an examination of the incentives and roles of a number of actors rather than those of states or central governments alone. Any complex system of governments requires institutional development to overcome the many collective-action problems through effective institutions. And, the development of effective institutions at any level is a process that takes time and is strongly affected by a variety of factors related to the resource (or problem at hand) and the individuals involved. Trying to jumpstart the process of institutional development through a formal policy of decentralization without a solid theoretical understanding of institutional development can retard rather than advance human well-being.

An important lesson of extensive research is that there is no single blueprint for an effective organization to solve similar problems, let alone substantially different ones. Enabling citizens and their officials to create collective-action organizations in the public and/ or private sphere at multiple levels takes considerable time and effort and will rarely approach either a fully centralized or a fully decentralized system. The choice is not simply between pure centralization and pure decentralization.

Further, decentralization is occurring in the context of large-scale social, political and natural processes over which local actors may have little or no control. These include globalization and integration of the global economy; the reorientation of global environmental politics in the wake of the emergence of the United States as the predominant international political actor; and global climate change and loss of biodiversity. We do not yet know how variations in these extremely prominent, macro-level factors affect the outcome of decentralization policies that many governments are attempting. And yet, our existing research points to the importance of institutionalizing decentralization reforms and involving local actors if decentralization policies are to generate greater local autonomy. The involvement of local actors should occur not just in the implementation but also in the initiation and design of decentralization policies.

Given that decentralization reforms in at least some countries have been underway for more than a decade and have produced visible local results, their measurement and analysis raises important questions about how we measure growth, sustainability and institutional change. National statistical measures of these changes scarcely register the important variations in performance that decentralization reforms introduce locally. National statistics, relying as they do on broad measures of average performance and deviations from that performance, do not provide much reason to pursue institutional change or attempt local development unless they can be reflected quickly in indicators of success. As citizens and scholars, it is important to begin the long and arduous process of thinking about measurements of environmental performance in which local changes can register as more than a minor blip.

Finally, it is important to sound a note of caution in assessing the broad topic of decentralization of environmental policies. Some forms of decentralized decision making about environmental issues may certainly be preferable on various ethnical and norm-ative grounds. It is essential, however, for scholars, public officials and citizens to recognize that decentralized decision making may lead to appealing outcomes as regards to poverty alleviation and environmental sustainability only when programs last for a long time and are designed specifically to reach this goal. Our empirical analysis from some very different cases indicates the overwhelm-ingly important role of politics in the initiation of decentralization reforms and in determining their impact. Indeed, overcoming the continuous problems of collective action faced in implementing decentralized efforts is also a thoroughly political process. We must think beyond the rhetoric of getting prices and institutions right. Effective decentralization is as much and more about encouraging processes that enable a different kind of politics. In this politics, local actors who are dependent on the resources whose disposition is at stake will play an important role. How the decentralization process is designed affects whose voices are heard at a local level as well as at larger scales.

Notes

1. See Peluso (1993) for an account and analysis of coercive forestry policies in Indonesia. The large literature on resistance shows the mechanisms that operate to cause centralized coercive control to fail. Scott (1985) remains the seminal text on the subject.
2. A recent report of the U.S. National Research Council summarizes extensive research that provides strong evidence that *no* single form of property owner-ship is associated with sustainable resource governance (see National Research Council, 2002; Dietz *et al.*, 2003).
3. Some criticisms of these initiatives can be found in Agrawal and Ostrom (2001).
4. For examples of works relying on a strategy of nomination to define decentral-ization, see Conyers, 1985; Rondinelli and Nellis, 1986; Rondinelli *et al.*, 1989; Samoff, 1989.
5. See Agrawal and Ribot (1999: 475–476), and Agrawal (2004) for a critique of such classificatory schemes.
6. Manor goes on to argue that decentralization likely occurs in this tripartite mixture whenever it offers promise. He also suggests, against *World Develop-ment Report 1997*, that such tripartite mixtures are reasonably common. See also Willis *et al.* (1999), who talk of political and functional decentralization as the two aspects of decentralization. They refer chiefly to fiscal measures in their discussion of functional decentralization.
7. For a similar criticism, see Agrawal and Ribot (1999: 474) and Agrawal and Ostrom (2001).

8. This discussion of the different types of property rights draws on and simplifies the scheme presented by Schlager and Ostrom (1992). Because of the questions addressed, they distinguished among five different classes of rights: access, withdrawal, management, exclusion and alienation. The following discussion includes access and exclusion, but as sub-classes of use and management rights respectively.

9. These three levels of analysis are further explored in Chapter 2 of Ostrom (2005).

10. Consider a non-random sample from some recent works. 'Democratization generally has assumed a central role in the developing world over the past decade in both reality and international donor thinking,' in Blair (2000: 21); 'In both developed and developing countries, recent decades have shown a tendency towards decentralization,' in De Vries (2000: 193); and, 'A significant development in Latin American politics in the last ten years has been the decentralization of government,' in Willis *et al.* (1999: 7).

11. Twenty-nine sets of users did not undertake any collective activity in regard to the forest they use. Seventy-five user groups had organized themselves sufficiently to hold at least some meetings, elect officials, and undertake at least some joint activities. Five formally-constituted user groups did not undertake any collective activities at all. The user groups included in the study ranged in age from 3 years to over 100 years.

REFERENCES

Agrawal, A. (2004). *Decentralization of Resource Policies in the Developing World, 1980–2005*. Presentation of book manuscript at the CHAOS-Cambridge University Press seminar series, University of Washington, Seattle.

Agrawal, A. and Chhatre, A. (2006). 'Explaining Success on the Commons: Community Forest Governance in the Indian Himalaya'. *World Development, 34*(1), 149–166.

Agrawal, A. and Ostrom, E. (2001). 'Collective Action, Property Rights and Decentralization in Resource Use in India and Nepal'. *Politics and Society, 29*(4), 485–514.

Agrawal, A. and Ribot, J.C. (1999). 'Accountability in Decentralization: A Framework with South Asian and West African Cases'. *The Journal of Developing Areas, 33*(Summer), 474–476.

Agrawal, A. and Yadama, G. (1997). 'How Do Local Institutions Mediate Resources? Market and Population Pressures on Forest *Panchayats* in Kumaon, India'. *Development and Change, 28*(3), 435–465.

Andersson, K.P. (2002). *Can Decentralization Save Bolivia's Forests? An Institutional Analysis of Municipal Forest Governance*. Doctoral dissertation. Indiana University, Bloomington.

———. (2004). 'Who Talks with Whom? The Role of Repeated Interactions in Decentralized Forest Governance'. *World Development, 32*(2), 233–249.

Binswanger, H. (1999). 'Technical Consultation on the Decentralization of Rural Development'. Proceedings Development Conference, Rome, December 16–18, 1997. Rome: FAO.

Blair, H. (2000). 'Participation and Accountability at the Periphery: Democratic Local Governance in Six Countries'. *World Development*, 28(Summer), 21–39.

Blomquist, W. (1992). *Dividing the Waters: Governing Groundwater in Southern California*. San Francisco: ICS Press.

Conyers, D. (1985). 'Decentralization: A Framework for Discussion'. In Abdul Hye Hasnat (ed.), *Decentralization: Local Government Institutions and Resource Mobilization* (pp. 22–42). Comilla, Bangladesh: Bangladesh Academy for Rural Development.

DeVries, Michiel S. (2000). 'The Rise and Fall of Decentralization: A Comparative Analysis of Arguments and Practices in European Countries'. *European Journal of Political Research*, 38(2), 193–224.

Dietz, T., Ostrom, E., and Stern, P. (2003). 'The Struggle to Govern the Commons'. *Science*, 302(December 12), 1907–1912.

Gibson, C., McKean, M., and Ostrom, E. (eds). (2000). *People and Forests: Communities, Institutions, and Governance*. Cambridge, MA: The MIT Press.

Gibson, C., Williams, J.T., and Ostrom, E. (2005). 'Local Enforcement and Better Forests'. *World Development*, 33(2), 273–284.

Hayes, T.M. and Ostrom, E. (2005). 'Conserving the World's Forests: Are Protected Areas the Only Way?' *Indiana Law Review*, 38(3), 595–617.

Lam, W.F. (1998). *Governing Irrigation Systems in Nepal: Institutions, Infrastructure, and Collective Action*. Oakland, CA: ICS Press.

Manor, J. (1999). *The Political Economy of Democratic Decentralization*. Washington, DC: The World Bank.

National Research Council. (2002). *The Drama of the Commons*. Washington, DC: National Academy Press.

Ostrom, E. (1990). *Governing the Commons: The Evolution of Institutions for Collective Action*. New York: Cambridge University Press.

———. (2005). *Understanding Institutional Diversity*. Princeton, NJ: Princeton University Press.

Ostrom, E., Gardner, R., and Walker, J. (1994). *Rules, Games, and Common-Pool Resources*. Ann Arbor, MI: University of Michigan Press.

Peluso, N. (1993). 'Coercing Conservation: The Politics of State Resource Control.' *Global Environmental Change*, 3(2), 199–218.

Poteete, A. and Ostrom, E. (2004). 'Heterogeneity, Group Size and Collective Action: The Role of Institutions in Forest Management'. *Development and Change*, 35(3), 435–461.

———. (2005). 'Bridging the Qualitative-Quantitative Divide: Strategies for Building Large-N Databases Based on Qualitative Research'. Paper presented at the 101st annual meeting of the American Political Science Association, Washington, DC, September 1–4.

Rondinelli, D., McCullough, J.S., and Johnson, R.W. (1989). 'Analyzing Decentralization Policies in Developing Countries: A Political-Economy Approach'. *Development and Change*, 20(1), 57–87.

Rondinelli, D. and Nellis, J. (1986). 'Assessing Decentralization Policies in Developing Countries: The Case for Cautious Optimism'. *Development Policy Review*, 4(1), 3–23.

Samoff, J. (1989). 'Decentralization: The Politics of Interventionism'. *Development and Change*, 21(3), 513–530.

Schlager, E. (1994). 'Fishers' Institutional Responses to Common-Pool Resource Dilemmas'. In Elinor Ostrom, Roy Gardner, and James M. Walker (eds), *Rules, Games, and Common-Pool Resources* (pp. 247–265). Ann Arbor, MI: University of Michigan Press.

Schlager, E. and Ostrom, E. (1992). 'Property-Rights Regimes and Natural Resources: A Conceptual Analysis'. *Land Economics, 68*(3), 249–262.

Scott, J.C. (1985). *Weapons of the Weak: Everyday Forms of Peasant Resistance.* New Haven: Yale University Press.

Shivakoti, G.P. and Ostrom, E. (2002). *Improving Irrigation Governance and Management in Nepal.* Oakland, CA: ICS Press.

Shivakoti, G.P., Vermillion, D.L., Lam, W.F., Ostrom, E., Pradhan, U., and Yoder, R. (eds). (2005). *Asian Irrigation in Transition: Responding to Challenges.* New Delhi: Sage Publications.

Tang, S.Y. (1994). 'Building Community Organizations: Credible Commitment and the New Institutional Economics'. *Human Systems Management, 13,* 221–232.

Varughese, G. and Ostrom, E. (2001). 'The Contested Role of Heterogeneity in Collective Action: Some Evidence from Community Forestry in Nepal'. *World Development, 29*(5), 747–765.

Willis, E., Garman, Christopher da C.B., and Haggard, S. (1999). 'Decentralization in Government: Latin America'. *Latin American Research Review, 34*(1), 7–9.

3 | THE EVOLUTION OF FOREST-RELATED INSTITUTIONS IN BHUTAN: ADAPTATIONS OF LOCAL PEOPLE TO THE RISING STATE

EDWARD L. WEBB and LAM DORJI

INTRODUCTION

Bhutan is a small country in the central Himalayas that has a rich history, substantial forests and a national government that is striving to pursue rational, equitable and sustainable development. Although Bhutan was only officially opened to outsiders in the 1970s, a well documented political history stretches back to the 1600s and reveals a close link with its abundant natural resources.

Forests cover more than 70 percent of the land. Forest resource use is part of the mixed subsistence farming system that closely links agricultural land with forests, from which users derive products and services. All rural villages in Bhutan depend on the forest for timber, fuel wood, fodder, leaf litter and water. Many forests are utilized for cattle grazing. In some rural areas, people hunt wild animals such as deer to supplement their protein needs. Non-timber forest products such as mushrooms and edible ferns not only supplement vegetables, but also provide people with alternative income. Leaf litter is collected for animal bedding and for generation of organic manure, which is a crucial resource for the farming system. Moreover, water is a very important forest product. The role of forests in maintaining a constant flow of water is very much within the knowledge of the local people and they regard water not just as an important resource but consider it as a forest product (Dorji, 2003).

With the opening of Bhutan to the outside world in the 1970s, a process of development was initiated that must be addressed by policy makers. About 79 percent of the population of Bhutan is dependent on forests. The importance of forests to all of Bhutanese society implies that a policy should be formulated to conserve forest resources while providing people with the rights to extract forest products. The history and present status can lead to predictions about the future of local management regimes and supply a foundation for both local and regional policy initiatives.

The purpose of this chapter is to discuss the links between the political history of Bhutan and the forest-related institutions in rural communities. Understanding how communities can or cannot adapt to emerging forest policies is an important component of long-term governance of natural resources.

Study Sites and Methodology

The data for this chapter were prepared after one year of fieldwork (Dorji, 2003) in 12 villages in the inner Himalayas of Bhutan (Map 3.1). The villages selected for this study were dispersed across the country in order to sample a spatially heterogeneous set of villages and to construct a composite history of forest institutions for Bhutan. All sites were located between 1,000 and 2,500 m above sea level, which is within the montane evergreen broadleaf forest as defined by Ohsawa (1991). The other two sites were located in temperate coniferous forest.

Six of the sites were established as long-term research sites, in which the complete International Forestry Resources and Institutions (IFRI) methodology was applied. In six other sites, a less intensive but complementary data collection methodology was utilized. In all 12 sites, additional survey methods were utilized to collect historical transect and conflict resolution data.

A Religio-political History of Bhutan

According to the Bhutanese chronicle *Lhoyi Chhoejung*, Bhutan was prehistorically (500 B.C.–600 A.D.) an extremely isolated place where there was no trade, communication or education. Each village was separated from the other by mountains and rivers and as a result had its own dialect, customs and culture. There was neither a formal religion nor any government. Therefore, taxation, law, revenue collection, or other aspects of a centralized

MAP 3.1

Map of Bhutan Indicating the 12 Villages of Study. The Six Villages Marked with a Square Were Those in Which a Full IFRI Study was Conducted; in the Other Six a Less-intensive, IFRI-compatible Study Was Initiated

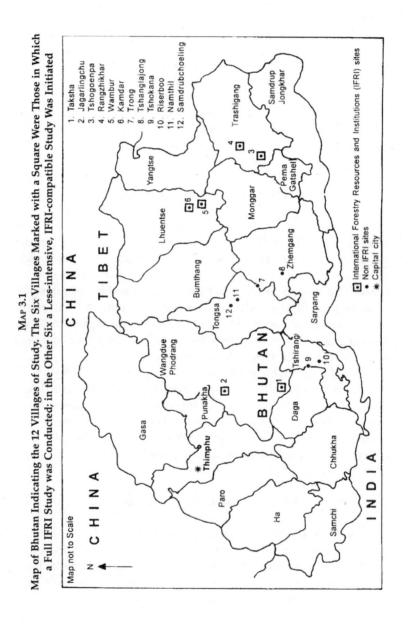

1. Taksha
2. Jagarlingchu
3. Tshogoenpa
4. Rangzhikhar
5. Wambur
6. Kamdar
7. Trong
8. Tshanglajong
9. Tshokana
10. Riserboo
11. Namthil
12. Samdrubchoeling

☐ International Forestry Resources and Institutions (IFRI) sites
• Non IFRI sites
✱ Capital city

government were absent. Population was very low and people lived in clustered villages with apparently little inter-village communication. However, at some point in prehistoric times, the Bon religion (Bonism) from Tibet spread into the central and southern parts of Bhutan (Hasrat, 1980). Bonism is characterized by mixed superstitious practices in which people worship deities representing manifestations of nature (such as the sun, moon, hills, mountains, trees, rivers, lakes, etc.). Witchcraft and magic played a predominant role in the rituals of Bonism. Local deities called *Gyap* and *Tsen* were worshipped in individual households, community monasteries and temples. Protectors of land and rocks known as *Lu Sadag* and evil spirits known as *Dhue* were constantly appeased. Sacrificial offerings of ox, sheep and poultry performed to worship local deities are still prevalent in many rural communities.

Tibetan Buddhism was introduced to Bhutan with the visit of the Guru Padmasambhava in 747 A.D. (Hasrat, 1980; Sinha, 1991). Historical records suggest that by then, some form of government existed with *Sindhu Gyap* serving as the King of Bumthang and *Debs* (petty kings) ruling different parts of eastern Bhutan independently. In western and central Bhutan, the influx of Tibetan Lamas (saints) in the 9th century continued for two centuries until Tibetan Buddhism and culture rose to dominance (ibid.).

Yet, the area that now comprises Bhutan remained a clan-based tribal region until the beginning of the 17th century, when in 1616 Zhabdrung Ngawang Namgyel (1594–1651) arrived in Bhutan and emerged as a consolidating religio-political ruler (Sinha, 1991). It was during the rule of Zhabdrung that many *dzongs*[1] were built and a dual system of government emerged. This dual system recognized two rulers over Bhutanese affairs: a *Druk Desi*, who headed the 'temporal rule', and the *Je Khenpo*, who presided over the 'spiritual matters of the region' (Dorji, 1995). The *Druk Desi* was recognized as the political ruler and was appointed by a four-member cabinet. During the dual system era of governance (1651–1906), 54 people served as *Druk Desi*, and 49 served as *Je Khenpo* (ibid.).

Although Zhabdrung apparently succeeded in establishing the first true political system over what is now Bhutan, those who followed as the *Druk Desi* generally could not function effectively.

This led to widespread conflict among factions vying for power (Das, 1974), culminating in several battles and eventually the emergence of Gongsa Ugyen Wangchuck, a leader who was unanimously elected the first hereditary King in 1907 (Planning Commission, RGOB, 2002). The hereditary monarchy has been in place since 1907, with later policies emanating from both the King's office and that of the elected governmental bodies.

While the combined religious and commercial interactions of the Bhutanese with Tibet, Assam and Bihar date back as far as the 12th century (Pommaret, 2000), the country essentially remained in self-imposed isolation until the second half of the 20th century. It was not until the reign of the third King Jigme Dorji Wangchuk that the country began to open up to the outside world (Hasrat, 1980; Planning Commission, RGOB, 2002).

Although the consolidation of the country and establishment of monarchy in 1907 provided the basis for increasing political stability, it was not until after 1950 under His Majesty Jigme Dorji Wangchuck that the government embarked on the concept of modern economic development with major economic, political and social reforms (Education Department, RGOB, 1997). The National Assembly was established in 1953 comprised of 105 elected representatives of the public, 10 elected representatives of the clergy and 35 representatives of the government. The Royal Advisory Council, consisting of representatives of citizenry and clergy, was established in 1965 to advise the King on matters of national importance, to act as a bridge between the King and the people and to ensure that the laws and decisions of the National Assembly were implemented. In 1968, the High Court, district and sub-district courts were established, the judiciary was separated from the executive and legislative branches and the cabinet was established (Planning Commission, RGOB, 2002).

Politics, Taxes and Forest Institutions before 1950s

There is a link between the religio-political history and the human-forest interface in Bhutan and the origins of this linkage reside in the taxation system originating with the government established by Zhabdrung in the 1600s. Not surprisingly, the establishment of a taxation system in Bhutan was driven by the local religio-politico regimes and ruling individuals, whose objective was to assume and maintain power. Although no specific writings exist on the subject, taxation probably evolved concurrently with the expansion of Buddhism in the 8th century through the rule of Zhabdrung, his reincarnations and *desids* who promulgated Buddhism. After Zhabdrung, the *desids* continued to promote Buddhism through construction of monasteries, *dzongs, stupas* and religious institutions (Hasrat, 1980). These structures provided a physical framework for the centralization of power in Bhutan, which may have lent support to the imposition of a formalized taxation system. Our interviews as well as other literature (Ura, 1995) revealed that local people's oral histories consistently traced the origin of taxes to Zhabdrung.

The seeds of the taxation system appear to have been sown early in the history of Bhutan, when the religious respect given by citizens to the elites was later converted into an obligatory tax. People offered their expressions of loyalty to Zhabdrung and other religious entities such as monasteries and monk bodies during the spread of Buddhism. These offerings were often in the form of agricultural products to gain blessings from the leaders. The religio-political elite not only accepted these offerings, but also subsequently enforced these in-kind offerings as a tax upon the populace.

There was a diversification in the way in which taxes could be paid. The first type of tax was called *wangyon. Wangyon* was an in-kind tax stemming from the earliest tributes to Zhabdrung, his various incarnations and the *dzongs*. The offerings of grains and farm products from the peasants were probably recorded and subsequently enforced as *wangyon*. Pain and Pema (2002) found that the logistics of the taxation system in the 17th century were described in contracts drawn between Zhabdrung and those who provided offerings. While some people paid annual *wangyon* in the form of farm and forest products, some devotees offered property such as land to monasteries and monk bodies. Second, *thojab* was a form of land tax that was based on the agricultural land holdings of a household, which had to be registered in the *dzong*. In other words, this was a wealth tax. Tax items differed from one place to another depending on the availability of resources in different places, and included grain, butter, oxen, animal skins and forest-based materials (shingles, bark, etc). Essentially, all necessary items required by the ruling regimes were garnered from local people in the form of tax.

The third form of taxation was labor. Labor activities included porterage, construction/repair and resource gathering. For porterage activities, each tax paying household was required to assist in transporting government consignments from one point to another, as arranged through the village. Ironically, the consignments often consisted of materials collected as taxes from communities (e.g., *thojab*). Construction/repair and maintenance activities included renovation of fortresses and the *dzong*, construction of roads and trails, and other activities as and when requested. Finally, households were required to provide labor for resource acquisition, such as tilling of agricultural land belonging to monasteries and local authorities, rice husking, cooking and herding (Ura, 1995). However, 'the privileged families, families of the higher incarnate lamas and the state officials were exempted' from the above taxes and obligations.

The porterage tax was revealed as a key factor in the formation of the most ancient forest institution of boundaries between village forest lands. Given the highly rural and remote settings of most villages, a series of villages would be involved before consignments reached the final destination. The places where consignments were dropped off by one village and received by the next village evolved into landmark boundaries between villages and the forests owned by the villages. Additionally, individuals representing local government authorities or aristocratic families often visited villages for purposes related to tax collection and/or to fulfill tasks assigned by their superiors. During such visits, it was also obligatory for villagers or their representatives to ensure a proper reception at certain places, to render hospitality and care during their stay in the village and to escort them to a place or point from where the representatives of the adjacent village would receive them and continue to render similar services. The process would go on until the official reached the final destination. Such reception and departure points also served as boundary references between villages. These required reference points for boundary demarcations between villages and they were supplemented with physical features such as streams or rivers, gullies, ridges, cliffs and foot-paths to clarify the boundaries off the main roads. As a result, the forested areas of Bhutan have been delineated through locally crafted institutional arrangements linked with the taxation system imposed by the religio-political elite.

The boundary institution became more important as the re-sources in the forest became more relevant for the payment of taxes (e.g., *wangyon*), and therefore, the evolution of these boundaries served to define rights—however loosely—among village commu-nities over the forest resources. Because these taxes included a wide range of edible and non edible products, the source of much of the materials was both the farm and the forest. In-kind taxes pertaining to products such as timber, shingles, fuel wood and bark from shrubs (e.g., *Daphne sp.*) had their sources in the forests.

Local people also refer to the history or traditional use of re-sources within certain boundaries in which they emphasized past prolonged usage as a basis for contemporary forest boundaries. Often implied in such claims is that they have nurtured and ren-dered care of the resources within the boundary. This does not imply a scarcity of the resource or the direct relevance of a limited resource for livelihood, but rather recognition of costs justifying use and exclusion rights.

We therefore argue that the formation of forest boundaries in rural Bhutan was initiated by the imposition of the taxation system by the ruling elite of ancient Bhutan. This may or may not have been coupled with a change in communities' perceptions of pos-sible scarcity (or future scarcity) of forest resources and ability to both fulfill subsistence requirements and pay hefty taxes to the *dzong*. In either case, we surmise that the emergence of ancient forest boundaries was at least in part the result of policy applied by local elites (i.e., a proto-government) and can therefore be seen as an adaptation of the community to a changing policy regime. This is not to say that boundaries were monitored and protected; indeed the boundary institution was a loose arrangement because of the abundance of forest in Bhutan. However, our interpretation is that local communities responded to the changing governance system by crafting institutions that established a framework of ownership and exclusion to some degree.

Forest Management Institutions
before 1950 not Related to Tax

While village boundaries were important in terms of political, administrative and tax purposes, there is no direct evidence to
suggest that boundaries evolved with a forest management objective (e.g., protection or regulated withdrawal). Yet, the Planning
Commission of Bhutan (2002) noted that 'even before the advent
of modernization in 1961, the country consisted of self reliant
subsistence communities, possessing well defined community-
based rules and institutions to facilitate the use of common resources.' Based on our field studies, we concluded the same: forest
management institutions do exist in rural Bhutan and did so long
before the rise of the modern Bhutanese state (Dorji, 2003; Dorji
and Webb, 2003). Therefore, an apparent puzzle arises: although
the government imposed no regulations on the use of forest resources and the resources themselves were abundant in the nearby
forests, many local forest institutions existed and continue today.
Why would institutions arise in a situation where resources were
salient, but not overtly scarce (cf. Gibson, 1999)? The purpose of
this section is to provide a hypothesis for the evolution of forest
management institutions in rural Bhutan and then to describe the
most relevant ones.

We hypothesize that the emergence of forest-related institutions occurred in part because forest resources, though available
in plenty, required a significant amount of time and effort to acquire. Any person who has walked in the forests of Bhutan (or the
Himalayas in general) will recognize the enormous amount of
effort required to obtain enough fuelwood, leaf litter and other
subsistence forest products. Hence, the collection strategy observed
in rural Bhutan is similar to the strategy seen in Nepal by Schweik
(2000): collection occurs more frequently near villages. Thus, even
though resources are highly abundant throughout Bhutan's forests,
local collection efforts would reduce the abundance of easily accessible products over time. Community collection near villages could
increase the possibility of resource conflict, demanding an institutional remedy. Reciprocating behavior, i.e., sharing and collective
management, would be an efficient proactive institutional response. We speculate that these linkages, although only based on

logic and not possible to prove historically, are a likely pathway for emerging forest institutions in a situation where resources are highly abundant overall, but resource acquisition is localized.

Today, we witness several ancient institutions that are related to sharing and helping each other within the context of forest resource allocation. Many communities have arrangements for water sharing during the cropping season; coordinated mechanisms to accomplish tasks such as house construction, cultivation and harvest; collective solutions exist for dealing with misfortunes such as a death in a family; participatory mechanisms are followed for hosting religious ceremonies and festivals that are strongly believed to be related to community welfare; and conflict-resolution processes are familiar to village members.

Dorji (2003) reviewed the forest-related institutions that exist today and before 1950. He concluded that most forest institutions related only to the part of the forest frequently accessed by villagers, a result that agrees well with optimal foraging theory. Forests far from the village were generally unregulated by village institutions. In those areas, no formal regulations pertaining to access, appropriation or management existed or exist today (see also Dorji *et al.*, 2006). In general, the reason for the lack of institutions regarding those forests is that they are less accessed and this remoteness precluded any need for regulation and hence no formal or informal institutions to be crafted. Nevertheless, despite the lack of formal and consistently applied institutional arrangements, those forests could still be governed by the tenets of Bonism, which state that guardian deities reside in the elements of nature and must be respected. Informal local religious practices that exist today are reported to be significant in conserving forests in rural areas (Allison, 2002).

On the other hand, forests close to villages were regulated by both formal and informal institutional arrangements. Rural livelihoods that were based on subsistence agriculture required a number of products that were obtained from the local forest. Not only were products necessary for subsistence agriculture, but also taxation increased the importance of having readily available forest products. Typically, households would extract products such as timber, fuelwood and non-timber forest products such as mushrooms, medicinal plants and fodder through forest grazing of livestock.

Research has uncovered several long-standing institutions that were present before 1950. These included *reesup, meesup, chusup* and *sokshings*. The institution of *reesup* was a customary practice whereby the community gave legitimacy to one individual (the *reesup*) to regulate forest products by ensuring equal and easy access to forest products based on community requirements. This institution was supported by the threat of social sanctions. Both customary rights and written agreements defined the terms, conditions and powers of the *reesup*, who was paid in kind and exempted from obligatory services to the community and the government after its emergence (Wangchuk, 2001). *Meesup* was the 'forest fire watcher', who would mobilize the community to fight forest fires (ibid.). Further, it was also his/her responsibility to find the culprit and report to the *dzong*. *Chusup* was the 'water caretaker'. The *chusup*'s responsibility was to ensure that households respected the traditional way for drinking water and to ensure proper distribution of water for irrigation among landowners.

The most widespread forest management institution in Bhutan is the *sokshing*. *Sokshings* are plots of forest specifically managed for the production of leaf litter and minor amounts of fuelwood (Wangchuk, 2001; Dorji, 2003; Dorji *et al.*, 2003). Most *sokshings* are small plots usually around 1 hectare in area (Wangchuk, 2001), located adjacent to the village, and heavily managed to maximize leaf litter production and fuelwood (Dorji *et al.*, 2003). Leaf litter from *sokshings* is mixed with cattle manure and used to fertilize crops. Given the major importance of agricultural output for subsistence practices of rural villages, consistent management practices and strong institutional arrangements have evolved for their governance.

Traditionally, a *sokshing* is owned by a household. Before 1950, the rights of ownership for an individual were complete (*sensu* Schlager and Ostrom, 1992), with the household given all rights of access, withdrawal, management, exclusion and alienation (Dorji *et al.*, 2006). The ownership rights allowed households to manage the forest in the way best for their livelihoods, while adhering to the local religious and social customs that prohibited clearcutting or unjustifiable cutting. Therefore, a consistent management system evolved whereby individuals managed the *sokshing* to contain only those tree species most valuable for composting:

usually *Quercus spp.* in the broadleaf zone. Moreover, silvicultural practices such as pruning encouraged leaf production by the trees. As a result, *sokshings* are highly productive leaf litter producing plots under the complete and mutually recognized ownership of one household or one community.

Institutions to resolve *sokshing*-related conflicts, although loose and informal, generally rested on the principal of face-to-face confrontation, with resolution based on utilization of strong social networks (Dorji, 2003; Dorji *et al.*, 2003). Because most households had a *sokshing*, we never encountered an individual who remembered or had heard of a *sokshing* conflict occurring, so in fact conflict-resolution institutions as reported to us may have included an element of *ad hoc* logic on the part of the respondents. Nevertheless, ownership rights were clearly recognized and respected by all members of the community.

Community *sokshings*, although less prevalent than individual *sokshings*, exhibit a wide array of institutions. Some villages have collective *sokshings* without any specified rules or norms and people simply go and collect leaf litter from the *sokshing* just as they would from non-*sokshing* natural forests. However, in most cases, *sokshing* rules are well defined, long-standing and passed down through generations as customary norms. For example, institutions can define the time and amount of litter to be collected by the community. Such is the case when a village celebrates 'ri tangni', which means 'releasing or opening the forest'. *Ri tangni* happens every year on a date determined by the villagers and is the only time in the year when all villagers have access to the forest. Access during *ri tangni* is unrestricted, so each household hires as many laborers as possible to maximize the leaf litter collection.

As a result of widely-recognized tenurial institutions combined with highly-evolved management systems, *sokshings* are keystones to the subsistence livelihoods of rural Bhutanese. When the appropriate indicators of management 'success' are used, *sokshings* exhibit clear signs of being well managed and appropriate for the purposes they are intended (Dorji, 2003).

Thus, forest-related institutions in Bhutan evolved in two manners. First, the institution of village forest boundaries evolved as a result of the external stress applied by the rising religio-political elite, which turned offerings of respect into a tax that exploited the farm–forest linkage. Boundaries evolved as an adaptation of local communities to more efficiently fulfill their imposed obligations to the rising state structure. Second, the forest management institutions evolved in response to the need for collective efforts to maintain and protect local forests for subsistence. We suggest that in the face of optimal foraging, ancient institutions such as *reesup, meesup, chusup* and *sokshings* may have evolved within the context of the ancient, pre-Zhabdrung agrarian society where local institutions would provide a framework for local forest use. It should be noted that some of the forest-related institutions are based on religious values and do not hold major significance for the conservation or appropriation of products from the forest.

In both boundary and forest management institutional setups, we are confident in concluding that the evolution and maintenance of institutional arrangements was greatly facilitated by the high levels of social capital exhibited by the close-knit communities of rural Bhutan (Dorji, 2003; Dorji *et al.*, 2003). Agreements across communities about boundaries and agreements within communities about *sokshings* have evolved over time in rural areas as a result of long-term negotiations, understanding and networking.

SOCIO-POLITICAL DEVELOPMENT AND FOREST INSTITUTIONS AFTER 1950

Bhutan's central government views forest as a national, cultural and environmental endowment. In pursuit of both utilization and conservation (a concept that is now called the 'Middle Path' of development), a forestry unit was created in 1952 under the Ministry of Trade and Industry. It was later upgraded to a department in 1961. With the start of the government's five year development plan in 1961, the planning process for national-level forest management in Bhutan also began. The initial placement of the forest department under the Ministry of Trade and Industry seemed to suggest that it was established with a commercial objective. However, a social forestry program was initiated simultaneously with the logging program, suggesting a balanced approach to forestry from the start. Logging activities were commercialized in 1984 under the Bhutan Logging Corporation (now Forest Development Corporation) of the Ministry of Agriculture. Later, the Forestry Department was transferred to the Ministry of Agriculture under which the Department grew into its present form. Currently known as the Department of Forestry Services (DoFS), the primary goal of the Department is the conservation of the environment and sustainable utilization of forestry resources. The principle objective is to ensure conservation of the environment, and second, to focus on the derivation of economic benefits from the forest through sustainable management. The DoFS with its line agencies achieves this through protection, extension/out-reach, management activities and *in situ* conservation activities.[2]

Several other governmental and non-governmental agencies were formed since the 1950s which have influence on forest-related policies. The principle policy-forming agency is the Ministry of Agriculture, within which the DoFS resides. Other governmental, non-governmental and international agencies have a significant influence on policy, either through policy formulation or conservation programs that aim to inform policy. Ultimately, however, the Ministry of Agriculture is the umbrella organization responsible for forestry policy and the DoFS under this ministry is the main implementing agency.

Three main policy trends were enacted since the 1950s that have influenced the people–forest interactions in Bhutan: (*a*) nationalization of forests; (*b*) formal definition of forests and the requirement of *sokshing* registration; and (*c*) land grant (*kidu*) formalization.

Nationalization of forests occurred in 1969 through the Bhutan Forest Act. This Act, much like Nepal's Forest Nationalization Act of 1957, expressly designated all forests outside of private tenure to be 'government reserve' forest and under the purview and management authority of the central government. Thus, all forests—including *sokshings*—immediately became *de jure* government forests and villagers no longer enjoyed unfettered and unregulated access to those resources (Dorji *et al.*, 2006). However, as will be discussed later, certain use rights were given over registered *sokshings*.

The Forest and Nature Conservation Act (1995) further delineated users' rights and requirements to government reserve forests. This Act requires local people to obtain a permit from the Forest Department to extract products from the forest. In recognition of the dependence of rural communities on forest products, the rules under this Act provide certain leverage to the rural populations in appropriating non timber resources for subsistence needs (Ministry of Agriculture, 2000). However, fuelwood or timber requirements are strictly regulated through the District Forestry Extension Officer and the territorial divisions of the Forest Department. In addition to requiring a permit to be secured for extraction of some forest products, the national government also levies a fee for those permits. Although the fee began as a nominal amount, it was revised upward according to the Forest and Nature Conservation Rules of 2000. This represents a high cost of compliance with new government policy, and it has been shown that such high cost resulted in user non-compliance in non-*sokshing* forests (Dorji *et al.*, 2006). Moreover, the imposition of heavy regulations and high costs served as a disincentive for the formation or maintenance of local institutions.

Another result of forest nationalization was that it extended to *sokshings* and, therefore, immediately changed the property rights regime over those important subsistence forest plots. Rather than full ownership, people with *sokshings* saw their property rights reduced to appropriation, *sensu* Schlager and Ostrom (1992) (Dorji *et al.*, 2006). This occurred because the right to alienation of that good (the *sokshing*) was denied to the appropriator by the government. While in practice this may be seen as a minor change since most people never relinquished their *sokshing* to another family, this change has resulted in contemporary changes in some people's behavior towards *sokshing*.

For example, people may modify their behavior towards *sokshings* if the government seeks to reclaim it from the household, which can legally occur under the 1969 Forest Act. This is a rather rare case, but it has occurred when the government has sought to expand existing government projects, or initiate a new project that will infringe on an existing *sokshing*. The government's reclamation of the *sokshing* has led in some cases to immediate short-term consumptive behaviors by appropriators. In one village, for example, the government reclaimed a *sokshing* in order to expand the boundaries of the village school. Confronted with the sudden loss of tenure, the *sokshing* appropriator immediately cut 14 trees in an attempt to glean timber benefits before losing the land. This behavioral change came largely from the lack of understanding about the governmental provisions; appropriators can in fact apply for a new *sokshing* if the current *sokshing* is reclaimed by the government. However, most of the village respondents were not aware of this provision.

The government countered the loss of alienation rights by passing legislation that formally recognized the existence of locally managed *sokshings*. With the formalization of land registration after the first National Assembly of 1953, *sokshings* were registered as part of a household or community's legal land register, indicating the legal recognition of people's utilization of a *sokshing* within the government managed forest. However, the Bhutan Forest Act of 1969 and corresponding clauses in the Land Act of 1978 introduced changes to this recognition.

The Land Act of 1978 provided a definition of *sokshing* that established certain use rights that were buttressed by legal policy. The Land Act defined *sokshing* as 'forest to be used as a source of leaf litter and fodder, [whereas] the owner has no right over the standing trees and land over which the *sokshing* is established' (Land Act 1978 as quoted by Wangchuk, 2001). While the traditional local institutions defining boundaries of *sokshing* were therefore legally recognized by the government, the nationalization ultimately restricted individual liberties regarding tree cutting. This restrictive policy has been reiterated in subsequent policies. Since the Forest Act of 1969 was written, there has been long-standing conflict between local people and the government, where citizens have been continuously seeking the re-establishment of full management rights (Pain and Pema, 2002).

The third major policy influencing people–forest relationships was the land *kidu* policy. Land *kidu* is a land grant from the King of Bhutan to needy families who directly apply to him for agricultural land. Through the office of one of the secretaries to His Majesty the King, the family or individual approaches His Majesty with an application that states his/her need and justifications for the *kidu*. An investigation or verification process is dispatched to the district and relevant agencies through the secretary's office. Based on the reports, the person may be granted the *kidu*. Because of the high priority of Bhutan's forest conservation policy, the government is reluctant to allocate forest land as a *kidu*. However, under certain circumstances, forest lands (such as registered *sokshings*) are also granted.

During recent years some people in urban settings have begun to value *sokshings* for their potential future commercial value rather than their current subsistence value. In urban and semi-urban areas, land is becoming a premium commodity, so a new strategy has evolved to exploit the land *kidu* system. One strategy to acquire new land has been to seek a *kidu* to convert a registered *sokshing* to another private land use. If a *sokshing* has no trees or is highly degraded, then it is available for conversion to agriculture through the land *kidu*. Therefore, a person with new agricultural land needs may cease rendering care and protection to the *sokshing* if it is believed that the land could be used for an alternative use. The *sokshing* proprietor would not actively cut trees in a *sokshing*, which would be clearly illegal and easily enforceable. Rather, the proprietor may initiate practices to accelerate secondary processes of degradation. In extreme cases, individuals may attempt to degrade the *sokshing* by way of setting fires or preventing regeneration, with the ultimate objective of obtaining rights to convert a *kidu*. Thus, *sokshings* may in some cases be seen as a 'back-up' resource for the future endeavors, rather than for the original subsistence purpose. Usually, the *kidu* allows a family to gain full ownership of a parcel of land and subsequently convert that area into agricultural use.

The modification of people's behavior towards *sokshings* has resulted from a loss of property rights through forest nationalization policy and increased economic opportunities for agricultural products or alternative land uses. However, the cases above are presently the exception rather than the rule. Very few instances of village–government conflict have been reported (although under-reporting may be occurring) and exploitation of land *kidu* loopholes seems to be restricted to areas near larger towns (e.g., Paro and Thimpu) where land pressure is higher and alternative land uses are more lucrative. It is important to be aware of the potential negative adaptations to emerging policy so that solutions may be designed at both the policy and the implementation levels.

On the other hand, the clear recognition of *sokshings* by the government as a legal and legitimate indigenous land use strategy in several policies since 1953 has measurably strengthened this form of property and allowed for local solutions to conflicts. For example, most conflict resolutions on *sokshings* begin informally at the local level and rely on local elders and leaders who work towards negotiation as a conflict-resolution approach. Traditional information and skills are employed to recognize proprietary rights over *sokshings*. Formal processes may become inevitable at times, but when that happens the courts rely on local information. The district level judicial court, which is the arena for formalized conflict resolution, recognizes and places a high level of importance on local institutional arrangements over *sokshings*. During conflicts regarding *sokshings*, the district courts seek local information by referring to internal agreements or by seeking explanations on village norms, traditions and culture. This often forms the basis of formalized judicial decisions. Therefore, rural villagers can enjoy predictable and secure rights over leaf litter and fuelwood through *sokshing* management with the support of the local government. This serves to countermand at least some of the tenure insecurity created by nationalization policy.

Thus, communities have not had to make major or extensive adaptations to the policy initiatives of the government since 1950. Although we have shown that indeed rural Bhutanese communities are flexible and adaptive when stresses are placed on existing institutional arrangements or the community in general (if no institutional arrangements exist), our analysis suggests that the policies of Bhutan's national government have succeeded in some fashion at maintaining institutional arrangements of rural Bhutanese society.

DISCUSSION AND CONCLUSIONS

This chapter has explored the relationship between the religio-political history of Bhutan, the policy initiatives of the centralized governments and the people–forest relationship over time. Through this analysis, we hypothesized that ancient local, community-based institutional arrangements evolved in one instance as a result of government's rise and early taxation policy, but in other cases as a result of institutional arrangements (forest boundaries) that ensured equitable distribution of benefits in managed forests near villages. In recent times, only minor modifications of people's behavior—not local institutions—have been documented as a result of the continuing development of Bhutan's central government. We have provided evidence that the low incidence of behavioral shift is due to the national government's clear recognition of the keystone role that *sokshings* play in the daily lives of rural Bhutanese society in spite of (*a*) policy that nationalizes forests and rescinds some traditional property rights and (*b*) land *kidu* policy that exposes *sokshings* to neglect as alternative land uses become more profitable in urban and semi-urban areas. This recognition by the government has allowed local solutions to be implemented within the larger policy umbrella of the national government.

But what about the future? Will it be possible to maintain the close and strong linkages between people and forests as Bhutan develops both politically and economically? Given the fact that the vast majority of people in Bhutan live in rural areas and are highly dependent upon forest products for their livelihoods, our analysis must suggest how these institutions can be supported by the central government. Moreover, given the fact that the array of forest-related institutions is small, adaptations to future policy may require the emergence of new institutions, rather than the modification of existing ones. Thus, policy makers should protect the inherent factors that maintain the potential for community-level collective action in the future.

The Government of Bhutan has declared its intention to develop according to the 'Middle Path' approach. This development philosophy rests on the idea that development should proceed in a controlled fashion that allows for maximum benefits to society while minimizing negative impacts. Laissez-faire development, while potentially bringing rapid economic growth, would likely be highly detrimental to the Bhutanese religion, culture, society, and livelihoods of farming communities. Remaining closed to the outside world is also untenable, as it would not allow for the society to take advantages of many beneficial opportunities offered internationally; moreover, technologies are already entering into Bhutanese society, so directed development seems to be the most appropriate response. Therefore, the Middle Path of development in Bhutan is an attempt to develop many sectors of society while maintaining key linkages with traditional lifestyles exhibited by the majority of society. When the Middle Path approach is viewed in conjunction with the 1995 policy that requires at least 60 percent of Bhutan to remain forested in perpetuity, it is clear that the maintenance of a strong people–forest relationship, which implicitly requires national support of local institutional arrangements, should be of primary importance to the policy-making body of Bhutan.

With this in mind, we present three central conclusions designed to facilitate proactive and mitigatory thinking on the part of policy makers, academics and development agencies.

1. **Maintaining social capital in rural Bhutan is a fulcrum of institutional strength and flexibility.**
   Local communities have shown an ability to adapt to early efforts to centralize power by the religio-political elite and craft relevant forest-related institutions apart from those efforts. Our thesis is that the institutional flexibility exhibited by communities is the result of low transaction costs derived from a high degree of social capital. Rural Bhutanese communities evolving and developing in relative isolation supported a high degree of familiarity, reciprocal trust and collective action among village members, a characteristic that persists to the present day.

   Development of Bhutan society can be seen as both a benefit to households as well as a potential threat to traditional village characteristics, particularly people–people and people–forest relationships. In terms of social capital and institutional flexibility, policy and development agencies should recognize that initiatives leading to a decline in social capital and/or an increase in transaction costs in rural areas could be detrimental to the historical flexibility exhibited in Bhutanese villages. There are several ways in which social capital may decrease, leading to a concomitant increase in transaction costs and loss of institutional flexibility. These include rural-to-urban migration, a reduction in the dependency of community members on collective or cooperative management, a reduction of community dependence on forests and agriculture for livelihoods and an increase in social conflict within villages (or, similarly, a reduction in reciprocal trust). Social conflict could arise as a result of many factors, but in particular we realize that a further reduction of tenure over forests and forest products could lead to an increase in social tensions among households trying to secure limited resources for livelihoods. Thus, the objective of this conclusion is to bring to the forefront a possible outcome of urbanization and loss of traditional village social networks. It is therefore recommended to duly consider the linkage between social capital and the ability to maintain robust and flexible forest-related institutions.

The Bhutanese government should provide forest management rights to communities, which will establish and strengthen incentives for long-term sustainable forest management and protection, and maintain social interactions and social capital. This can be achieved by activities to promote the exercising of the community forestry rights as provided in the 1995 Forest and Nature Conservation Act, and 2003 Forest and Nature Conservation Rules.

Finally, an improvement in basic services to rural communities could serve as a mechanism to reduce rural–urban migration rates. Determining what services rural communities want or need is a challenging task and requires a significant bottom-up extension effort. Indeed, the government has already achieved an extraordinary goal with its bilateral international partnerships, which have built clean water facilities, educational facilities and health facilities in all corners of the country. However, with the inevitable development of the country, the interest to migrate to city centers will likely increase, particularly in younger generations. Therefore, new governmental services designed to promote stable rural or semi-rural livelihoods could be pursued.

2. **Nationalization of non-*sokshing* forests may be leading to non-compliant behavior.**
Much of this chapter discussed the importance of the fact that the state policy recognizes the history, importance and

institutions governing *sokshing* forests. However, the vast majority of Bhutan's forest is outside of *sokshings*. In this chapter, as well as in other papers (e.g., Dorji *et al.*, 2006) it has been argued that the contemporary nationalization policy imposed restrictions that are costly to comply with. Non-compliant behavior in non-*sokshing* forest does occur in the form of illegally felled trees. The challenge is not to try and prevent people from cutting trees, which is allowed even today with a permit, but to craft policy that allows local institutions to be built so that protection and responsible management is endorsed by the users, rather than the Forest Department.

One option for non-*sokshing* forest conservation is to strengthen the emerging community-based forest management strategy, through which local needs such as timber and non-timber forest products could be met through community institutions and mechanisms of enforcing access, withdrawal, management, exclusion and alienation rights. In Nepal, the government learned through bitter experience that the central government was not capable of maintaining all forests (Gautam *et al.*, 2004). People dependent on the resource must be incorporated into forest management and conservation strategies, even if the forest is state forest. Moreover, relinquishing management rights of at least part of the of non-*sokshing* forests to communities would strengthen their responsibility and long-term interests towards sustainable forest management and conservation, possibly leading to improved management.

3. *Sokshings* **need further protection.**
   We have shown that although the nationalization policy produced a disincentive towards long-term sustainable forest governance by communities, the government also crafted a policy that allowed households to hold proprietary rights over traditional *sokshings*. Moreover, the judicial system and *dzongkhag* administrations informally recognize and respect local arrangements over *sokshings* in their deliberations. Thus, the local recognition of traditional *sokshing* arrangements, as well as a progressive national policy maintaining most use

rights has been a crucial element of maintaining institutional and management stability towards forests.

However, there is no policy that requires local governments to incorporate local institutions in judicial decisions or conflict resolution. This arrangement by the local judicial system is a courteous measure afforded to the local communities by the local administration. The fact that deferring to local community arrangements increases the fairness and acceptance of decisions by local people does not guarantee that this informal institution between local government and rural communities will continue.

Therefore, it would be advisable for policy makers in Bhutan to consider drafting a policy that fully recognizes local institutional arrangements that can be incorporated into the local governance structures of the national government. Such a measure would legitimize the existence of local institutional arrangements in terms of their capacity to manage forests and resolve conflicts. Moreover, it would provide greater security to rural communities through the explicit recognition of local institutions.

As long as the *sokshings* remain relevant to the agricultural livelihoods of farmers, the present policy should explicitly support long-term local management. Maintaining the relevance of *sokshings* can be accomplished by encouraging organic farming systems and discouraging use of fertilizers and pesticides. This would help maintain the strong linkage between *sokshing* management and agricultural productivity, helping to keep the *sokshing* as an important component of Bhutanese rural life.

However, in developing areas where alternative land uses of *sokshings* may lead to negligent behavior towards *sokshings* and attempts to exploit land *kidu* loopholes, protection over the forest in *sokshings* must be strengthened. This can be done by (*a*) initiating policy reforms under which a *sokshing* forest should be reverted to closed canopy natural forest if the *sokshing* is degraded, rather than allow it to be considered for *kidu*, (*b*) mapping the boundaries of *sokshing* in the national or local register and (*c*) increasing the rigor with which land *kidu* grants are evaluated, ensuring that the land under application is not a *sokshing*.

ACKNOWLEDGMENTS

This chapter is an extension of research conducted by Lam Dorji, supported by a grant to the Asian Institute of Technology from the Austrian government. Clark C. Gibson, William R. Burch, Jnr and Ambika P. Gautam made very insightful comments to earlier versions of this chapter.

NOTES

1. *Dzong*: a fortress that serves as both the administrative center and the residence of the monks for a district.
2. Protection: Protection against encroachment and illegal felling, protection against fire hazards, effective surveillance and preventive measures against insect and disease epidemics. Extension: activities to create awareness about fire hazards; afforestation programs; protection from encroachment in *sokshing* and *tsamdrog*; management of community and private forests; allocation of dry wood and sanctioning of subsidized timber for rural house construction. Management: to conserve and manage forestry resources on a sustainable basis for local as well as commercial consumption by harvesting based on the principle of scientific management. *In situ* conservation: establishment of protected areas to conserve the unique biodiversity and ecosystems of the various ecozones in the country.

REFERENCES

Allison, E. (2002). *The Dharma, Deities, and La Dam: An Exploratory Study of the Role of Religion in Environmental Conservation in Bhutan*. Dissertation. Yale University, School of Forestry and Environmental Studies.

Das, N. (1974). *The Dragon Country: The General History of Bhutan*. New Delhi: Orient Longman.

Dorji, C.T. (1995). *A Political and Religious History of Bhutan*. Delhi: Prominent Publishers.

Dorji, L. (2003). *Assessing the Evolution, Status, and Future Implications of Forest Resources Management in the Inner Himalayas of the Kingdom of Bhutan*. Doctoral dissertation. Asian Institute of Technology, Bangkok.

Dorji, L. and Webb, E.L. (2003). 'Evolution of Political Economy and Forest Management in Bhutan'. Paper presented at the conference on Politics of the Commons: Articulating Development and Strengthening Local Practices. Chiang Mai, July 11–14.

Dorji, L., Webb, E.L., and Shivakoti, G. (2003). 'Can a Nationalized Forest Management System Uphold Local Institutions? A Case of Leaf Litter Forest (*Sokshing*) Management in Bhutan'. *Asian Studies Review*, 27(3), 341–359.

————. (2006). 'Property Rights, Incentives and Forest Management in Bhutan'. *Environmental Conservation*, 33(2), 141–147.

Education Department, Royal Government of Bhutan. (1997). *A History of Bhutan, Provisional Edition: Coursebook for Class X*. Thimphu: Curriculum and Professional Support Section, Education Department.

Gautam, A.P., Shivakoti, G.P., and Webb, E.L. (2004). 'A Review of Forest Policies, Institutions, and Changes in the Resource Condition in Nepal'. *International Forestry Review*, 6(2), 136–148.

Gibson, C.C. (1999). 'Forest Resources: Institutions for Local Governance in Guatemala'. In J. Burger, E. Ostrom, R.B. Norgaard, D. Polansky, and B.D. Goldstein (eds), *Protecting the Commons* (pp. 71–89). Washington, DC: Island Press.

Hasrat, B. (1980). *History of Bhutan: Land of the Peaceful Dragon*. Thimpu: Royal Government of Bhutan, Education Department.

Ministry of Agriculture, Royal Government of Bhutan. (2000). *Forest and Nature Conservation Rules of Bhutan 2000*. 2 vols. Thimphu: Ministry of Agriculture.

Ohsawa, M. (ed.). (1991). *Life Zone Ecology of the Bhutan Himalaya*. Chiba University, Laboratory of Ecology.

Pain, A. and Pema, D. (2002). 'Continuing Customs of Negotiation and Contestation in Bhutan'. *Journal of Bhutan Studies*, 2, 219–227.

Planning Commission, Royal Government of Bhutan. (2002). *Ninth Plan Main Document (2002–2007)*. Thimphu: Planning Commission.

Pommaret, F. (2000). 'Ancient Trade Partners: Bhutan, Cooch Bihar and Assam (17th–19th Centuries)'. *Journal of Bhutan Studies*, 2(1), 30–53.

Schlager, E. and Ostrom, E. (1992). 'Property Rights Regimes and Natural Resources: A Conceptual Analysis'. *Land Economics*, 68(3), 249–262.

Schweik, C. (2000). 'Optimal Foraging, Institutions, and Forest Change: A Case from Nepal'. In C.C. Gibson, M.A. McKean, and E. Ostrom (eds). *People and Forests: Communities Institutions, and Governance* (pp. 99–134). Cambridge: The MIT Press.

Sinha, A.C. (1991). *Bhutan: Ethnic Identity and National Dilemma*. New Delhi: Reliance Publishing House.

Ura, K. (1995). *The Hero with a Thousand Eyes—A Historical Novel*. Thimpu: Center for Bhutan Studies.

Wangchuk, S. (2001). 'Local Resource Management Institutions: A Case Study on Sokshing Management'. *Journal of Bhutan Studies*, 3(1), 1–47.

4 | Integrating Informal with Formal Forest Management Institutions for Sustainable Collective Action in India

RUCHA GHATE and DEEPSHIKHA MEHRA

Introduction

Since a decade and a half of policy change in India, 'participatory' forestry has been gradually maturing. With three subsequent government resolutions,[1] each one more liberal than the earlier, and some evidence of successful implementation of participatory efforts, indications are that finally co-management of forestry resources is becoming acceptable at various levels of governance. Although 'participatory' forestry is a modern concept, 'community' management has a long history in the Indian context, which developed social laws and norms that made sure that extraction by human beings did not hinder the natural growth of the forest. Yet, the first policy statement of British India in 1894 considered forest communities as 'intruders' and 'aliens' over the state property and forest lands were transformed into mere sources of revenue for the British Government (Rangarajan, 1996), even at the expense of forest area allocated to villagers' use.

After India's independence in 1947, forest dwellers and the social workers working among them expected a basic restructuring of the forest policy combined with re-recognition of tribal rights over forests in the new forest policy of the Indian Government (Ghate, 1992). Yet the government of free India adopted all the basic principles laid down by the British. Prolonged protests by activists, academia, politicians and communities at large, and realization of its own inability to maintain desired level of forest cover single-handedly through the 'policing forest department', compelled the government to adopt a more accommodative approach in the form of the Forest Policy of 1988 and its Joint Forest Management (JFM) program in 1990. Fiscal crisis, structural adjustment, economic liberalization policies, pressure from donor agencies for greater accountability and transparency, the recognition of the failure of past approaches by state agencies and the demonstration effect of successful pilot efforts by non-governmental organizations (NGOs) or other government agencies in other sectors (Thompson, 1995) were other important reasons for the government's shift from a century-old centralized management system to decentralized participatory management. Under JFM, partnership between the Forest Department (FD) and local communities is based on joint management objectives in which communities are expected to share both responsibilities and benefits that would be generated. Responsibilities involve helping the FD to manage the forest and in turn the benefits they get are usufruct rights and sharing of revenue from the sale of timber. In a way, it is partially promoting common-property regimes as a means of restraining degraded forests and building up a community resource base (McKean, 2000).

Some communities, however, did not wait for the government to bring in necessary policy changes and had started protecting forests within their village jurisdiction prior to policy initiatives. Almost two decades before the advent of JFM, community-initiated and NGO-promoted collective-action-based resource management had emerged intermittently throughout the country. Several studies indicate the existence of such communities who had consciously maintained and managed the forests within their village boundaries at their own initiative in India in the distant as well as the recent past (Gadgil and Berkes, 1991; Gadgil and Guha, 1992; Gadgil and Subhash Chandra, 1992; Ghate, 2000, 2004; Guha, 1983; Roy Burman, 1985; Sarin, 1996). Many informal networks of NGOs also sprouted in the 1980s in order to facilitate the processes of decentralized management with or without government support. Thus, there are three distinct ways in which collective-action-based institutional arrangements have emerged in India in the past three decades: community-initiated, NGO-promoted and state-sponsored JFM.

Historical and contemporary evidence suggests that resource users can often create institutional arrangements and management regimes that help them allocate benefits equitably, over long time periods and with only limited efficiency losses (McKean, 1992;

Ostrom, 1992a, 1992b; Agrawal, 1999). Investigating the question of why some communities organize themselves to solve the problems of institutional supply, while others in similar circumstances do not, has led to an enormous literature on issues and factors that may be conducive to collective action (Agrawal, 2002). Communities may organize themselves for collective efforts to manage resources that are scarce as well as salient for the community (Gibson and Becker, 1999). In the Indian context, despite a hostile atmosphere, some communities have opted for self-governance of forests to meet their sustenance needs. This is mainly because forest is the 'lifeline' for the millions of biomass-dependent Indians living in rural areas in general and those living in and around forests in particular. Realizing the fact that they themselves are the primary sufferers of forest degradation, these communities have protected forests within their village boundaries by restricting use within the community. Some attempts have been informal and based on mutual understanding alone, while others have been much more explicit with a formulated rule structure regarding inclusion or exclusion of participants, obligations of participants, appropriation strategies, monitoring, and sanctions and conflict resolving mechanisms.

Similarly, NGOs have encouraged communities to manage their own resources through extension activities. In India, NGOs have gained credibility in the forestry sector mainly because of the unpopular and restrictive role of the FD. Even in the initial stages of the participatory approach adopted by the FD, local communities found it hard to believe that the department was willing to accept them as partners in forest management. Under these circumstances, in many places NGOs have played a crucial role of facilitator in bridging the gap (Varalakshmi and Kaul, 1999). In the process of devolution in India, one can visualize NGO participation in fostering 'community-based forest management', where they will help in building community stakes in common property resources (CPRs), rebuilding social capital to facilitate CPR management, and promoting bottom-up approaches to natural resource management strategies (Jodha, 2002). The Government of India too has recognized the positive role that NGOs can play. The recognition has come in the form of mandatory involvement of NGO representative in the JFM committee (via its circular no. 6.21/89-FP-dt.1.6.1990). Extending the role further, NGOs are now being increasingly involved right from the first stage of preparation of micro-plan at village level, to monitoring and evaluation in states like Andhra Pradesh.

Evolutions of these diverse approaches to CPR conservation—all with the objective of managing forests through collective action—have common objectives of strengthening the ecological security and meeting subsistence biomass needs of the local people. However, they have different implementation strategies and mechanisms, and therefore exhibit different strengths and weaknesses. If the role played by factors that ensure sustainability of collective action in each of these can be understood, it would help in modifying forest policy so that future forest management projects can develop an appropriate implementation strategy to best meet the contextual circumstances.

This chapter presents three case studies representing the three institutional arrangements (community-initiated, JFM-initiated, and NGO-promoted) to understand which attributes have contributed to collective action in central India. We have differentiated between 'participation' and 'collective action'. Under JFM, the 'participatory management' proposed by the government is not necessarily based on collective action. It could be imposed on a community or remain just on paper (Lele, 1998). Without conviction and commitment, 'participation' in such programs could be devoid of real interest on behalf of FD as well as the communities. On the other hand, community-based autonomous collective efforts suffer the likelihood of non-sustainability in the absence of legitimate sanctions and provisions (Ghate, 2000; Lele, 1998; Sarin, 1995; Sundar, 2000; Sundar et al., 2001).

To evaluate the institutional variations among the three case studies, we use Institutional Analysis and Development (IAD) framework. The IAD analytical framework is coupled with multi-criteria analysis (MCA) to compare the collective action attributes across the three cases.

STUDY SITES

This study was undertaken using three representative villages from Gadchiroli district of Maharashtra State, India. Despite the fact that Gadchiroli holds the major proportion of forest in the state, the per capita income of Gadchiroli district is 48 percent less than the state average. The total geographical area of the district is 14,412 sq km, i.e., 4.7 percent of the state. Approximately 61.3 percent of the state forest revenue comes from this district. Only 0.99 percent of the state's population resides in this district, 38 percent of which is tribal and highly dependent on forest for sustenance (for location of study sites see Map 4.1).

MAP 4.1
Map of India

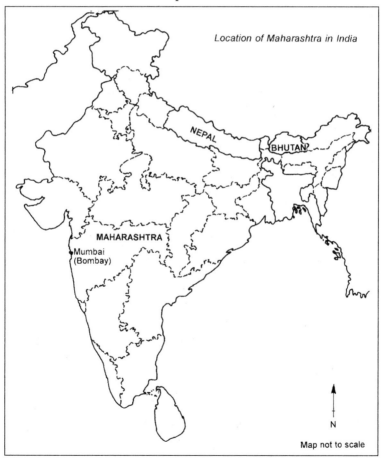

Location of Maharashtra in India

Map not to scale

Methods

Collective Action Sustainability Indicators

Among the writings of many scholars, Robert Wade, Elinor Ostrom, Jean-Marie Baland and Jean-Philippe Plateau are significant because of their analyses of large number of sustainable management efforts and identification of factors conducive to CPR management. Wade's (1994) work examined how corporate institutions arise in villages, what accounts for their success in resolving common dilemmas and why they may be successful in managing the commons. According to Wade, small group size, clear boundaries, and ease in monitoring and enforcement are some of the 14 conditions that determine the effectiveness of rules. On the basis of 14 case studies, Ostrom enumerated eight design principles that are 'essential elements or conditions that help to account for the success of these institutions in sustaining the CPRs and gaining the compliance of generation after generation of appropriators to the rules in use' (1990: 90). They are: clearly defined boundaries, congruence, collective-choice arrangements, monitoring, conflict-resolving mechanisms, minimal recognition of rights to organize and nested enterprises. Baland and Platteau (1996: 175) reviewed studies on commons and found that small size of a user group, proximity to the resource, homogeneity among group members, effective enforcement mechanism and past experience of co-operation were some factors necessary to achieve sustainable co-operation. Characteristics of the resource as substantive factors affecting the effectiveness of institutions governing the commons are also varied. Volatility and unpredictability in resource flow (Wade, 1988), mobility of the resource (Naughton-Treves and Sanderson, 1995) and stationarity and storage (Blomiquist et al., 1994) are some of the aspects in addition to the 'attribute of the resource' and 'attributes of appropriators' (Ostrom, 1999). The roles of technology, population pressures, property rights regimes and heterogeneity are some of the variables studied by different scholars.

After review of literature on commons and collective action, the following variables were chosen as relevant and sufficiently indicative of 'sustainability' of collective action in the context of our study sites:

1. Equitable distribution of benefits.
2. An indigenously developed conflict resolution mechanism.
3. Preference for the future.
4. Existence and use of social capital.
5. Monitoring of resource use and sanctioning of rule breakers.
6. Coordination between formal and informal institutions.

With the help of these six parameters, a comparison was made between three institutional structures to find which institutional arrangements are conducive to sustainable collective action.

Data Collection

The data for the study were collected through two main methodologies. First, we used research instruments developed by the International Forestry Resources and Institutions (IFRI) research program. A set of 10 pre-structured questionnaire was filled in using rapid appraisal and traditional interview method. A subset of the total IFRI database for the study sites was used for the analysis here. Second, we conducted focused group discussions, team observation and key informant discussion.

Analysis of the data was undertaken within the IAD framework. The IAD framework identifies major types of structural variables that are present to some extent in all institutional arrangements, but whose values differ from one type of institutional arrangement to another (Ostrom, 1999). The IAD framework recognizes three levels of activities: operational, collective choice and constitutional level. Operational activities have been defined as day-to-day activities of forest users and others as to when, where and how to withdraw products or otherwise use the forest, how to improve the condition of the forest, monitor the action of others, impose sanctions and rewards, and/or exchange information. Collective-choice activities are the policy-making activities of users, user group officials and others about operational activities. The decision-making activities about who will make the rules have been defined as the constitutional-choice activities (Ostrom, 1998). For the purpose of this study, activities at constitutional level are the initiation of the JFM program and the issuance of government order and its guidelines as suggested in the 1988 Indian Forest Policy that has promoted participatory forest management. Collective-choice activities are the activities taken up by a group or an elected committee of a formal or informal forest association like the Forest Protection Committee (FPC). The operational activities are the activities carried out by the community as a whole to manage and protect the forest in the form of rules, sanctions, monitoring, etc. In normal course, once the government has decided on a program like JFM (constitutional level), the implementing agency, i.e., the FD selects villages and helps in formation of FPC (collective level), which is responsible for making working rules (operational level) for the whole community.

Multi-criteria Analysis (MCA)

Using relevant questions from IFRI questionnaire and through group discussions with the communities, numeric scores for each of the six qualitative attributes (multiple criteria) were determined for analyzing the most suitable institutional structure for the sustainability of collective action. We are aware of the fact that although MCA helps in adding varying qualitative attributes, it involves discriminatory judgment to be made by the researcher. MCA aggregates data on individual criterion to show overall performance of the options chosen. This method involves implicit and explicit aggregation of the performance of each option, attribute or variable to produce a performance matrix. With the help of a simple linear additive evaluation model, which combines option's values on the many criteria, one overall value is calculated. To ensure objectivity and to avoid individual bias, we made use of all the relevant questions from IFRI protocols, which are standardized question sets used by researchers across countries. Each group discussion with the communities was followed by discussions amongst the members of our research team constituting of economists, political scientists, sociologists and botanists to capture various perceptions before making any judgment on the performance of institutions.

Each of the six attributes were assigned a score from 0–100, based on the strength of that attribute (100 being strongest). Thus, the maximum any institutional structure (JFM, NGO or community-initiated system) could score from the combined six attributes was 600. Both the methods of data collection were given weightage according to the number and directness of the questions in each method to effectively identify the relative existence or absence of a particular attribute and its elements. The scores of the two methods were totalled to arrive at one score for each attribute in each institutional structure. Final scores of all variables/attributes for each institutional structure were aggregated to arrive at the final result depicting the performance of the institutional structures on the six parameters indicating sustainability of collective action.

RESULTS

The results of this research are presented in two main sections. First, we discuss the historical context of forest management in the three villages, as revealed through the interviews. Thereafter, we present the results of the MCA. The geographical, social, economic and demographic profiles of these case studies are given in Table 4.1.

Case Study 1: Village Deulgaon—
A Community-initiated Attempt

Salience and scarcity of its forest resource and the ill effects of degradation of forest on other natural resources prompted forest conservation in this village. Indiscriminate felling of trees by neighboring villagers was worrying the people of Deulgaon for a long time. Moreover, activities of contractors extracting valuable *tendu* (*Diospyros melanoxylon*) leaves were also adding to their concern. *Tendu* is found in abundance in the forest of Gadchiroli and its leaves in dry form are used for making a local style of cigarette called *bidi* (tobacco is rolled in these leaves). The practice is that the FD designates the job of *tendu* leaf collection to contractors by floating tenders and it is expected that local wage labor would be hired for the job. But in case of Deulgaon the contractors neither

TABLE 4.1

Profiles of Three Study Villages, Gadchiroli District, Maharashtra State, India

	Deulgaon (Community-initiated)	Ranwahi (NGO-promoted)	Markegaon (JFM Program)
Latitude	20°15'16.0' latitude	N 20°30'22.8' latitude	20°14'42.3' latitude
Longitude	80°1'41.4' EO longitude	80°21'37.7' EO longitude	80°19'59.6' EO longitude
Mean sea level	230 meters ASL	250 meters ASL	250 meters ASL
Location	18 km from Dhanora, the sub-district (taluka) of Gadchiroli district of Maharashtra	25 km from Kurkheda town, the sub-district of Gadchiroli district of Maharashtra	5 km from the sub-district center that is Dhanora in Gadchiroli district of Maharashtra
Geographical area	718.48 ha	924.43 ha	530.29 ha
Forest area	601.37 ha	641.71 ha	431.44 ha
Per capita forest	3.5 ha	2.4 ha	2.7 ha
Population	173	393	161
Number of households	33	81	32
Three main ethinc/ caste groups	70% Gond (tribals) 30% Kunbi (OBC)	96% Gond 1% Scheduled Caste 1% nomadic tribe	100% Gond
Languages spoken	Marathi and Gondi	Marathi and Gondi	Marathi and Gondi
Literacy	51%	62.84%	48%
Houses	Mud and brick with tiled or thatched roofs	Mud, brick and concrete houses with tiled roofs	Mud and brick with tiled or thatched roofs

Main occupation	Agriculture	Agriculture	Agriculture
Landed	33 households	62 households	30 households
Landholding (average)	2 acres	4 acres	4 acres
Crops grown	Paddy, *tur*, *lakhori* (pulse), *jawar*, *chana*, etc.	Paddy, *chana* and *tur*, *cilliy* (cash crop)	Paddy, *tur*, *mung*, *urad*, beans, *kurat*
Own crop consumed	8–9 months	8–9 months	8 months
Forest dependence	Fuelwood, fodder, timber, wildlife, minor forest products like *awala* (phyllanthus emblica), *hirda* (terminalia chebula), *moha*, *tendu* leaves and *char*	Fuelwood, fodder, timber, bushes, grasses, leaves (*tendu*), water, wildlife, fruits, vegetables, bamboo, *Moha* flower, gum, etc.	Fuelwood, fodder, timber, bushes, grasses, leaves (*tendu*), water, wildlife, agricultural implements, hunting gears, herbs to make pesticides for crops, storage utensils, kitchen implements, livestock sheds, furniture, toys, headgears for marriage purposes and other items like carved pillars made especially for marriages, grain crushing implements, etc.

employed locals for leaf extraction, nor did they leave any trees for the villagers to harvest leaves from.

The community members of Deulgaon remained mute spectators to these activities in the forest because they were not sure whether the forest was within their village boundary. This was because no land survey had taken place since 1922. Immediately after a land survey in 1988, the local Police *'patil'* (a person in the village nominated by the Police Department) and a local resident spoke to the community and built consensus to stall the activities of outsiders. It was in 1990, after many informal meetings, that the community decided to take steps to not only stop neighboring villagers from harvesting from Deulgaon forest, but to impose restrictions on themselves as well.

The villagers decided to protect the forest within their administrative boundary. It was decided unanimously that each household would harvest according to its genuine subsistence requirement and would not sell any forest product. Moreover, simple operational-level rules were formulated initially regarding quantity of forest products to be harvested, monitoring of compliance to rules, sanctioning of rule breakers and arbitration of dispute among local users. Monetary sanctions were introduced for felling of valuable trees like *tendu, moha* (*Madhuca longifolia*) and other trees such as gum yielding species. Most importantly, daytime patrolling by the community members was introduced. Two persons (both male and female members) from two households were sent on patrol on rotational basis throughout the year. All these activities were adopted without a formal association or governing body in Deulgaon. The informal efforts of the community continued in the form of 'protection' and 'self-restriction'. Natural regeneration was supported by protection alone, as they had no access to funding or technical know-how to artificially increase the stock and quality of regeneration.

In 1998, Deulgaon was given an offer by the FD to join the JFM program. A visit by the Range Forest Officer to the village generated interest within the community to consider joining JFM. After several internal community meetings discussing the pros and cons of joining JFM, a consensus was reached and the villagers decided to register under JFM. The expected benefits to the community included employment generation from plantation activities taken up by the department, 50 percent of the proceeds from the sale of timber harvested from the plantations, a share of fines collected from illegal harvesters when caught by the community and incentive money coming at the outset of JFM activities as a fund at the disposal of the community.

The same year a Forest Protection committee was set-up under JFM. In 2000, it was formally registered under the name of 'Samyukt Van Vyavasthapan Samiti' (Joint Forest Management Committee). A plantation on 85 hectares of forestland was established with the department's assistance, where species that the forest lacked or the villagers desired were planted. The community was also provided incentive money, which it used for the construction of a community hall.

At present, the formalized governance structure in Deulgaon is as per JFM regulations, but the spirit and the indigenously developed methods of functioning have remained as earlier. Following the procedure of institutional set-up under JFM, an executive committee is elected and a general body is formed. The executive body constitutes of seven men and three women and the general body includes one man and one woman from each household. Meetings of the forest association take place once per month and are generally well attended. The agenda of the meetings revolves around all forest-related activities, similar to the informal discussions that took place before the advent of JFM. Suggestions from all members are invited but unanimity on acceptance of these suggestions remains an important factor. For example, if any household requires more than its daily subsistence need of a forest product, such as need for fuelwood for a special occasion, a written request has to be submitted at the monthly meeting. Decision to accept or reject the request is then taken unanimously. Due to growing clarity of purpose over the years and strict implementation of the rules with monetary sanctions right from the beginning, compliance has remained high. A sliding scale penalty structure has been built wherein the fine increase is concomitant with the frequency of the infraction.

Although the community has continued with its own rule structure that has evolved over the years, it has also adopted some of the rules prescribed under JFM. For example, trees only of a certain minimum girth can be harvested, thus protecting smaller trees and ensuring sustainability. For fuelwood, only dead wood and fallen branches are to be collected. Sale of timber, fuelwood and fodder is not allowed. Since the procedure for framing of rules has remained same as earlier, almost everyone in the community is aware of these rules and find them clear to understand, flexible to the needs of the people, fair and legitimate.

In case of persistent non-compliance, the rules require that the offender be taken to the police, though not to the FD. Ever since the formation of the FPC, communication and coordination with the FD has not been very good. This is mainly because there is no cooperation from FD in sanctioning pilferers of forest products from neighboring villages. The community reported to us that instances have occurred when some poachers were caught by the community and taken to the local FD office with the seized products along with the equipment used by the poachers, but the department released the culprits along with the equipment. Despite such discouragement, the people of Deulgaon have continued with their efforts to protect their forest.

Case Study 2: Village Markegaon—
JFM-initiated Collective Action

For Markegaon, a small tribal village, access to forest and forest products has always been easy due to low population density and abundance of forest surrounding the village. Thus, the need for forest protection and restrictive use of forest products has never been a priority. However, one citizen of Markegaon became concerned that the forest quality could not be maintained with a constant population increase in the surrounding villages. Yet, even after two years of effort he could not convince the community to take up forest protection work and restrict self-use. It was only after the village was covered under JFM (constitutional level) and the incentives offered—a fund for the community and employment for plantation work in the village—that the community initiated protection through the formation of an FPC in 1997. In the first meeting of the FPC, the villagers decided to lay restrictions at the operational level, one on grazing (*Chara Bandi*) and the other on tree felling (*Kurhad Bandi*).

The forest association was formally registered in the year 2000. An executive committee of the association was formed. At the time of our survey there were eight men and three women elected members in this committee. The general body consists of one male and one female adult from each household. Under JFM, meetings of FPC are to be held once a month, but in Markegaon they typically take place once every three months. The attendance in those meetings is about 50 percent despite a community-accepted provision of a fine for those not attending two consecutive meetings.

Decisions in the meetings are normally taken regarding poaching of bamboo and thefts in the plantation areas. Suggestions are invited from members for improvements to be made in vigilance or in restrictive rules; although during our field visits no suggestions had been recorded from any member. Payment of fines also takes place during these meetings. Members of the association carry out voluntary protection activities, which involves three persons from three households by rotation for a 12-hour vigil. The forest association has a written statement of its mission and objectives, which is based on the Forest Policy of the Government of India, 1988.

JFM does not have any standard rules for governance that can be applied across villages. As per stipulations, the operative rules are to be made by the members of the forest association in the presence of a forest department official to ensure that the rules are in line with the objectives of JFM. Such rules were made in Markegaon gradually over a six-year period regarding harvesting of forest products for subsistence needs, a complete ban on harvesting by outsiders, restricting the sale of forest products and voluntary patrolling on rotational basis. However, due to lack of active support from the forest department in fixing of penalties or dealing with infractions, implementation of the rules is proving to be ineffective.

During one of our recent visits, it was found that the association is becoming more active and is formulating more self-restrictive rules without being prompted by the FD. The FPC of a neighboring village and a local NGO appear to be the motivating factors. The rules now include ban on cutting of new trees, especially valuable trees like *tendu*, *awala* and *moha*; restricting timber use by allowing only one pole per year per family for house construction and permission to collect only fallen wood and stems for fuel, with the quantity being restricted to one cartload per year. The penalty structure has improved as well.

Nevertheless, infractions to the rules take place as people collect more than the defined limit. Leniency in penalties is observed in cases where the offender(s) continue to be let off in the first couple of instances. This happens mainly because the community knows well that although they are protecting the forest, it belongs to the government. The FPC is aware that unless the FD backs the committee's decisions they have no legal standing. Indifference of the FD official, the Forest Guard who is the *ex officio* secretary of the FPC, has weakened the collective-level activities. Any representative of the FD rarely attends meetings of the forest association. As a result the community is not completely aware of the provisions of JFM and the department is not aware of the decisions taken by the association. The 'jointness' in day-to-day decision making is missing. This state-initiated collective action is progressing at a slow pace.

Despite these challenges, the villagers feel that registration under JFM has been beneficial to them, as without it they never would have started the protection work. It is due to JFM that the villagers have come to know the importance and techniques of stopping forest fires and have received funds for various developmental works.

Cast Study 3: Village Ranwahi—An NGO-initiated Effort

Ranwahi is the largest and the oldest village among the three case studies. Here, the seeds of forest protection were sown by a local NGO named Amhi Amchya Arogya Sathi (AAA). It began with a 'sakhi mela' (an all women get-together) that was organized in 1995 by one member of the AAA. Many women from nearby provinces came for the *mela*. Each woman representative was asked to share the positive and negative developments in her village. A woman representing the village of Ranwahi spoke of the problems that they had to face due to indiscriminate felling by timber contractors and neighboring communities. She was impressed by the experiences of other villages that had taken initiative in forest protection. After returning to the village, she narrated her experiences to some fellow villagers who then collectively decided to work towards convincing the community to take up forest protection. Simultaneously, the efforts by the NGO continued in this direction. Some time later, another member of AAA called a meeting of the community and spoke to the villagers about the need of forest protection, the program of JFM and its advantages. Convinced of the need for forest protection, the community reached a consensus and applied to the FD to be included in JFM, thereby ensuring constitutional backing to their activities. After receiving the application, the Deputy Conservator of Forest sent his deputy to hold a meeting with the people of Ranwahi and to get an indication of their commitment.

In the meantime, the community started protection work on its own. Protection was mainly designed against poachers of forest products from the neighboring villages. Ironically, while outsiders were prevented from harvesting from this forest, wasteful harvesting by the Ranwahi community continued. This situation remains so even today. Encouraged by the suggestions from the AAA, some villagers tried to estimate the usage of forest products by each household and found that extraction was way beyond the actual requirement. It was then decided by the community that this had to stop immediately and that the community members would collect only what was genuinely required. Subsequent discussions and decisions took place either during the 'gram sabha' (village meetings) that were held at regular intervals, or during informal meetings as and when needed.

Initially, only male members from each household could participate in the meetings. On the suggestion by AAA, women were also encouraged to participate. The community started 24-hour monitoring of the forest. These activities continued until 1998, when the FPC was informally set up under the JFM. In 2001 it was formally registered.

Under its formal set up, an executive committee and a general body of the association were formed with representation from different sections of the community. Since then, monthly meetings of all members are held and are attended by almost all the members of the association. In these meetings, normally the decisions about the extra requirements for forest products are made. Forest patrolling for monitoring of forest use by outsiders is taken very seriously, and if any irregularity is found, it is brought to the notice of the committee. Strategies to deal with the problem are also taken up for discussion. Conventionally, all decisions are taken unanimously. Conflicts within the group have decreased over the years and this may be due to leniency shown in imposing penalties.

The association carries out its activities with the help of all its members. In case of forest activities taken up by the FD, the members work on daily wages. Guarding of forests continues to be on voluntary basis, as was done prior to joining the JFM program. At the time of the research, the community was contemplating an arrangement wherein the FD would be assigning a lump sum amount for protection work, which would be distributed among the households through the association.

Other than protection, the association also sometimes undertakes activities such as determining who is authorized to harvest forest products, monitoring conformance to rules, sanctioning rule breakers, among others. It also looks into distribution of revenue earned through forest contracts amongst households in accordance with the work done.

To ensure smooth functioning of the forest-related activities, the association has formulated the rules under the guidance of AAA. Therefore, almost all members are aware of the rules and perceive them as fair and legitimate. The rules include a ban on felling of trees for fuelwood. In case of timber for construction of houses, 10 poles per year per household are permitted. Up to 50 poles can be harvested after permission is sought from the committee. Over and above this limit, poles have to be bought at the rate of Rs 5 per pole. In case of fodder, there is no limit fixed on the quantity that can be harvested and open grazing is generally practiced except for designated areas such as the 60-hectare plantation set up under JFM.

The members of the user group generally follow the rules, but infractions take place as fuelwood or timber is often collected in excess of the limit. For such infractions the provision is to pardon the offender on the first and second instances with a warning and expel the offender from the association on the third instance. However, the community has not faced this situation yet. Although the FD officials are not called to enforce penalties on the community members, whenever neighboring villagers are caught stealing from the Ranwahi forest they are taken to the range forest office where a fine is imposed and a certain percentage is shared with the association. This is indicative of the good relations that the community of Ranwahi has with the FD. Ranwahi also has the advantage of the constant presence and guidance from AAA through its volunteers. Along with the guidance from forest officials on forest governance and improvement techniques, the Ranwahi community benefits from income-generating activities such as forest nurseries with a buy-back guarantee from the department. With the help of the NGO, some 'study groups' on wildlife, agriculture, medicinal plants and trees are set up. These are indirectly helping the community members to realize the benefits available to them through forest conservation and sustainable management. As a result, the level of awareness regarding their rights is high.

PERFORMANCE OF THE THREE VILLAGES

In this section we present how the three villages have fared under the six selected parameters of sustainable collective action (Table 4.2).

Equitable Distribution of Benefits

Since the three villages began protecting their forests, forest produce has been used by the villagers only for subsistence and not for commercial use. The basic understanding among the villagers is that each household should get according to its subsistence need. Agriculture being the dominant occupation for the three rural communities, people's needs for forest products such as fuelwood, fodder, timber and non-timber forest products, such as fruits, roots and medicinal herbs, are similar across villages. Therefore, to understand the arrangement for distribution of benefits, whether equitable or not, we considered peoples' perceptions regarding benefit distribution under each institutional arrangement.

We could surmise from the discussion with the villagers in Deulgaon that there are adequate restrictions (i.e., appropriate rules along with their strict implementation, etc.) on the quantity of a forest product that could be harvested by any household. Deulgaon is the only village among the three that actually imposes

TABLE 4.2
Variables and Scores of Multi-criteria Analysis

Variables/Attributes Chosen to Analyze Sustainable Collective Action	Criterion for Higher Scoring	Total Scores Assigned	Weights/Scores to Each Method[1] of Data Collection		Total Scores for Community-initiated Village: Deulgaon	Total Scores for JFM-promoted Village: Makegaon	Total Scores for NGO-promoted Village: Ranwahi
			IFRI[2]	GD&O[3]			
Distribution of benefits	Equitability of distribution	100	40	60	80	48	70
Conflict-resolving mechanism	Indigenously-developed conflict-resolving mechanism	100	60	40	90	40	22
Preference for future	Lower discount rate	100	50	50	58	45	31
Social capital	Existence and use of social capital	100	40	60	68	25	32
Monitoring of resources use	Effective monitoring	100	60	40	77	37	54
Coordination between formal and informal institutions	Effective coordination	100	60	40	51	35	73
Total		600	310	290	424	230	315

Notes: [1] Criterion for assigning weights to a particular method under a particular variable = Number of questions covered plus directness and effectiveness of the questions to reflect the attributes/sustainability variable.
[2] International Forestry Resources and Institutions (IFRI) method.
[3] Group Discussions and Observations method.

a fine on breaking of any such rule. Since no one is allowed to collect more than what is required for household use, the community perceives that benefit distribution is equitable.

In Ranwahi, the community imposes restrictions in order to ensure equitable distribution of benefits. There is a provision for graduated sanctions for persistent infractions as well, but we found that they are not implemented seriously. Answers to questions about how rules are made, who participates in rule making and how people felt about the rules have revealed that some members of the community are somewhat dissatisfied with the implementation of the rules. This is mainly because, as mentioned by some community members, over harvesting by some—usually the more powerful—goes on unrestricted and these persons are always pardoned if caught.

In Markegaon, JFM has not address the issue of intra-community distribution of benefits. Rules in this regard are to be framed and implemented by the community members, including how to deal with infractions (which are supposed to be accomplished under the guidance of FD). Sharing of revenue from harvesting of timber is contemplated between the FD and the community as a whole. The MOU does not address intra-community differences. Thus, Markegaon has scored the lowest on equitable benefit sharing.

An Indigenously-developed Conflict-resolution Mechanism

Conflict resolution was explored through IFRI questions related to incidence of infractions, the nature of infractions, rules and punishments related to infractions and whether infractions have increased or decreased over time. Through these questions we inquired whether conflict-resolving mechanisms in the three case study villages were indigenous or provided by an outside agency.

Deulgaon is the only village that has an indigenously-developed conflict-resolving mechanism. In making rules as well as in dealing with infractions, Ranwahi is influenced by the NGO and its philosophy of leniency. In Markegaon, the rule-book states that every resolution of conflict has to be done with the help of the *ex officio* secretary of the association.

Responses to questions about whether the level of conflicts has remained same or increased over the past year and whether conflict has been disruptive of normal activities revealed that the indigenous mechanism had proved to be effective in Deulgaon. There, conflicts have decreased over the years and have been solved in ways that are not disruptive of normal activities. In Markegaon and Ranwahi, the extent of conflicts have remained more or less the same. As mentioned earlier, in Ranwahi infractions are not strictly penalized in order to avoid antagonizing anyone within the community. However, this leniency has resulted in dissatisfaction among those people who follow the rules strictly. JFM-supported Markegaon expects the department to play the role of mediator for resolution of conflicts, which is highly dependent on the active interest of the *ex officio* member. In the absence of this (*ex officio* FD representative), Markegaon is not able to deal with the conflicts effectively. During group discussions, an attempt was made to find the level of awareness, extent of participation and compliance of rules. On all these counts, Deulgaon has fared better than the other two communities.

Preference for Future

Time preference is important because it influences the economic efficiency of resource investments and inter-generational equity. In the present context, it is difficult to use a precise discount rate to show a community's preference for future for two reasons. First, collective action for forest management is limited to protecting the forest and not to harvesting the forest commercially. Therefore, efficiency and incremental ratios as calculated for commercial enterprises, where it is possible to make decisions on the basis of then prevailing prices and likely prices in future, are not relevant here. Indeed, the communities in our study area (including the JFM village) do not have authority to make decisions regarding commercial matters. Second, our discussions with the community members repeatedly showed that for them non-use value of forest (i.e., posterity, religious beliefs, existence, etc.) is as important as economic value. It is therefore difficult for respondents to ascribe a specific monetary or discount value to the forest and its products. Value for this attribute is therefore based on the intensity of peoples' feelings regarding protection, as reflected in the survey. In case of JFM, the value is given on the basis of the provisions in the scheme.

It is clear from the study that the communities have attempted to restrict the use of forest products and have reduced their needs based on the forest. Moreover, they have expressed (*a*) readiness to invest today both in terms of labor and money to protect the forest for the future, (*b*) strong cultural views of the forest and (*c*) high awareness of the effects of degradation of forest on other resources. The strength of these three aspects have been used to record the scores for the MCA.

The Deulgaon community began protecting the forest nearly eight years before JFM came to the village. This is important because it is only after JFM that the community received funds for various developmental works. Up to that time, the community had voluntarily spent time and energy in patrolling the forest and restricting its use. However, they were not able to integrate techniques to improve the productivity of the forest by taking up plantations, or reduce their needs on forest products by opting for alternatives, until the JFM program came to their village and brought funds.

In contrast, Markegaon reaped JFM benefits earlier in the evolution of forest management. Funds and expertise have been available to improve productivity through species mix and techniques to reduce the need for forest products by providing alternatives like bio-gas. In cases where project implementation requires funds (e.g., for infrastructure development), the JFM model has scored higher. Ranwahi community exhibited a strongly economic view of the forest and the community protected the resource particularly for the market value of the forest products. Thus, the community has taken steps to restrict use of the forest, although the implementation is not very successful. As a result, Ranwahi has scored lowest on this criterion.

Existence and Use of Social Capital

Social capital consists of the stock of active connections among people: the trust, mutual understanding and shared values and behavior that bind the members of human networks and communities that make cooperative action possible (Cohen and Prusak, 2001). Usually, social capital grows over a considerable period of time as a community shares and learns from common experiences from which understanding and norms evolve. The village histories of Deulgaon and Markegaon were volatile. In- and out-migrations have taken place until very recently.

Although the entire population of Markegaon belongs to the *Gond* tribe, this homogenous and indigenous population has scored the least in terms of social capital. This village exemplifies the impact of erosion of social capital due to centralization of ownership and management of the natural resource. The surrounding forests had been neglected, even abused, by the locals in the past after losing all stakes in them. Under the JFM arrangement as well, the FD as an institution has not made any efforts to enhance and incorporate social capital as a necessary ingredient for effective management of forest. Thereby, the FD has taken no initiative in promoting operational rules for regulating the community's exploitation of the resource. There is little interaction of the department with the community members, resulting in many incidences of infractions and poor awareness regarding provisions and restrictions under JFM.

Deulgaon has scored well in terms of social capital, because people interact often with each other about both community and forest matters. With no outside support whatsoever, the Deulgaon community has been meeting frequently, both formally and informally, to discuss problems related to its forest. This has helped in evolving mutual understanding. Only after detailed discussions are decisions made, and these decisions are taken unanimously. Since the entire community is involved in decision making and rule making, not only is the general awareness within the community regarding rules high, but also the members consider the rules legitimate. The incidence of infraction by community members is quite low. Due to shared understanding regarding need for protection from the neighboring villages, strict vigilance is maintained by the community members. This is despite the fact that the population is ethnically heterogeneous.

In case of Ranwahi, we found that people interact with each other on issues related with the community in general and that the NGO is at least partially responsible in bringing the community together. While this result indicated that the NGO is promoting sustainable collective action, the emphasis by the NGO seems to be greater on the activities related to its own project portfolio, rather than the community's agenda. Responses to various questions reveal that many people are not aware of the rules that govern forest use. The level of active participation of all the community members in the meetings is also low. Most of the infractions are pardoned simply because of the fear that they might cause conflicts within the community, thus diluting the authority of the officials of the local forest association and its effectiveness. Hence, while Ranwahi's social capital has been assessed as greater than Markegaon, it is substantially less than that of Deulgaon.

Monitoring of Resource Use

Monitoring here refers to the rules that regulate forest use by the community members themselves and protection from poachers. The mode and extent of monitoring can be reflected in number of infractions, penalties and guards, the timing of patrolling and the method of dealing with poachers when caught. This attribute is important because it indicates how willing the community is to invest in the form of time and effort. Especially, in cases where funding is not provided for employing paid guards, the households have to take turns in patrolling, as is reportedly been done in all the three case study villages.

IFRI has many direct questions dealing with monitoring of resource use. It includes questions like the number of guards appointed; their method of selection; the types of penalties imposed on infraction(s) for the first time, second time or more; about the records thereof; alternative action taken in case of non-payment of fine; ways of restoration of harvesting rights once lost; frequency of general body meetings and the attendance in these meetings. Information has also been collected to learn whether the communities are aware of the internal or external thefts, whether women are included in the monitoring work, the duration of guard duties, and whether the number of thefts have reduced over time.

The data on these aspects reveals that Deulgaon community is very serious in dealing with both internal and external infractions. They impose fines even on the first-time rule breaker, be it a community member or an outsider. The Deulgaon community is also, unlike the other two, particular about maintaining records of penalties and fines. The commitment on the part of the Deulgaon community to comply with the rules laid out for forest use, to attend general body meetings and to approach external officials to impose penalties when required, are all indicators of serious monitoring. This intensive monitoring has resulted in decreased incidences of infractions over the years.

Markegaon was found to be less strict in imposing penalties on both internal rule breakers and outsiders. Community members do not patrol at night. Since the forest protection work was introduced in Markegaon only after it was covered under JFM, the community thinks that formulation of rules, implementation, dealing with infractions and patrolling is the job of the FD. Moreover, the community does not feel an urgent need for strict monitoring because the village is located in the heart of rich forest where pressure from neighboring communities is also low. As a result, Markegaon has scored low on monitoring.

In case of Ranwahi, compliance of rules by the community itself is quite poor, but the community shows no leniency in dealing with poachers from outside. Awareness regarding infractions is mainly regarding encroachments by neighboring villagers. Both Ranwahi and Markegaon seem to be quite casual in monitoring of use by their own community members, which reflects in the status of their forests as well (Ghate and Nagendra, 2005).

Coordination between Formal and Informal Institutions

Our analysis has found that the most important factor for sustaining collective action is coordination between formal and informal institutions. Community efforts alone may not prove to be effective if they are not backed by a formal organization. For example, infractions as defined by the informal organization may not hold much value without legal sanctity provided by the government. Similarly, any formal attempt towards protection of forests unless accepted by the locals, would prove to be equally ineffective. In the three case studies, the extent of cooperation differed across the institutions.

We asked questions about the type of activities undertaken together by the Forest Department and the local community; the type, extent and quality of coordination between the two; the relationship with each other; and conflicts between the two groups. From the description of villages it is quite clear that coordination between the FD and the people of Ranwahi is the highest, followed by Deulgaon and Markegaon.

The NGO has played a key catalytic role in improving awareness level within Ranwahi, encouraging it to initiate resource management and at the same time to ensure legal backing to the efforts by bringing in JFM. Joint forest activities such as plantations, protection and monitoring against neighboring villagers is well coordinated in Ranwahi. The community has frequent meetings with the Forest Guard who occasionally inspects the forest.

In Deulgaon, the situation is different, as the community has to sort out all the infractions either by itself or through the state police. It receives very little help from the FD because the community feels that the department would not cooperate with the community in nabbing poachers. Moreover, the community does not receive its share of money collected through fines from the poachers by the FD. This was an indictor of absence of backing by the department to the community's activities.

In case of Markegaon, contrary to expectation, there is very little coordination between the local community and the FD. There is no help to the local community in case of monitoring or protection work. In case of plantation activity undertaken under JFM as well, the community is not consulted regarding selection of species to be planted.

Results of the Multi-criteria Analysis and IAD Framework

Based on the earlier discussion on the performance of the three villages on the sustainability variables/indicators, a performance matrix has been constructed from the aggregation of scores under each attribute (Table 4.2). Scores in the table reflect the performance of the three institutional structures against the six selected parameters that are considered conducive to collective action. Similarly, institutional analysis is also presented in a tabular form in Table 4.3 and is discussed in this section. Deulgaon as a community-initiated forest management institution has scored highest because of its better performance on all parameters due to the freedom it enjoyed in crafting its operational-level activities. The exception has been the parameter of 'coordination', due to lack of constitutional-level backing. Ranwahi community has scored the highest on this parameter.

Since the Deulgaon community evolved operational level activities like the rule structure by itself as and when the need arose, their understanding and compliance is much better. Although the

TABLE 4.3

Performance Matrix Using Institutional Analysis and IAD Framework

Community/ Institutional Level Activities	Constitutional	Collective	Operational
Deulgaon	Not in the beginning	Among the group—yes. Little role of the forest department	Good
Markegaon	Yes	No coordination, forest department not active	Rules present, but low adherence to rules
Ranwahi	Yes	Coordination by the NGO	Rules partially implemented

community had not directly addressed equity in benefit sharing, mutual understanding and cognisance given to genuine household needs and strict monitoring of adherence to rules kept the members satisfied in that regard. It is through collective decision that this community has consciously invested time and effort to continue the sustainable supply of forest products. The history of Deulgaon community shows that the village has not been a cohesive group coexisting for a long time. The community settled in its present form within the past 60 years. This fact further highlights the achievement of the community in building social capital. However, to begin with there was no constitutional-level backing to the collective efforts, because the government had not yet adopted JFM. Even after inducting Deulgaon into the JFM program, the collective-level activities which need support from the FD are weak due to lack of coordination between the department and the community.

Performance of the JFM village Markegaon is lowest despite the fact that the collective action has had constitutional-level backing right from its genesis. Apathy of the concerned local forest officials who are supposed to be directly responsible for helping the community in collective-level decision making, like monitoring, is an important reason for poor performance of Markegaon. Social capital seems to have eroded over time, which is reflected in lack of mechanism for conflict resolution, equitable benefit distribution and low preference for future. The FD, which could have put in efforts to revive social capital, has not done so for various possible reasons. It could have invested in reviving traditional practices and helped in building dormant social capital (Grootaert and Narayan, 1999), thereby improving operational-level activities for the success of JFM. In JFM, like any other state-driven government programs, implementation is highly personalized and depends upon personal view and convictions of the local implementing officers. A disinterested forest official responsible for implementation of JFM can restrict activities to the minimum that is required under the law. Communities that would benefit from greater support would tend to suffer in that case, which may have been the situation with Markegaon.

NGOs can play a useful role in transferring advantages of a formal set-up to communities by linking constitutional-level activities with operational-level activities. However, NGOs are driven by their own agenda and have their own limitations. This can interfere with collective-level activities like adherence of rules and conflict resolution. In case of Ranwahi, since the NGO is not directly involved in forestry-related work and does not want to antagonize any community member (which could hamper activities of its own interest), leniency in dealing with infractions is reflected in the overall performance of the institution.

CONCLUSIONS

The three case studies reiterate the necessity of integrating the three levels—constitutional, collective and operational—in institution building for sustainability of collective action. In our study, the community-initiated effort seems to be most effective in sustaining collective action because of the autonomy it enjoyed in forming operational-level rules.

In case of NGO-promoted forest management effort, it can be surmised that communities might be receptive to ideas from an agency that they trust. Yet, much of the success would depend on the commitment and priorities of particular NGOs. Therefore, this institutional arrangement may not provide unique solutions for uniform application. Moreover, such efforts may suffer from limitations of technical skills and finance. It would be unwise to assume that self-motivated communities or NGOs exist in large numbers and will solve the problems of equity, efficiency and sustainability in natural resource management through collective action.

In the absence of tenure and without the legal backing for dealing with disputes and infractions, sustainability of informal collective efforts is questionable (Ghate and Mehra, 2004). This is one important reason why an increasing number of communities in India are applying for JFM, although it is a quasi-legal arrangement. In the given situation in India today, collective action can be most sustainable under state initiatives such as JFM if it can solve the problem of integration of the three institutional levels. If the state-run initiative at constitutional level can develop a mechanism that provides more autonomy to the local communities in dealing with operational-level activities and ensure that the implementing agency, i.e., the FD is motivated and skilled in collective-level working, the broad objective of sustaining natural resources through collective action can be achieved.

MAP 4.2
Map of Maharashtra State

Location of Sample Villages in Maharashtra State

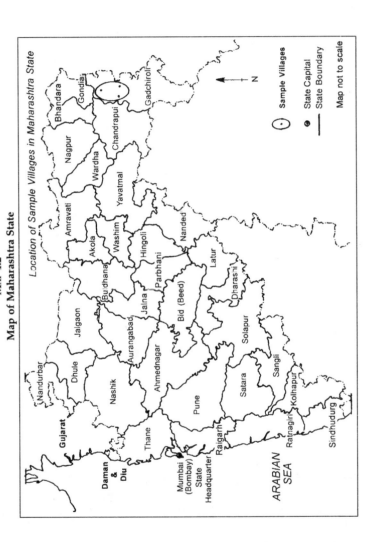

Sample Villages

State Capital

State Boundary

Map not to scale

Map 4.3
Map of Gadchiroli District, Maharashtra

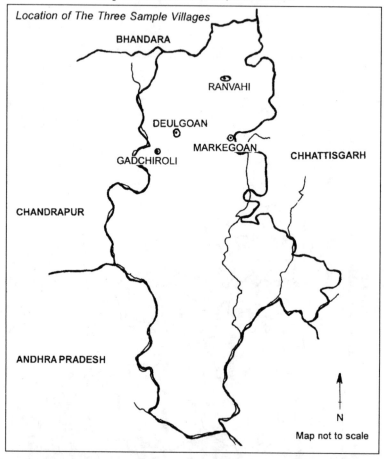

The present centralized system operating in a top-down manner cannot independently evolve appropriate strategies while operating in the midst of the complicated community–forest relationship that exists in India. Rather than restricting the choice between either 'state' or 'village community' with or without NGO support, there is need for situation-specific coordinated efforts in which forest areas are protected for multiple objectives by incorporating positive aspects of existing institutional structure. Under the reformed version of JFM, leaning towards Community Forest Management, there is great potential for getting the best out of communities as well as NGOs. It is the spirit and quality of implementation by the FD that would determine whether responsive and flexible informal institutions can be integrated to ultimately succeed in sustainable forest management.

ACKNOWLEDGMENTS

This chapter is based on a research project funded by the South Asian Network for Development and Environmental Economics. We are grateful to Professor Partha Dasgupta, Gopal Kadekodi and Priya Shaymsundar for their valuable suggestions for the chapter. We are grateful to the members of the three communities for their enthusiastic cooperation each time we visited them.

NOTE

1. No. 6.2/89-Forest Policy, June 1, 1990; No.22-8/2000-JFM(FPD), February 21, 2000; Strengthening of JFM Programme, Guidelines, by MoEF, on December 24, 2002.

REFERENCES

Agrawal, A. (1999). *Greener Pastures: Politics, Markets and Community among a Migrant Pastoral People*. Durham, NC: Duke University Press.
———. (2002). 'Common Resources and Institutional Sustainability'. In Elinor Ostrom, Thomas Dietz, Nives Dolsak, Paul C. Stern, Susan Stonich, and Elke U. Weber (eds), *The Drama of the Commons*. Washington, DC: National Academy Press.
Baland, J. and Platteau, J. (1996). *Halting Degradation of Natural Resources: Is There a Role for Rural Communities?* Oxford: Clarendon Press.
Blomiquist, W., Schlager, E., Yan Tang, S., and Ostrom, E. (1994). 'Regularities from the Field and Possible Explanations'. In Elinor Ostrom, Roy Gardner, and James Walker (eds), *Rules, Games, and Common-Pool Resources* (pp. 301–316). Ann Arbor, MI: University of Michigan Press.
Cohen, D. and Prusak, L. (2001). *In Good Company. How Social Capital Makes Organizations Work*. Boston, MA: Harvard Business School Press.
Gadgil, M. and Berkes, F. (1991). 'Traditional Resource Management Systems'. *Resource Management and Optimization*, 8(3–4), 127–141.
Gadgil, M. and Guha, R. (1992). *This Fissured Land: An Ecological History of India*. New Delhi: Oxford University Press.

Gadgil, M. and Subhash Chandra, M.D. (1992). 'Sacred Groves'. *Indian International Centre Quarterly*, 19(1–2), 183–87.

Ghate, R. (1992). *Forest Policy and Tribal Development*. New Delhi: Concept Publishing Co.

———. (2000). 'The Role of Autonomy in Self-organizing Process: A Case Study of Local Forest Management in India'. Working Paper No. W00-12. Workshop on Political Theory and Policy Analysis, Indiana University, Bloomington.

———. (2004). *Uncommons in the Commons: Community Initiated Forest Resource Management*. New Delhi: Concept Publishing Co.

Ghate, R. and Mehra, D. (2004). 'The Land on which the Forest Stands is not Ours, So What? Forest Products are ours! A Study of Three Collective Action Based Forest Regimes Operating Without Land Tenure'. *Forests, Trees and Livelihoods*, 14(2,3,4), 91–108.

Ghate, R. and Nagendra, H. (2005). 'Role of Monitoring in Institutional Performance: Forest Management in Maharashtra, India'. *Conservation and Society*, 3(2), 509–532.

Gibson, C. and Becker, D. (1999). 'The Lack of Institutional Demand'. In Clark Gibson, Elinor Ostrom, and Margaret McKean (eds), *People and Forests: Communities Institutions and Governance* (pp. 135–162). Cambridge: The MIT Press.

Grootaert, C. and Narayan, D.C. (1999). *Local Lustitutions, Poverty and Household Welfare in Bolivia*. Washington, DC: The World Bank.

Guha, R. (1983). 'Forestry in British and Post-British India—A Historical Analysis'. *Economic and Political Weekly*, XXVIII(44), October 29.

Jodha, N.S. (2002). 'Natural Resource Management and Poverty Alleviation in Mountain Areas: Approaches and Efforts'. Conference Paper Series No. 11. International Conference on Natural Assets organized by the Political Economy Research Institute (PERI) University.

Lele, S. (1998). 'Why, Who, and How of Jointness in Joint Forest Management: Theoretical Considerations and Empirical Onsights from the Western Ghats of Karnataka'. Paper presented at Crossing Boundaries, the seventh annual conference of the International Association for the Study of Common Property, Vancouver.

McKean, M.A. (1992). 'Management of Traditional Common Lands (Iriaichi) in Japan'. In D. Bromley (ed.), *Making the Commons Work: Theory, Practice and Policy* (pp. 63–93). San Francisco: Institute for Contemporary Studies.

———. (2000). 'Common Property: What is it, What is it Good for, and What Makes it Work?'. In Clark Gibson, Margaret McKean, and Elinor Ostrom (eds), *People and Forests: Communities, Institutions, and Governance*. Cambridge, MA: The MIT Press.

Naughton-Treves, L. and Sanderson, S. (1995). 'Property, Politics and Wildlife Conservation'. *World Development*, 23(8), 1265–1275.

Ostrom, E. (1990). *Governing the Commons: The Evolution of Institutions for Collective Action*. Cambridge: Cambridge University Press.

———. (1992a). *Crafting Institutions for Self-Governing Irrigation Systems*. San Francisco, CA: ICS Press.

———. (1992b). 'Policy Analysis of Collective Action and Self-Governance'. In William N. Dunn and Rita Mae Kelly (eds), *Advances In Policy Studies Since 1950*. Policy Studies Review Annual (vol. 10, pp. 81–119).

Ostrom, E. (1998). 'Institutional Analysis. Design principles, and Threats to Sustainable Community Governance and Management of Commons'. In Erling Berge and Nils Christian Stenseth (eds), *Law and the Governance of Renewable Resources: Studies from Northern Europe and Africa* (pp. 27–53). Oakland, CA: ICS Press.

———. (1999). 'Institutional Rational Choice: An Assessment of the Institutional Analysis and Development Framework'. In Paul A. Sabatier (ed.), *Theories of the Policy Process* (pp. 35–71). Boulder, CO: Westview Press.

Rangarajan, M. (1996). *Fencing the Forest: Conservation and Ecological Change in India's Central Province, 1860–1914.* New Delhi: Oxford University Press.

Roy Burman, B.K. (1985), 'Issues in Environmental Management Cantering Forest, Role of Tribal Communities'. *South Asian Anthropologist, 6*(1), 41–48.

Sarin, M. (1995). 'Joint Forest Management in India: Achievements and Unaddressed Challenges'. *Unasylva 180, 46*(1), 30–36.

———. (1998/1996). 'From Conflict to Collaboration: Institutional Issues in Community Management'. In M. Poffenberger and B. McGean (eds), *Village Voices, Forest Choices* (pp. 165–203). New Delhi: Oxford University Press.

Sundar, N. (2000). 'Unpacking the "Joint" in Joint Forest Management'. *Development and Change, 31*(1), 255–279.

Sundar, N., Jeffery, R., and Thin, N. (2001). *Branching Out: Joint Forest Management in India.* New Delhi: Oxford University Press.

Thompson, J. (1995). 'Participatory Approaches in Government Bureaucracies: Facilitating the Process of Institutional Change'. *World Development, 23*(9), 1521–1534.

Varalakshmi, V. and Kaul O.N. (1999). 'Non-governmental Organisations: Their Role in Forestry Research and Extension'. *The Indian Forester, 125*(1), 37–44.

Wade, R. (1994). *Village Republics: Economic Conditions for Collective Action in South India.* Oakland: ICS Press.

5 DECENTRALIZATION POLICY AND REVITALIZATION OF LOCAL INSTITUTIONS FOR PROTECTED AREA CO-MANAGEMENT IN WEST SUMATRA, INDONESIA

YONARIZA and GANESH P. SHIVAKOTI

INTRODUCTION

Unlike many countries in Asia where forest management is usually under a forest department and protected areas management falls under the Ministry of Environment, in Indonesia both forest and protected area management fall under the Department of Forestry. As such, forestry policies must also include policies related to protected area management. The Indonesian government has classified forest area by function into: (*a*) protection forest, (*b*) conservation forest, (*c*) production forest, (*d*) limited production forest and (*e*) conversion forest. The first two categories of forest fall under protected areas. Because forest management policy includes protected areas, it is important to measure how local communities surrounding protected areas respond to the evolving protected area policies. The success and failure of forestry policy will affect forest condition in protected areas as a function of local people and external actors' compliance or non-compliance with emergent forestry policies.

There has been an enormous literature dealing with how the centralized model of forest management implemented during the New Order Regime since the late 1960s in Indonesia has caused forest degradation and has diminished local participation in forest management. During the New Order period, forest area in Indonesia declined from 150 million hectares in 1960 to only 90 million hectares in the year 2000 (Lindayanti, 2002; FWI/GFW/WRI, 2002). Centralized management not only caused forests to become the subject of exploitation but also marginalized local institutions managing the forest.

The Basic Forestry Law No. 67 of 1967 and the Village Administration Law No. 5/1979, enacted during the New Order Regime, have directly resulted in the loss of local control over forest resources and reduced the role of local institutions in managing forests.

The Forestry Law gave the state the power to control all of the forests of the country that could be concessioned out for forestry activities, with no mention of local people's rights over forest resources. The Village Administration Law was enacted to implement Java's *desa* system of governance by terminating the existing diversity of local village institutions in the country, including those dealing with forest resources. This pattern of universal centralized management of forest model confirms the earlier finding that the historical emergence of colonial powers and nation states and their assumption of authority over most common lands and natural resources led to the demise of traditional Natural Resources Management (NRM) systems (see Chapter 1, Borrini-Feyerabend *et al.*, 2000).

There was resistance against the village reorganization to adopt the Javanese model in many provinces, as there was a fear that the adoption of the *desa* system would significantly alter traditional governance arrangements all over the country. In West Sumatra, for example, this law was implemented in 1983, four years after enactment, and created more than 3,000 *desa* units from the previous 530 *nagari* units. Thus, the adoption of the *desa* system involved the splitting of each *nagari* into 4–5 *desa* administrative units. Hence, *nagari* government was abandoned.

From the central government's perspective, having one standard village administration unit for rural development planning and financing simplified matters (for detailed discussion, see Kato, 1989). But, as a consequence of centralized forest governance and management, several problems emerged, including stripping of local control over forest resources (Lindayanti, 2002); the creation of open access forests resulting from the government's incapacity to protect the forest in protected areas (Haeruman, 2001); an access gap between forest concession companies and local stakeholders (Barr, 1998); dissatisfaction among those marginalized communities (Rhee, 2000); and increased illegal logging in protected areas (Barber and Talbott, 2003; Hiller *et al.*, 2004; Laurance, 2004; McCarthy, 2002; Ravenel, 2004). These consequences may have been predictable, however, because 'destruction or degradation of forest resources is most likely to occur in those forests where those involved have not established an effective local governance mechanism' (Ostrom, 1999).

After the collapse of the New Order Regime in early 1999, the succeeding regime changed the policy by adopting administrative decentralization for many sectors of government. The decentralization policy opened up opportunities for governments at the provincial and district levels to readopt their local village administration, arrangements abandoning the homogenized *desa* administration system. In West Sumatra Province, the regional government revitalized village level governance by returning to the *nagari* government system in early 2001. This decision was based on the idea that the *nagari* is not only simple as an administrative unit, but also it is a sociocultural unit with its own political and judicial apparatus; it is an institution where rules and roles are clearly defined (Kato, 1978).

Decentralization offered new space for *nagari* innovation. We argue in this chapter that *nagaris* tended to respond to protected areas management policy differently, depending on the incentives for participation. Given the level of incentives and local socioeconomic conditions, decentralization could trigger local actions and creativity. In this chapter, we focus on the dynamics of forest management in protected areas after enactment of decentralization laws and revitalization of *nagaris*. Specifically, we seek to answer the following questions:

1. What are the recent policy milestones in Indonesia related to protected area management after decentralization?
2. Has regional autonomy triggered the local initiative to grow?
3. Has decentralization in West Sumatra revitalized the *nagari* role in forest management?

4. What are the implications for co-management of protected areas from the collective action point of view?

There is voluminous literature that analyzes forest management in Indonesia under the centralized management model and there is also a growing literature base examining the situation of forest management after the implementation of regional autonomy in 2001 (e.g., Aden, 2001; CIFOR, 2002; Dewi *et al.*, 2005; FWI/ GFW/WRI, 2002; McCarthy, 2004; Obidzinski, 2004; Sudana, 2004). But there has been little attempt to explore whether regional autonomy and forest policy could provide incentives for local participation in guarding protected areas and ultimately in creating a co-management situation. This study is an endeavor to fill that gap.

In the next section, we review recent forest and protected areas governance and management policies in Indonesia. After a brief discussion on field research methods, we review the district level government's response to revitalization of the *nagari* administration system. We then examine the effect of *nagari* revitalization and *nagari* involvement in forest protection and management.

We have also assessed the level of local knowledge on the existence of protected areas and local initiatives to curtail illegal logging in those areas. We interpret variable responses by different communities towards forest protection based mainly on incentives and how co-management mechanisms have evolved over time. Finally, we put forward policy implications of these findings for effective community-based resource management.

POLICY CHANGES FOR PROTECTED AREAS IN INDONESIA

Current forest governance and management in Indonesia is guided by Law No. 41/1999 issued during the government administrative transition. This law explicitly articulated decentralization and local people's empowerment and the drafting of the law included the participation of civil society groups (Lindayanti, 2002).

Article 6.1 of the law outlines three main forest functions: conservation, protection and production. Production forests perform the main function of producing forest products; protection forests protect life-supporting systems for hydrology, prevent floods, control erosion, prevent sea water intrusion and maintain soil fertility; and conservation forests enclose an area with specific characteristics to preserve the ecosystem and its species. As noted earlier the protection and conservation forests fall under the category of a protected area. Article 7 further divides conservation forests into (*a*) nature reserve forests (forests having the main function of preserving plant and animal diversity and its ecosystem and also as the place for life-supporting system) and (*b*) nature preservation forests (a forest having the main function of protecting life-supporting system, preserving species diversity of plants and animals and sustainable use of biological resources and its ecosystem). Our study site was classified as a nature reserve.

The central government still holds significant control over certain aspects of forest management. Part Three of the Law, Article 4, gives authority to the central government to regulate and organize all aspects related to forests, forest areas and products, to assign the status of a certain area as a forest or a non-forest area, to regulate and determine legal relations between man and forest, and to regulate legal actions concerning forestry.

The role of the local government in managing forests can be seen in Chapter VIII of the law on the delegation of authorities, where Article 66 specifies that while implementing forest administration, the central government must delegate some authority to the local government. Furthermore, these roles of local government must be bounded by central government regulation. As a manifestation of this article, the government has issued three government regulations (GR): GR No. 34/2002 on forest management and forest management planning, forest utilization; GR No. 44/2004 on forest planning; and GR No. 45/2004 on forest protection. These regulations stipulate the role of local government in many aspects of forest management. In essence, there is delegation of authority to local governments to manage forest areas within their jurisdiction by following the guidelines provided by the central government.

The current forestry law also recognizes the role of local people in forest and protected area management, thus providing room for the local community to participate. Chapter IX of the law is devoted to community customary law. Similalry, Article 69 emphasizes that communities shall be obliged to participate in maintaining and preventing forest areas from disturbance and damage, and to implement forest rehabilitation. The community can also request assistance, guidance and support from non-governmental organizations, other parties or the government. Community roles are further elaborated in Article 70, emphasizing their importance in co-management[1] of forestry resources.

Thus, the decentralization law, enacted in 1999 and revised in 2004, transferred authority of managing natural resources such as forests and protected areas to autonomous local governments. This authority can be regarded as a compulsory obligation in controlling the environment and managing natural resources such as forests and protected areas. In order to examine how local governments and people have responded to policy changes, we examined whether and how the revitalized *nagari* administration has been involved in the management of one important protected area in West Sumatra.

STUDY AREA OVERVIEW AND METHODS

Barisan I Nature Reserve is a protected area encompassing 74,000 hectares in West Sumatra province (Map 5.1). This is a long-established protected area dating back to Dutch colonial times in the early 20th century. According to the IUCN protected areas classification, this site belongs to category VI, which by definition contains predominantly unmodified natural systems managed to ensure long-term protection and maintenance of biological diversity, while at the same time providing a sustainable flow of natural products and services to meet community needs (IUCN, 1994). The government of Indonesia, however, considers this area as a nature reserve forest, which, as described earlier, means that it should be a forest area having the main function of preserving plant and animal diversity and ecosystems and also as the place for life-supporting systems (Forestry Law No. 41/1999).

Map 5.1
Barisan I Nature Reserve, West Sumatra, Indonesia

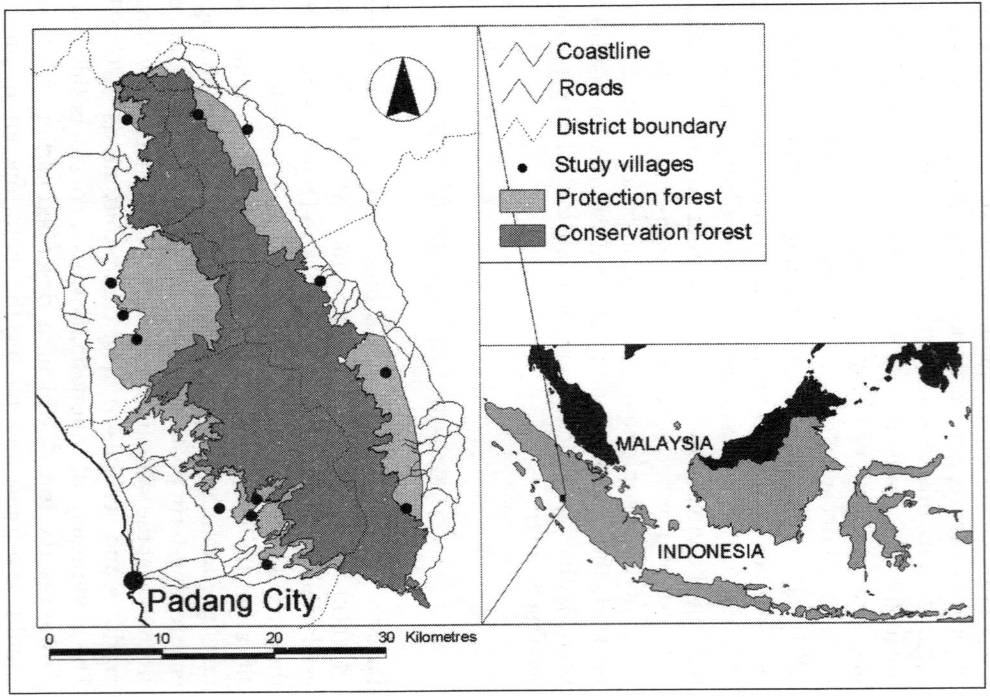

The reserve straddles four autonomous districts: the urban area of Padang city (the capital of West Sumatra Province), the peri-urban area of Padang Pariaman district in the western part, accessible rural areas of Tanah Datar district and poorly accessible rural areas of Solok district in the southern and in the eastern parts. Thus, the villages surrounding Barisan have a varying degree of market access and physical settings.

Barisan I Nature Reserve has important environmental functions such as maintaining water quality, supplying water to Singkarak Lake where a 154 MW hydroelectric power plant operates, supplying water to a number of small-scale irrigation systems surrounding the forest reserve and supplying piped water to villages and towns.

Physically, this reserve represents a contiguous forest that, according to recent forestry law, requires a complex system of forest management. It has a core conservation area where the central government is responsible for management. Under current decentralization law, the part surrounding the core area is within the authority of district government. Outside of that is a buffer region communal forest under management of the 23 surrounding *nagaris* that have traditional claims of rights inside the protected area.

We selected 11 out of 23 *nagaris* surrounding the reserve for detailed study. These *nagaris* were purposively selected based on the number of forest-related activities, including farming, fuelwood collection, non-timber forest product collection, hunting and trapping and timber felling. Based on their physical location and accessibility, these *nagaris* were further divided into urban (three in Padang), peri-urban (three in Pariaman), accessible rural (two in Tanah Datar) and poorly accessible rural (three in Solok). Within these 11 *nagaris*, we purposively selected 17 sub-villages (*jorong*) and 10 percent of the households (N = 299) for a household survey. Background information such as household size, land holding, education level and occupation of respondents were collected (Table 5.1). The respondents' education level across all sites did not vary; in contrast, however, the majority of urban households depended on off-farm activities for their livelihood, whereas the

Table 5.1

Characteristics of 299 Sampled Households and their Respondents in 11 Villages Surrounding Barisan I Nature Reserve, West Sumatra, Indonesia

Physical Setting	Number of Households	Level of Education of Respondents			Respondents Involved in Farming	Average Household Size	Average Irrigated Land Holding (ha)	Average Dry Land Holding (ha)
		Illiterate	Elementary School	High School +				
Urban (Padang)	70 (100.0)	8 (11.4)	33 (47.1)	29 41.4	30 (42.9)	6	0.26	0.59
Peri-urban (Pariaman)	75 (100.0)	2 (2.7)	57 (76.0)	16 (21.3)	45 (60.0)	5	0.41	1.11
Rural good accessibility (Tanah Datar)	74 (100.0)	5 (6.8)	37 (50.0)	32 (43.2)	46 (62.2)	5	0.64	0.86
Rural poor accessibility (Solok)	80 (100.0)	6 (7.5)	52 (65.0)	22 (27.5)	58 (72.5)	6	0.45	0.88
Total	299 (100.0)	21 (7.0)	179 (59.9)	99 (33.1)	179 (59.9)			

Note: Figures in brackets are percentages.

peri-urban and rural areas were farm oriented. Similarly, the size of the land holding for urban dwellers was nearly half of the other residents in rural areas.

GOVERNMENT DECENTRALIZATION AND THE REVITALIZATION OF *NAGARI* ADMINISTRATION

Law No. 22/1999 was intended to reduce centralization and the authoritarian government model during the New Order Regime and to acknowledge social, political and cultural diversity in the country. In West Sumatra, the process of decentralization has a particularly dynamic and interesting character where, along with the general decentralization of central political authority and economic resources to the districts, a fundamental restructuring of local village government was initiated (Benda-Beckmann and Benda-Beckman, 2001). The policy of regional autonomy has been taken up as 'to return to the *nagari*'. Some district governments, in turn, decentralized some of the authority to *nagari* government. There is a great expectation that by implementing multilevel decentralization, government at all levels will be more responsive towards local needs and hence participation will increase (ibid.).

However, local responses to decentralization vary across spatial and infrastructural dimensions at the macro, meso and micro levels. The district heads and parliamentarians have (re)acted with quite variable speed and enthusiasm to these developments. Recent research reports show that in two districts, Limapuluh Koto and Solok, energetic district heads have undertaken a number of initiatives to implement the new structure as soon as possible, in particular, revising their district administrative structures and pushing forward the return to the *nagari* system. They were quick in promulgating their own district regulations and Solok district was ready to start as soon as the provincial regulation became effective in January 2001 (ibid.). With regard to protected area management, Solok district is also far ahead of other districts by starting several initiatives, which we discuss in detail in the following section.

District Government Initiative

Solok district has made a systematic effort to maintain its several protected areas. The District Forestry Service issued a decree on establishment of a Community Forest Guarding Unit (CFGU), starting from the year 2003. At Barisan I Nature Reserve, the district government set up CFGU in four *nagaris* consisting of the *nagari* head, the chief of youth, the chief of the *adat* council and the respective sub-village heads who are assigned and recruited to guard the forest. Their tasks were to patrol the forest and to detect any threat such as forest fire, illegal logging, fauna hunting and illegal collection of forest products. The CFGU had to report to the district government each case of default found in their respective villages. This dramatically reduced illegal timber felling. The district government followed up reports by taking necessary action, coordinating forest patrols and helping to prevent forest fires by coordinating with the central government forestry unit in the district.

CFGUs have worked quite well in each *nagari* of Solok district. In *nagari* Koto Sani, this unit stopped tree cutting for canoe making in the protected area. In *nagari* Batang Barus, the CFGU informed its community members regarding the importance of forests, got the users involved in forest patrol and sent periodic reports to the district forestry services. However, while some *nagaris* have taken the initiative to safeguard the protected areas in their vicinities, others have not been so successful and hence the forest condition varies across *nagaris*. We therefore examine, in the following section, how the revitalized *nagari* administration responds to the decentralization opportunities by examination at the household level.

Nagari Initiative and Community Perception of Participation in Protected Areas Management

During our field survey we found that some village CFGUs took additional steps to protect the forest of the Reserve. In turn, this had a positive impact on forest management within protected area. In poorly-accessible rural areas of Solok district, nearly half of the households reported some positive impact with regard to forest management after a return to *nagari* administration system (Table 5.2).

TABLE 5.2
Perceived Presence of Local Forest Guards and Forest Regulations from Sampled Households near Barisan I Nature Reserve

Physical Setting	Number of Households	Perceived Impact of Nagari Revitalization on Forest Management			Nagari Activities	
		No Impact	Do Not Know	Positive Impact	Local Forest Use Regulation	Local Forest Guard
Urban	70	69	1	0	0	0
(Padang)	(100.0)	(98.6)	(1.4)	(0.0)	(0.0)	(0.0)
Peri-urban	75	39	25	11	4	3
(Pariaman)	(100.0)	(52.0)	(33.3)	(14.7)	(5.3)	(4.0)
Rural good accessibility	74	52	17	5	0	0
(Tanah Datar)	(100.0)	(70.3)	(23.0)	(6.8)	(0.0)	(0.0)
Rural poor accessibility	80	26	16	38	38	19
(Solok)	(100.0)	(32.5)	(20.0)	(47.5)	(47.5)	(23.8)
Total	**299**	**186**	**59**	**54**	**42**	**22**
	(100.0)	**(62.2)**	**(19.7)**	**(18.1)**	**(14.0)**	**(7.4)**

Note: Figures in brackets are percentages.

In contrast, in urban, peri-urban, and accessible rural areas, households revealed a lower impact of *nagari* revitalization in managing forests.

To those who mentioned a change in forest protection since *nagari* revitalization, we asked what activities *nagaris* had been taking with regard to the protected area. Two main responses included guarding and regulating forest use (Table 5.2). This implies that the communities were already participating in two important aspects of forest conservation. For example, *nagari* Koto Sani in Solok district had implemented *nagari* regulations regarding forest, i.e., (a) villagers were allowed to cut timber for their own use, (b) if timber was for sale within *nagari*, there was a tax levied by Nagari Council for IDR 50,000 per m³ and (c) no timber transport was allowed outside the *nagari*.

Similarly in *nagari* Jawi-Jawi of district Solok, a *nagari* regulation was proposed to not allow any further logging and forest clearing for agriculture. It was mentioned in the regulation that people who were currently farming in the protected areas were allowed to continue but no more expansion would be allowed. Even though this regulation will still need district government approval, at the local level it had taken effect: no more forest clearing had been carried out and farmers followed the regulation.

In *nagari* Guguak Malalo, a highly accessible rural *nagari* forest regulation was designed for ecological protection. The villagers wanted to protect the forest from landslides threat within the periphery of their villages. The main instrument for this regulation was to ban (a) tree cutting, (b) shifting cultivation and (c) animal hunting.

Padang Laweh Malalo *nagari* was quite distinct as far as conservation forest is concerned. The *nagari* administration negotiated with the regional government forestry department to readjust the protected area boundary to put headwater forest under *nagari* control. By putting this area under community control, the villagers felt more secure that the forest where water sources were found would be better protected as compared to a forest under state control, while lacking sufficient controlling mechanisms.

Aside from drafting *nagari* regulations to protect forests, some *nagaris* came forward to protect their forest. There were attempts by local people to stop illegal logging in *nagari* Talang of Solok district, where youth reported cases of illegal logging carried out by ex-police officers and other officials working for the *nagari* government. In *nagari* Saningbakar along Singkarak Lake, it was reported that in order to rehabilitate critical forest areas, migrants from this *nagari* mobilized and invested as much as IDR 153 million for rehabilitation.

LOCAL KNOWLEDGE ABOUT EXISTENCE OF THE PROTECTED AREA

The effect of *nagari* revitalization on protected area management can also be seen from local knowledge on the existence of the protected area. We found out that the majority of households (70.9 percent) were aware of the existence of Barisan I Nature Reserve; however, there was variability among these households about the perceived rights and responsibilities to manage forest resources. The majority of the respondents did not know who had the authority over the protected area. When asked about the ownership and management of forest resources nearly all respondents from urban and peri-urban households thought that these resources were controlled by regional and/or district administrations. In rural Solok district, however, more than a quarter of the respondents said that it was the *nagari* that had the authority over protected areas. This shows the active role taken by the *nagari* in guarding protected areas in the rural setting (Table 5.3).

CURTAILING ILLEGAL LOGGING

We also sought the opinion of respondents on the impact of *nagari* administration on illegal logging. We asked if there had been a reduction in the number of households involved in illegal logging. Our household survey found that 56 out of 299 households were involved in timber felling in protected areas (Table 5.3), with the fewest households engaged in illegal logging coming from

TABLE 5.3
Perceived Existence of Protected Area, Authority over Protected Areas, and Number of Households Involved in Timber Felling in Barisan I Nature Reserve

Physical Setting	Number of Households	Perceived Existence of Protected Area			Perceived Authority over Protected Areas			Number of Households	
		No	Exists	Do not Know	Government	Nagari	Other	Currently Involved in Timber Felling	Previously Involved in Timber Felling
Urban (Padang)	70 (100.0)	20 (28.6)	42 (60.0)	8 (11.4)	25 (35.71)	1 (1.43)	44 (62.86)	15 (21.4)	17 (24.3)
Peri-urban (Pariaman)	75 (100.0)	8 (10.7)	55 (73.3)	12 (16.0)	38 (50.67)	3 (4.00)	34 (45.33)	17 (22.7)	25 (33.3)
Rural good accessibility (Tanah Datar)	74 (100.0)	8 (10.8)	58 (78.4)	8 (10.8)	30 (40.54)	4 (5.41)	40 (54.05)	21 (28.4)	34 (45.9)
Rural poor accessibility (Solok)	80 (100.0)	14 (17.5)	57 (71.3)	9 (11.3)	16 (20.00)	21 (26.25)	43 (53.75)	3 (3.8)	37 (46.3)
Total	299 (100.0)	50 (16.7)	212 (70.9)	37 (12.4)	109 (36.40)	29 (9.70)	161 (53.90)	56 (18.7)	113 (37.8)

Note: Figures in brackets are percentages.

poorly accessible rural Solok. In contrast, the numbers were higher in the urban area of Padang, the peri-urban area of Padang Pariaman and the accessible rural areas of Tanah Datar. The responses from the same households, however, showed that prior to *nagari* revitalization, the number of households involved in timber felling varied little across rural and urban respondents (Table 5.3). The reason for stopping timber felling in protected areas was due to the ban on timber felling since *nagari* revitalization.

Factors Influencing Local Participation

Why is the rural area of Solok district different from the rest of districts surrounding Barisan I Nature Reserve and why have some *nagaris* taken the initiative to get involved in protected area management? Why were these kinds of initiatives absent in the previously centralized model of protected area management? What are the incentives for local governments to get involved in managing protected areas? In order to seek answers to these issues, we have to examine the current government decentralization policy and how the financial burden is shared between central and district governments in Indonesia.

With the implementation of decentralization, the government adjusted how the financial burden was allocated. After decentralization, a higher percentage of collected natural resources tax was returned to the provincial and district governments than before the new policy. This was a significant change in the relocation of tax collected under the decentralization law. Formerly, Indonesia had the most centralized taxation system in the world (Simanjuntak, 2001).

Solok district has received enormous benefit from decentralization. For example, surface water for hydropower plants is a taxable natural resource. With the introduction of Law No. 34 on tax and retribution enacted in the year 2000, 70 percent of all natural resources revenue, including surface water tax, was to be returned to the district government. The district government, in turn, should allocate 10 percent of the amount to the village-level government.

The National Power Corporation (PLN) as the operator of Singkarak Hydro Electric Power Plant pays an amount of IDR

1.8 billion (US$ 180,000) per year as surface water tax (*Mimbar Minang*, 2003) to the central government, of which 70 percent is returned to district governments where the natural resources are located. The surface water tax received by the district government from Singkarak Power Plant has created the incentive to get involved in protected area management. Using this money, the district government persuaded the *nagari* government to protect forests and finance the operation of a *nagari* forest guard task force. The Solok district government has enjoyed this tax return since the implementation of government decentralization law in 2001 and this has helped enhance protected area management by supporting guards through the implementation of effective monitoring mechanisms. In order to maintain sustainable water supply to Singkarak Lake, the district government was triggered to take an active role in preserving the remaining forest.

DE FACTO PARTICIPATION AND CO-MANAGEMENT

What we have seen from these case studies is that in response to the decentralization policy, some communities have taken active roles by protecting the forest and others have played a passive role by not taking any action at all. We can see the importance of decentralized governance and user participation in the co-management of natural resources (da Silva, 2004). A basic principal of decentralization is to bring the government closer to people. According to the World Bank (1999), co-management partly supports and partly presupposes decentralization and vice versa, which means that both co-management and decentralization are interlinked and depend on each other in order to succeed. Other related literature emphasizes that the need for co-management is to reduce the cost and thus increase efficiency (see Chapter 2, Jones and Burgess, 2005). Partnerships with local communities may reduce enforcement costs (da Silva, 2004).

One major justification among co-management proponents is that increased stakeholder participation will enhance the efficiency and perhaps the equity of the intertwined common property resource management and social systems (Castro and Nielsen, 2001).

However, our findings show that the perceived incentives in terms of material benefit is paramount in co-management. This confirms earlier findings that incentives are a vital aspect of getting people to negotiate, reach to an agreement and to continue participating (Castro and Nielsen, 2001). Our analysis of household responses showed that if the benefits—from guarding forests—are high then communities will come forward to co-manage the resource.

DISCUSSION AND CONCLUSION

The issues we posited earlier in this chapter were:

(a) What are the recent policy milestones in Indonesia related to protected area management after decentralization?
(b) Has regional autonomy triggered the local initiative to grow?
(c) Has decentralization in West Sumatra revitalized the *nagari* role in forest management?
(d) What are the implications for co-management of protected areas from the collective action point of view?

We have shown that since the adoption of the decentralization policy in 1999, the government of Indonesia enacted forestry laws in the same year, together with administrative decentralization and community empowerment. Taken together, these policies provide room for local government and local communities to participate in protected area management.

However, our data show that the responses of regional and district government to decentralization policy and protected area management varies considerably. If we look at the lower level of administration, the revitalization of *nagari* institutions in West Sumatra has resulted in varying degrees of participation in forest management, depending on the initiative taken by the higher levels of government, incentives available and community-specific context.

The important policy implications from this study can be summarized as follows. First, there is variation in community and district government responses to decentralization policy with regard to forest management according to community setting, incentives available and level of dependence on resources. Therefore, decentralized policies should have room for local initiatives and their specific context in implementation of forest management policies.

Second, decentralization policy does open room for local participation to grow. However, the participation only happens if there are foreseeable benefits accruing to participation that are clearly envisioned by the users. To get communities involved in protecting forests, the incentive mechanism should go beyond trees and forest land to include local endowments and ecological benefits that are highly valued by the local community.

Third, decentralization and revitalization of local institutions like *nagaris* in West Sumatra and many other similar village-level institutions in Indonesia does not guarantee correction and improvement to resource management. These policies depend on several factors such as the ecological setting, dependence on forest resources, rules, roles and modes of benefit and cost sharing, and local leadership. These critical issues are important lessons to understand the coping mechanisms of local people from diverse settings as evidenced from our study under changing policy perspectives. This can set forth guiding principals for drafting dynamic policies on issues of natural resources governance and management, including forestry.

Note

1. Defined as 'the sharing of responsibilities, rights and duties between the primary stakeholders, in particular, local communities and the nation state; a decentralized approach to decision making that involves the local users in the decision-making process as equals with the nation state' (World Bank, 1999).

References

Aden, J. (2001). *Decentralisation of Natural Resource Sectors in Indonesia: Opportunities and Risks*. EASES Discussion Paper Series. September, Washington, DC: The World Bank East Asian Environmental and Social Development Unit. Available on-line: http://www.gtzsfdm.or.id/documents/dec_ind/gv_pa_doc/Decent_ of%20Natural.pdf, accessed on 3/31/2004.

Barber, C.V. and Talbott, K. (2003). 'The Chainsaw and the Gun: The Role of the Military in Deforesting Indonesia'. *Journal of Sustainable Forestry, 16*(3–4), 137–166.

Barr, C.M. (1998). 'Bob Hasan, the Rise of Apkindo, and the Shifting Dynamics of Control in Indonesia's Timber Sector'. *Indonesia, 65*, 1–36.

Benda-Beckmann, F. and Benda-Beckmann, K. (2001). *Recreating the Nagari: Decentralization in West Sumatra*. Max Planck Institute for Social Anthropology Working Paper No. 31. Halle: Max Planck Institute for Social Anthropology.

Borrini-Feyerabend, G., Farvar, M.T., Nguinguiri, J.C., and Ndangang, V.A. (2000). *Co-management of Natural Resources: Organizing, Negotiating and Learning-by-Doing*. Kasparek Verlag, Heidelberg: GTZ and IUCN.

Castro, A.P. and Nielsen, E. (2001). 'Indigenous People and Co-management: Implications for Conflict Management'. *Environmental Science & Policy, 4*, 229–239.

CIFOR NEWS online. (August 2002). 'Illegal logging in Indonesia'. *CIFOR NEWS online*, 30. http://www.cifor.cgiar.org/publications/pdf_files/News-30.pdf, accessed on 9/2/2005.

da Silva, P.P. (2004). 'From Common Property to Co-management: Lessons from Brazil's First Maritime Extractive Reserve'. *Marine Policy, 28*, 419–428.

Dewi, S., Belcher, B., and Puntodewo, A. (2005). 'Village Economic Opportunity, Forest Dependence, and Rural Livelihoods in East Kalimantan, Indonesia'. *World Development, 33*(9), 1419–1434.

FWI/GFW/WRI. (2002). *The State of the Forest: Indonesia*. Bogor: Forest Watch Indonesia, and Washington, DC: Global Forest Watch.

Haeruman, H. Js. (2001). 'Financing Integrated Sustainable Forest and Protected Areas Management in Indonesia: Alternative Mechanisms to Finance Participatory Forest and Protected Areas Management'. International Workshop of Experts on Financing Sustainable Forest Management, Oslo, January 22–25. A Government-led Initiative in Support of the United Nations IPF/IFF/UNFF Processes.

Hiller, M.A., Jarvis, B.C., Lisa, H., Paulson, L.J., Pollard, E.H.B., and Stanley, S.A. (2004). 'Recent Trends in Illegal Logging and Brief Discussion of Their Cause: A Case Study from Gunung Palung National Park, Indonesia'. *Journal of Sustainable Forestry, 19*(1–3), 181–212.

IUCN. (1994). Guidelines for Protected Area Management Categories. CNPPA with the Assistance of WCMC. Gland, Switzerland and Cambridge, UK: IUCN.

Jones, P. J.S. and Burgess, J. (2005). 'Building Partnership Capacity for the Collaborative Management of Marine Protected Areas in the UK: A Preliminary Analysis'. *Journal of Environmental Management, 77*, 227–243.

Kato, T. (1978). 'Change and Continuity in the Minangkabau Matrilineal System'. *Indonesia*, April 25, 1–16.

———. (1989). 'Different Fields, Similar Locusts: Adat Communities and the Village Law of 1979 in Indonesia'. *Indonesia, 47*, 89–114.

Laurance, W.F. (2004). The Perils of Payoff: Corruption as a Threat to Global Bio-diversity'. *Trends in Ecology & Evolution, 19*(8), 399–401.

Lindayanti, R. (2002). 'Shaping Local Forest Tenure in National Politics'. In Nives Dolsak and Elinor Ostrom (eds), *The Commons in the New Millennium.* Cam-bridge, MA: The MIT Press.

McCarthy, J.F. (2002). 'Power and Interest on Sumatra's Rainforest Frontier: Clien-telist Coalitions, Illegal Logging and Conservation in the Alas Valley'. *Journal of Southeast Asian Studies, 33*(1), 77–106.

———. (2004). 'Changing to Gray Area: Decentralisation and the Emergence of Volatile Socio-legal Configurations in Central Kalimantan, Indonesia'. *World Development, 32*, 1199–1233.

Mimbar, M. (2003). 'Demo menuntut pembukaan pintu air (Protest for Lifting up Water Gate)'. *Mimbar Minang*, January 14.

Obidzinski, K. (2004). 'Illegal Logging and the Fate of Indonesia's Forests in Times of Regional Autonomy'. Paper presented at the Tenth Biennial Conference of the International Association for the Study of Common Property (IASCP), Oaxaca, August 9–13.

Ostrom, E. (1999). *Self-Governance and Forest Resources.* CIFOR Occasional Paper No. 20. Bogor: Center for International Forestry Research (CIFOR).

President of the Republic of Indonesia. (1990). Conservation Act No. 5/1990. Jakarta: State Minister for State Secretary of the Republic of Indonesia.

———. (1998). Government Regulation No. 68/1998 on Nature Reserve and Nature Conservation. Jakarta: State Minister for State Secretary of the Republic of Indonesia.

———. (1999a). Forestry Law No. 41/1999. Jakarta: State Minister for State Sec-retary of the Republic of Indonesia.

———. (1999b). Local Government Act No. 22/1999. Jakarta: State Minister for State Secretary of the Republic of Indonesia.

———. (2002). Government the Regulation No. 34/2002. Jakarta: State Minister for State Secretary of the Republic of Indonesia.

———. (2004a). Financial Balance Act No. 33/2004. Jakarta: State Minister for State Secretary of the Republic of Indonesia.

———. (2004b). Government Regulation No. 44/2004. Jakarta: State Minister for State Secretary of the Republic of Indonesia.

———. (2004c). Government Regulation No. 45/2004 on Forest Protection. Jakarta: State Minister for State Secretary of the Republic of Indonesia.

———. (2004d). Regional Autonomy Act No. 32/2004. Jakarta: State Minister for State Secretary of the Republic of Indonesia.

Ravenel, R.M. (2004). 'Community-based Logging and *De facto* Decentralisation: Illegal Logging in the Gunung Palung Area of West Kalimantan, Indonesia'. *Journal of Sustainable Forestry, 19*(1–3), 213–237.

Rhee, S. (2000). '*De facto* Decentralization during a Period of Transition in East Kalimantan'. *Asia-Pacific Community Forestry Newsletter, 13*(2), 34–40. Available online: http://www.recoftc.org/documents/APCF_Newsletter/13_2/Defacto_rhee.pdf

Simanjuntak, R. (2001). 'Local Taxation Policy in the Decentralizing Era'. Paper presented at the Domestic Trade, Decentralization and Globalization, a One Day Conference, Jakarta, April 3.

Sudana, M. (2004). 'Winners take All. Understanding Forest Conflict in the Era of Decentralisation in Indonesia'. Paper presented at the Commons in an Age of Global Transition: Challenges, Risks and Opportunities, the tenth conference of the International Association for the Study of Common Property, Oaxaca, August 9–13.

World Bank. (1999). *Report from the International CBNRM Workshop*. Washington, DC, May 10–14, 1998. Available online: http://www.worldbank.org/wbi/conatrem/

6 EVOLUTION, IMPACTS AND CHALLENGES OF COMMUNITY-BASED FORESTRY IN NEPAL

AMBIKA P. GAUTAM and GANESH P. SHIVAKOTI

INTRODUCTION

It has been more than two decades since Nepal formally adopted the concept of participatory forest management through the formulation of *Panchayat* Forest (PF) and *Panchayat* Protected Forest (PPF) Rules in 1978. Since then, there have been a number of changes in forest policy. Community-based forest management evolved from limited participation of local agencies in forest management in some areas to being the most prioritized forestry program of the government during the period (Acharya, 2002; Bartlett, 1992). There has been increasing handover of public forest lands to the local communities under the community and leasehold forestry programs implemented by the government with support from various bilateral and multilateral donor agencies. Several studies have shown that these programs have met with some notable successes in terms of improving the biophysical environment, uplifting rural livelihoods and institutional development, particularly in the Middle Hills where the programs have been extensively implemented (Collett *et al.*, 1996; Gautam *et al.*, 2002a; Virgo and Subba, 1994; Jackson *et al.*, 1998; Sterk, 1998; JTRCF, 2001; Webb and Gautam, 2001). Because of these achievements, community-based forest management in Nepal, particularly the community forestry program, has been able to draw considerable attention of scholars, development agencies and environmental activists during the last decade.

All is not green, however, with Nepal's community forestry. For example, there are wide differences in the success of the community forestry program among the *terai*,[1] Middle Hills and high mountain regions (JTRCF, 2001). Studies have also pointed towards some limitations of the present model of community forestry as the sole resource management alternative even for the Middle Hills (e.g., Jackson *et al.*, 1993; Gautam, 2002). Several anomalies and misconduct within community Forest User Groups (FUGs) have been reported particularly from the *terai* (Baral and Subedi, 2000). The recent changes in the government forest policy, particularly the provisions related to the sharing of income from community forests with the national and local governments and a ban on handing over of contiguous large blocks of forests in the *terai* and inner-*terai* to the local communities, have created mistrust and conflict between the government agencies and the FUGs (Gautam *et al.*, 2004).

This chapter first presents a brief overview of the evolution of community-based forest management in Nepal. Impacts of the community-based forest management on the biophysical environment, changes on the availability of essential forest products to the user households due to changes in forest condition and adaptation strategies of the households to changing availability of the forest products have been analyzed in a mountain watershed in Central Nepal. We report that the community-based forest management programs had several positive impacts on the forest and the people of the study area, but the programs also had some limitations and may face challenges ahead. The findings are expected to contribute in the identification of prevailing gaps in forest policies and implementation strategies related to community-based forest management in Nepal and other Asian countries, which can be useful to adapt the existing systems to suit the local contexts for continued benefit of the local people and supporting ecosystems.

EVOLUTION OF COMMUNITY-BASED FOREST MANAGEMENT IN NEPAL

Community-based management of forest, in the form of traditional or indigenous systems, has a long history in the hills of Nepal (Arnold and Campbell, 1986; Fisher, 1989; Messerschmidt, 1993). These systems were operational under different types of institutional arrangements at different times and locations. *Talukdari,*[2] *kipat,*[3] and religious forest management systems are some examples. Some of the rules adopted by these indigenous systems of forest management include harvesting only selected products and species, harvesting according to the condition of product, limiting amount of product and using social means of monitoring (Arnold and Campbell, 1986). Some types of indigenous forest management systems continue to exist in many places despite a widespread perception that nationalization of forests in 1957 destroyed these systems.

Community forestry as a formal national forest management strategy was conceived in 1976 after the government drafted a national forestry plan in that year. The plan for the first time recognized the role of local communities and specifically emphasized local participation in forest management. This change in policy was the result of the government's realization that forests can not be managed without the cooperation of local communities (Shrestha, 1996). To implement the concept laid down by the plan, the Forest Act of 1961[4] was amended in 1977 to define the new categories of forests to be managed by local communities, religious institutions and individuals. Operating rules for PF and PPF were prepared in 1978, which allowed local government units known as *panchayats* to manage barren or degraded lands for forest production. PFs were limited to degraded forest areas (about 125 hectare) entrusted to a village *panchayat* for reforestation and use. PPFs were existing forests handed over to a village *panchayat* for protection and proper management under a shareholder arrangement regarding the distribution of income from the sale of forest products. PPFs were limited to about 500 hectares in each *panchayat* (Kanel, 1997). A further provision of leasehold forestry was made in the rules under which limited degraded forest was given to individuals or agencies for reforestation and production of forest products. These amendments in Forest Act and Regulations represent a major shift in Nepal's forest policy although the partnership between the Forest Department and the *panchayat* was generally not successful (see Pokharel, 1997).

The major thrust to the community forestry program came through the Master Plan for the Forestry Sector of 1989. The plan recognized community and private forestry as the largest among the six identified primary forestry programs and encouraged transfer of forests to local communities for active management and use. It gave a clear direction to the development of the community forestry program by emphasizing the need for establishing FUGs as the appropriate local institutions responsible for the protection, development and sustainable utilization of forests and for developing an operational management plan by communities as a prerequisite to handing over forests for their use. It also emphasized the need for retraining the entire forestry staff for their new role as advisors and extension workers (HMGN/ADB/FINNIDA, 1989). The formulation and implementation of the Master Plan can thus be considered as a turning point in the history of forestry sector policy in Nepal.

The eighth five-year plan (1992–97) strongly supported a user group-based community forestry program as recommended by the Master Plan. It also emphasized the need for further intensification of people's participation in forestry management practices by implementing leasehold forestry for environmental conservation and economic benefit of local people living below the poverty line. These objectives of the leasehold forestry program were to be achieved through intensive management of degraded forest patches including agroforestry and horticultural forestry (HMGN, 1992).

Despite the clear direction provided by the Master Plan, the community forestry program could not gain momentum until the promulgation and enforcement of new forestry legislation (including the Forest Act of 1993 and Forest Regulation of 1995) in 1995. This was partly because of the lengthy and complicated procedure in handing over of a forest to the local communities. The emphasis of the Master Plan for user group-based forest management could not be materialized during the first few years of its implementation because it made it impossible to ignore the village *panchayats* in community forestry arrangements until the official ideology in favor of the *panchayat* system collapsed in 1990 (Fisher, 2000).

The current forestry legislation strongly supports the Master Plan policy of user group-based forest management. The forest handover procedure has been simplified by authorizing the local district forest officer to handover any part of a national forest to the local FUG for management and use as a community forest. The Forest Act of 1993 identifies the FUG as a semi-autonomous local entity that can price, sell and transport surplus forest products independently anywhere within the country. The income generated can be used by the FUG in any community development activity after setting aside 25 percent of the income for forest development. The response to these positive changes in legislation has been encouraging in the favor of community-based forest management. The community forestry program has dramatically expanded in terms of both spatial coverage and number of forests handed over to local communities. Records available at the forest department show that a total of 14,337 registered FUGs, including 1.65 million households, already existed in the country (as of November 30, 2006) managing 1.22 million hectares of designated community forest land (about 20.5 percent of the country's forested area), mostly in the Middle Hills. Many FUGs have now moved into intensive forest management for the purpose of producing surplus for sales.

The government has made some changes in forest policy recently. One of the important components of the new policy includes a collaborative management of contiguous large blocks of forests in the *terai* and inner-*terai* as national forest while setting aside barren lands, shrublands and isolated forest patches for handing over as community forests (HMGN, 2000). The Forest Department also issued a circular in September 2000 prohibiting the extraction of any forest product from a community forest, even for meeting subsistence needs, unless a forest resource inventory and assessment of annual increment has been made. These changes in forest policy have met with intense opposition from the Federation of Community Forest Users in Nepal. It is not quite clear why the government, after having met with a certain degree of successes from the community forestry program, came up with these new policy provisions. Whatever the reason, the new policy is likely to destroy the mutual trust and collaboration between communities and the forest bureaucracy that has been built up after more than two decades of the implementation of the community forestry program.

IMPACTS OF COMMUNITY-BASED FORESTRY ON FOREST AND THE LOCAL PEOPLE

With the objective of understanding whether, and if yes how, the implementation of community-based forest management policy had impacts on the condition of the resource and availability of essential forest products for the local people, a case study was conducted in a 153 sq km watershed in central Nepal, using a combination of research methods and techniques. The hypothesis was that implementation of the community-based forest management strategy (including community forestry and leasehold forestry) has improved forest condition and availability of forest products to the user households.

STUDY AREA

The study was conducted in the Upper Roshi watershed located within Kabhrepalanchok district in the Middle Hills of Nepal (Map 6.1). The watershed is reasonably representative of the Middle Hills in terms of its topography, climate, forest types and cover, local economy and forest use. This is one of the pioneer areas for implementing the government-sponsored community forestry program in Nepal, with continuous donor support since 1978. Leasehold forestry is another form of the community-based forest management program implemented by the government since 1992. According to the records available in local district forest office, a total of 2,135 hectares of public forest land in the watershed was being managed by 63 FUGs consisting of 6,808 households under the community forestry program by the end of 2000. Another 110 hectares of degraded forest was managed by small local groups of people living below the poverty line under the leasehold forestry program.

METHODS

The study used a multi-scale and integrated approach of data collection and analysis. The trends of changes in forest cover and other major land cover/land uses in between 1976 and 2000 and

M𝖠𝖯 6.1

Location of the Upper Roshi Watershed in Kabhrepalanchok District, Nepal

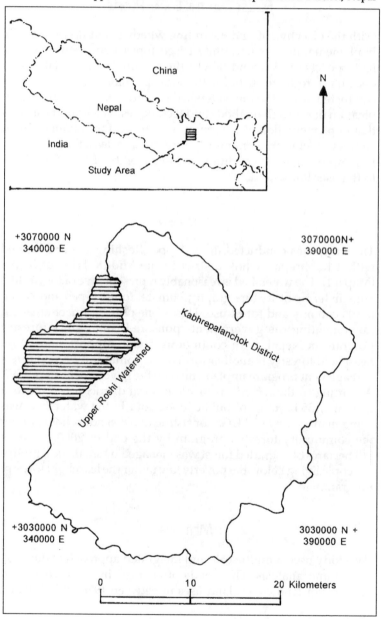

relationships between forest cover change and governance arrangement were analyzed at the watershed level using remote sensing and geographic information systems (GIS) technologies. Three satellite images including a Landsat Multi-spectral Scanner satellite image from 1976, a Landsat Thematic Mapper satellite image from 1989 and an Indian Remote Sensing satellite image from 2000 (IRS-1C, LISS-III) served as the main data sources. Black-and-white aerial photographs of 1:50000 scale, topographic maps and primary data in the form of the ground-truth information required for the classification and accuracy assessment of IRS image, as well as forest level information on forest types, condition and history of land use provided by the local people were used. Important steps involved in mapping land cover/land use types and detection of changes in forest cover over the period have been shown in Figure 6.1.

The study identified three major types of forests in the study area based on the governance arrangements: community forests, semi-government forests and government forests. Community forests, as defined in this study, include formally registered community forests and leasehold forests managed by local user groups formed under the community forestry and leasehold forestry policies of the national government. Forested areas that were legally under the authority of the district forest office but with *de facto* control and claim of ownership by local communities and/or municipalities have been defined as semi-government forests. Those local collective efforts in the semi-government forests had received informal recognition by the concerned government authorities. Forested areas under the direct control of the district forest office and without any form of collective action by the local people were categorized as government forests.

Continuing the investigation on the role of governing institutions in determining forest condition, we further analyzed the relationship between forest governance and biological condition of eight forests within the watershed. Homogeneity in ecological condition across sites and ease of identifying forest users and patterns of forest use were the criteria used in site selection. Six of the selected forests were community forests and the remaining two were semi-government forests. Primary data from those sites were collected using International Forestry Resources and Institution (IFRI) research protocols (see IFRI, 2001 for details) and

Figure 6.1
A Simplified Procedure Used in Land Use Mapping and Changes Detection

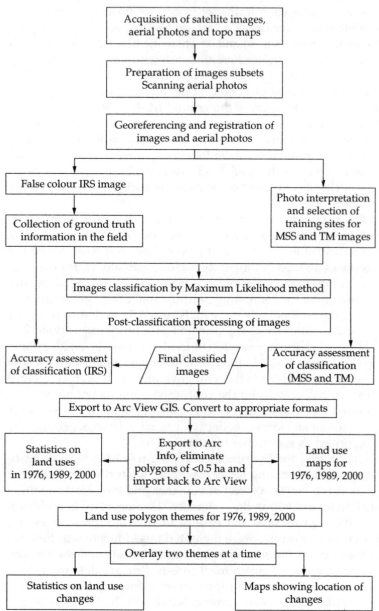

household surveys at some sites. Four dependent variables, including basal area of trees, density of trees, density of saplings plus shrubs and richness of plant species, were chosen to represent forest condition in the analysis. The significance of difference in mean plot values of the dependent variables between the two groups of forest (community and semi-government) was analyzed using a t-test or its non-parametric equivalent depending upon the nature of distribution of the variable values across the forest plots.

The effects of changes in forest condition on the availability of four essential forest products (firewood, timber/poles, fodder and leaf litter) and adaptation strategies of the households to the changing availability of the forest products were analyzed using primary data/information collected through semi-structured interviews with 106 household heads selected randomly from 16 forest user groups within the watershed. The household selection process is presented in Appendix 6.1.

RESULTS AND DISCUSSION

Changes in Forest Cover

The results show that forest area (both broadleaf and coniferous) in the watershed increased and upland agriculture and grassland areas declined between 1976 and 2000. Shrublands decreased during the first period (1976–89) but increased during the second period (1989–2000), while lowland agricultural area expanded during the first period. The trend was reversed during the second period (Table 6.1; Maps 6.2 and 6.3).

Further investigation on changes in forested area of the watershed (forest plus shrublands) revealed that of the total 6,658.2 hectares of forest and shrub area in 1976, 64.3 percent remained unchanged, 12.6 percent improved (shrublands in 1976 converted to forest in 2000), 4.1 percent deteriorated (forest in 1976 converted to shrub-lands in 2000), and 19.1 percent converted to other use in between 1976 and 2000. The high conversion of forested area to other use was, however, compensated by gain from the other use and there was an overall 7.6 percent net gain in forested area during the period.

TABLE 6.1
Cover and Change in Cover of Different Land Cover Types across Three
Time Periods in Upper Roshi Watershed, Kabhrepalanchok District, Nepal

Land Use Class	Percent Cover			Percent Change in Cover		
	1976	1989	2000	1976–1989	1989–2000	1976–2000
Broadleaf forest	31.1	32.4	33.2	+4.1	+2.6	+6.8
Conifer forest	3.7	5.3	6.7	+44.2	+26.4	+82.2
Shrublands	8.6	4.6	6.7	–46.1	+45.0	–21.8
Grasslands	3.1	1.5	1.3	–49.8	–16.7	–58.2
Lowland agriculture	10.3	13.2	11.9	+28.2	–9.4	+16.2
Upland agriculture and other	43.2	42.9	40.0	–0.7	–6.7	–7.4

Note: The total watershed area is 15,335 hectares.

Associations of Forest Cover Change and Present Condition with Governance

A GIS overlay of the polygon theme showing location and extent of changes in forest cover with the polygon theme of forest governance arrangement showed that the proportional net improvement as well as gain to the forested area between 1976 and 2000 was highest in the semi-government forests followed by the community forests (Table 6.2). The government forests, which were located mostly in the southern high mountains (comprising around 50 percent of the total forested area), remained relatively stable during the period although deterioration was substantially higher compared to the improvement in elevations above 2,300 m (Gautam, 2002).

The finding that forest regeneration was higher in the semi-government forests compared to the community forests indicates less importance of legal transfer of resource ownership for successful forest conservation at the local level when the collective efforts of local users and their *de facto* rules have received informal recognition by the concerned government authorities. In fact, the community forests and some of the semi-government forests in the study area were quite similar in terms of forest use pattern and monitoring systems. The two groups of forests, however, differ in terms of forest maintenance activities. Silvicultural treatments such as bush clearing, thinning, pruning and enrichment planting were regularly being done in most of the community forests but not in the semi-government forests. Another notable difference between the two forest types in this watershed was the involvement of local

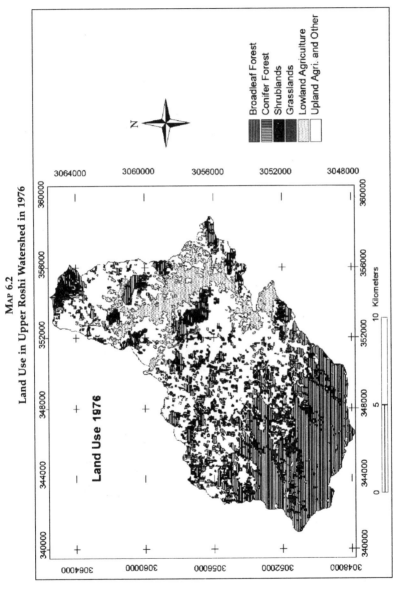

MAP 6.2
Land Use in Upper Roshi Watershed in 1976

Land Use 1976

Broadleaf Forest
Conifer Forest
Shrublands
Grasslands
Lowland Agriculture
Upland Agri. and Other

N

0   5   10 Kilometers

MAP 6.3
Land Use in Upper Roshi Watershed in 2000

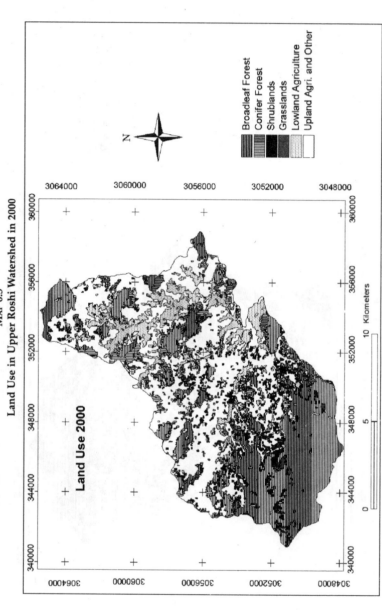

Land Use 2000

Broadleaf Forest
Conifer Forest
Shrublands
Grasslands
Lowland Agriculture
Upland Agri. and Other

Table 6.2

Changes in Forested Area between 1976 and 2000 for Geographical
Spaces in Upper Roshi Watershed that were under the Three
Governance Arrangements in 2000

Governance Type	Forested Area in 1976 (ha)	Percentage of Forested Area in 1976 Compared to the Area in 2000				
		Unchanged	Improved	Deteriorated	Lost to Other Use	Gained from Other Use
Community	1,516.1	62.3	28.4	2.1	7.2	28.8
Semi-government	327.9	45.3	37.5	0.9	16.2	39.3
Government	3,433.6	82.7	5.4	3.7	8.2	10.7

municipalities in forest conservation in most of the semi-government forests. When viewed from this point of view, the finding of this study indicates that a joint effort by forest user groups and local agencies improves the prospects for successful forest conservation at the local level particularly in urban and semi-urban areas (see also Webb and Khurshid, 2000).

The relatively stable condition of the government forests was because of the general remoteness of these forests from the settlements and lower extraction pressure compared to other forests, rather than effective monitoring or enforcement by the forestry staff. Interviews with the local forestry staff and the local people revealed that forested areas under the direct control of the district forest office were virtually open access as the forestry staff members have been mostly engaged in the community forestry activities after the implementation of community forestry program in the district.

The results show that the community forestry and leasehold forestry programs were unsuccessful at reaching more than 50 percent of the total forest area, most of which was located in southern high mountains. This situation remained despite favorable policy and continuous donor support for more than two decades for the implementation of the community forestry program. A major challenge to extending community forestry in the southern mountains is the difficulty in identifying traditional users and their use patterns (prerequisites for community forest handover). The general remoteness of the forests and difficult topography with steep slopes are other limitations for the villagers in managing these forests as community forests. The District Forest Office has committed its limited human and financial resources to the implementation of community forestry and leasehold forestry programs, rather than management of forests under its direct control. Due to absence of monitoring and management, the high elevation forests, which generally have higher commercial and biological values compared to low elevation forests (Dinerstein, 1998; Jackson *et al.*, 1993), have started deteriorating rapidly in recent years (field observation). Deteriorating trends of those forests was also evident from a substantial (45 percent) increase in shrub area of the watershed in between 1989 and 2000 as found in this study and higher rates of forest deterioration compared to improvements above 2,300 m (Gautam, 2002).

The results of the analysis on the relationship between forest governance and biological condition of the forests show that the density of saplings plus shrubs and average richness of plant species per plot were significantly higher in the community forests than the semi-government forests. The community forests also had a higher average density of trees than the semi-government forests although this difference was not statistically significant. The two groups of forests had similar average basal areas of trees (Table 6.3).

The differences in species richness and the density of saplings and shrubs between the community and semi-government forests

TABLE 6.3
Comparison of Mean Values of Selected Forest Characteristics between Community and Semi-government Forests of Upper Roshi Watershed, Nepal

Dependent Variable	Community (N=161)	Semi-government (N=70)	P value	Stat test
Basal area of trees (m²/ha)	7.3	7.4	0.777	Mann-Whitney
Density of trees (number/ha)	414	398	0.785	Mann-Whitney
Density of saplings plus shrubs (number/ha)	2,477	1,415	0.018	Mann-Whitney
Richness of plant species (number of species/plot)	11.7	10.4	0.006	t

Note: N denotes the number of forest plots.

might have resulted from species manipulation by user groups through silvicultural treatments such as bush clearing, thinning, pruning and enrichment plantation in the process of forest management plan implementation. Bush clearing, which was being done regularly in most of the community forests, may also have created favorable conditions for the germination of tree seeds and growth of seedlings, thus contributing to the increase in the number of smaller individuals in community forests compared to the semi-government forests. The same did not happen in semi-government forests because of the absence of an officially approved forest management plan and lack of technical support from the forestry staff required for implementing such forest maintenance activities.

As the community forests and semi-government forests included in this study are located in very similar ecological and socio-economic settings, the findings of the second analysis presented above suggest a relative superiority of local institutions in the community forests over the semi-government forests. This conclusion is based on the assumption that the initial conditions (at the commencement of community-based management) of the community and semi-government forests included in this study were similar. The absence of time series data on the biological condition of those forests did not allow for quantitative detection and comparison of changes over time between the two groups of forests.

Changes in Forest Product Availability and Adaptation by Forest-Dependent Households

The ease with which the four main forest products were available to the households at the time of the study (2001) and 20 years prior varied with the type of product. Fodder and timber were ranked by a majority of respondents as the scarcest forest products, both at present as well as 20 years earlier. Leaf litter was the only product easily available to the majority of households at the time of the study. Availability of firewood was intermediate (Table 6.4).

The availability of the forest products to the households during the two periods was compared statistically using a Wilcoxon Signed Ranks test.[5] The results show that the availability of leaf litter and firewood was significantly greater in 2001 than 20 years earlier, while availability of fodder (including leaf fodder and grasses)

TABLE 6.4

Percentage of Respondents Ranking the Availability of Essential
Forest Products at Present (A) and 20 Years Ago
(B) in Upper Roshi Watershed, Nepal

	Firewood		Fodder		Timber and Poles		Leaf Litter	
Product	A	B	A	B	A	B	A	B
N	101	87	95	84	106	92	95	84
Easily available	3.0	11.5	0.0	7.1	0.0	0.0	22.1	13.1
Available	44.6	20.7	10.5	30.9	10.4	10.9	52.6	20.2
Hardly available	46.5	41.4	12.7	28.6	15.1	14.1	15.8	36.9
Not available	5.9	26.4	76.8	33.4	74.5	75.0	9.5	29.8

decreased significantly during the same period. Availability of
timber and poles was only marginally higher in 2001 compared
to the availability 20 years earlier (Table 6.5).

TABLE 6.5

Percentage of Responses Indicating Changes in the Availability of
Main Forest Products in 2001 Compared with 20 Years Ago

Product	N	Increased	Decreased	Remained the Same	Assy. Sig. (2-tailed)
Firewood	87	51.7	21.8	26.4	0.018
Fodder	84	7.1	56.0	36.9	0.000
Timber and poles	92	26.1	21.7	52.2	0.744
Leaf litter	84	57.1	9.5	33.3	0.000

According to the respondents, though getting fodder and timber was difficult in both the periods, the reasons leading to those
difficulties were different. Twenty years earlier, most of the forests
were degraded and were not able to produce required products.
Although the condition of many of the forests had improved by
2001, there had not been a concomitant increase in the availability
of timber and fodder to the user households because of the restrictions imposed by the user groups themselves on the harvest of
these products. The respondents' perceptions were supported by
observations in the field and informal interviews with FUG leaders.
For example, eight of the 16 interviewed community forests had
good stocking of timber trees. However, limited harvesting of timber for subsistence use was being allowed by FUGs from only three
forests. Similarly, while about half of the user groups had good

stocking of fodder trees in their forests, none of them allowed harvesting of leaf fodder (personal observation). Since grazing and harvesting of leaf fodder from community forests was banned by the respective FUGs, grass collected occasionally was the only fodder that was available from the forests to the user households (Gautam, 2002).

Our experience and the interviews with the users indicate that the local FUGs in the study area (and the hills in general) have generally adopted protection-oriented and rigid rules to prevent the harvesting of timber and leaf fodder after they took over the forest from the government. This may be due to a limited knowledge about actual yields and responses of forest to intervention and a result of the concern of the user groups about the risk of degrading the forest. It may, however, also indicate a change in the community forest management objectives of the FUGs from the initial objective of meeting subsistence requirements towards timber production for commercial purposes at present.

The decrease in fodder availability from the forests is also attributable to the fact that either part or all of many of the forests are pine plantations, which sustain low levels of fodder species. Pines, which have no value for fodder and are poor firewood, were actively promoted in the study area as species of choice in government plantations during 1970s and 1980s, without giving due consideration to the diverse product requirements of the local people. Most of these plantations were later handed over to FUGs as community forests (Gautam and Webb, 2001).

The data suggest that even for products that had been increasingly available to the households over the 20-year study period, there were large gaps between the supply of products from forests and households' subsistence requirements. When asked whether the quantity of forest products available from the community forest was sufficient to meet their household needs, 70 percent of the respondents said that the quantity of firewood available was insufficient and 46 percent said leaf litter was insufficient (Gautam, 2002). For a majority of the respondents who could not fulfill their household needs from the community forest private land was the most important alternative source for fulfilling the deficit of forest products (Table 6.6).

Table 6.6
The Most Important Alternative Source for
Meeting the Forest Product Deficit

Product	N	Government Forests	Own Private Land	Buy from Others and Market	Use Substitute
Firewood	71	12.7	52.1	5.6	29.6
Fodder	83	9.6	55.4	2.4	32.5
Timber and poles	92	15.2	45.7	39.1	0.0

Note: Numbers are percentage of respondents (N).

The results presented indicate that in addition to community forests, private sources of forest products are making a substantial contribution to the rural livelihoods of community and leasehold forestry users in the study area. The findings also show that use of substitute fuel and fodder is becoming common for many households who have opportunities of getting those substitutes and can afford to buy them. The two most common fuel substitutes, according to the respondents, were sawdust from local sawmills followed by kerosene oil. Dried paddy-straw bought mainly from neighboring areas of Bhaktapur district was the most common product used as substitute for green fodder.

The increasingly important role of private forestry in the watershed is not a surprise considering the fact that there had been a two- to three-fold increase in tree cover on sloping terraces of Kabhrepalanchok district in between 1964 and 1988 (Carter and Gilmour, 1989) and that trend is expected to have continued after 1988 as well. Whether the community forestry program influenced the planting of trees on private land is not clear. The change in dependency towards private resources is important for meeting increasing demands and reducing the pressure on forestland. There is, however, a concern that increasing dependency of land-rich farmers on private resources may favor the present protectionist approach in community forest management, which could lead to marginalization of poorer members of the user group who do not have sufficient private land to grow trees and also cannot afford alternatives. If this happens, the poorer members will be forced to buy trees from their land-rich neighbors or illegally extract forest products from the community or government forests to meet their subsistence requirements.

CONCLUSIONS AND POLICY IMPLICATIONS

Forest policy in Nepal evolved continuously in favor of community-based forest management over the last two-and-half decades. This change in forest management from fully centralized control of the resource towards a more participatory approach had many positive impacts on the forest and the local people as evidenced by the findings of the case study presented in this chapter. Forest cover in the study area increased after the implementation of the community forestry and leasehold forestry programs and the biological condition of the community-managed forests was improving. One important development on the institutional front over the last two decades was that the concept of the FUG as the responsible local organization entrusted to manage and use forests has been strongly embedded within the institutional structure of the national forest governance system.

The positive changes in forest cover and condition provide some evidence of ecological sustainability of the resource and the findings also signify to some extent the success of forest conservation efforts by local communities and the agencies involved. The results thus provide evidence for a relative superiority of community-based forest governance in the hills compared to complete government control of the resource.

The results of this study also point towards some limitations of the present models of community-based forest management systems as the sole resource management alternatives for all the accessible forests in the hills as envisaged by the Master Plan. Some of the issues surrounding the community forestry and leasehold forestry programs, challenges likely to be faced by these programs in near future and their implications for forest policy can be summarized as follows.

Coordination between the FUG and Local Municipality

The existing forest policy and forestry legislation of Nepal recognize the user groups formed under the community forestry program as autonomous local entities responsible for the management and use of local forests. The relationship of an FUG with other local agencies (e.g., Village Development Committee or municipality) has not been specified in the Master Plan as well as in the current forestry legislation. The finding of this study that the proportionately highest level of forest improvement and gain took place in semi-government forests, however, indicates that a joint effort by forest user groups and local agencies improves the prospects for successful forest conservation at the local level, particularly in urban and semi-urban areas. The results thus provide a basis for questioning the appropriateness of existing policy, especially when viewed in the context of existing conflict between the Forest Act of 1993 and the Local Governance Act of 1997.

Tenure and Forest Condition

The finding that forest improvement and gain was higher in the semi-government forests compared to the formal community forests indicates that formal handover of forest ownership is not a major factor determining successful forest conservation at the local level when the rights to organize and manage forests for the community benefits have been recognized (even informally) by concerned authorities. In other words, *de facto* rules are more important than *de jure* rules in our study area and this may be applicable to other local settings. The finding that the community forests were generally better in biological conditions over the semi-government forests, however, do not fully support the above conclusion and indicates the relative superiority of institutional arrangements in community forests compared to the semi-government forests. The inconsistency in the findings from the two analyses indicates that the outcomes from local forest management initiatives may be more dependent on the local institutional arrangements that regulate forest use and maintenance of the resource than on the type of property rights arrangements.

Passive Approach to the Management of Community Forests

The results of this study show that the community forests were not able to meet a substantial proportion of the users' forestry-related household requirements, particularly for fodder and timber, despite a general improvement in forest condition over the last few decades. One of the reasons leading to this situation was a passive (i.e., protection-oriented) approach adopted by most of the FUGs in the management of community forests. According to Arnold (1998), such a conservative approach in the management of community forests is common in the Middle Hills of Nepal. There could be several reasons leading to the adoption of the protectionist approach in community forest management by FUGs but their concern over the risk of degrading the resource may be the most important one. The decrease in fodder availability from the forests is also probably attributable to the fact that many community forests in the study area are pine plantations that sustain low levels of fodder species.

The protectionist approach of community forest management has not only affected the general availability of products to the user households but also may have serious equity implications for community forest management. The negative effects arising from such an approach are found to be more direct to the poorer users, particularly land-poor households, because there will be less opportunity for private forestry to supplement restricted/ protected community forest products (Gautam *et al.*, 2002b). Moreover, lack of disposable income will prevent a household from purchasing the required product from a secondary source. A protectionist approach of forest management by the FUGs thus might further marginalize more forest-dependent households without providing them alternatives. This may eventually result in inequity within communities and could also be a potential threat to the long-term sustainability of the community forestry program. Lack of timber availability resulting from a protectionist approach by the FUGs may also place the remaining national forest areas (i.e., open-access forest) under increasing extraction pressure as communities seek out alternative sites for timber collection. In this context, optimum utilization of the community forests with due consideration to the requirements of poorer and disadvantaged households is one of the key issues that needs consideration in the management of community forests in future. This could possibly be achieved through effective training and extension activities that increase the confidence of FUGs on yield-based active forest management.

Further research should investigate the impacts of changes in forest product availability on different socio-economic groups within the user groups. Private forests constitute an important source of subsistence products in the study area, but how private forestry is emerging to cope with the challenges arising from changing dependencies of rural households between community, government and private resources is not properly known. This is thus another important area to be addressed by future research.

Limitation of the Present Community Forestry

The findings indicate that the community forestry and leasehold forestry programs along with the informal local arrangements played important roles in improving forest condition in some parts of the watershed. However, the existing models of the programs were unsuccessful in reaching more than 50 percent of the total forest area, most of which was located in southern high mountains. One of the major factors responsible for this outcome could be the inability of the existing community-based forest management policy and operational procedures to acknowledge the high difference in biophysical, socio-economic and demographic conditions between the lower hills and the elevated mountains in the southern part of the watershed. Such a situation exists in other parts of the Middle Hills as well. This gap in forest policy has raised concern over the future of high elevation forests, which have extensive coverage in the Middle Hills as a whole but remain largely open access. Although more research is needed before making any recommendation on the appropriate governance regime for the high elevation forests of the Middle Hills, the findings of this study reinforce our conclusion that existing policy needs to be revised to make it more flexible to contextual factors and to not adhere to a 'blueprint' approach in the implementation of the community forestry policy.

Appendix 6.1

Sampling Procedure Involved in the Selection of Respondents for the Household Survey

A list of forest user groups in the watershed was prepared on the basis of the record of formalized community and leasehold forest user groups available at the District Forest Office, Kabhrepalanchok. From the list, 16 (19.7 percent) user groups were selected randomly for the survey. All the member households from the selected user groups formed the population of the study. The sample size was determined by using the equation for sampling developed by Arkin and Colton (1963), for 0.05 probability level, a reliability of ±4 percent and an expected rate of occurrence of 95 percent:

$$n = [NZ^2 \, p(1-p)]/[Nd^2 + Z^2 \, p(1-p)],$$

where n is the sample size, N is the total population (households), p is the estimated proportion of the population included, and d is the level of precision.

The sample was distributed among the selected forest user groups on a proportional basis using the following formula:

$$n1 = (N1 * n)/N,$$

where n1 is the size of the sub-sample in a particular user group; N1 is the total number of households in that user group; n is the sample size; and N is the total population.

Households from each user group were randomly selected. The open-ended interview was designed to elicit maximum information from the respondents.

Acknowledgments

Financial support for this research was provided by DANIDA through a doctoral research grant to Ambika Gautam under Integrated Watershed Development and Management Program of the Asian Institute of Technology, ANUTECH Pty Ltd., Australia via Nepal Australia Community Resource Management Project, Kathmandu, and a MacArthur grant made available via the Workshop in Political Theory and Policy Analysis at Indiana University. We thank the Center for the Study of Institutions, Population, and Environmental Change, funded by National Science Foundation grant SBR-9521918, at Indiana University for sharing Landsat satellite images of 1976 and 1989.

Notes

1. Low flat land in the southern part of the country.
2. *Talukdars* were local headmen during the period of rules by the *Ranas* who had the responsibility of regulating forest use.

3. A form of land tenure in which land was regarded as the common property of the local ethnic group and was managed from within the ethnic tribal's organization (Fisher, 1989).
4. The first comprehensive forestry legislation promulgated after the nationalization of forests in 1957. The Act divided forests into different categories and strengthened the role of Forest Department in forest conservation.
5. This test makes no assumptions about the shapes of the distributions of the two variables and takes into account information about the magnitude of differences within pairs and gives more weight to pairs that show large differences than to pairs that show small differences.

References

Acharya, K.P. (2002). 'Twenty-four Years of Community Forestry in Nepal'. *International Forestry Review*, 4(2), 149–156.

Arkin, H. and Colton, R. (1963). *Table of Statistics*, 2nd Edn. New York: Barnes and Noble.

Arnold, J.E.M. (1998). *Managing Forests as Common Property*. FAO Forestry Paper 136. Rome: Food and Agriculture Organization of the United Nations.

Arnold, J.E.M. and Campbell, J.G. (1986). 'Collective Management of Hill Forests in Nepal: The Community Forestry Development Project'. In *Proceedings of the Conference on Common Property Resource Management*. Washington, DC: National Research Council, National Academy Press.

Baral, J.C. and Subedi, B.R. (2000). 'Some Community Forestry Issues in the Terai, Nepal: Where do We Go from Here?'. *Forest, Trees and People Newsletter*, 42, 20–25.

Bartlett, A.G. (1992). 'A Review of Community Forestry Advances in Nepal'. *Commonwealth Forestry Review*, 71(2), 95–100.

Carter, A.S. and Gilmour, D.A. (1989). 'Increase in Tree Cover on Private Farmland in Central Nepal'. *Mountain Research and Development*, 9(4), 381–391.

Collett, G., Chhetri, R., Jackson, W.J., and Shepherd. (1996). *Nepal Australia Community Forestry Project Socio-economic Impact Study*. Canberra: ANUTECH Pty Ltd.

Dinerstein, E. (1998). 'A Biodiversity Assessment and Gap Analysis of the Himalayas'. In *Report on the International Meeting on Himalaya Ecoregional Cooperation*, held during February 16–18, in Kathmandu, Nepal. The United Nations Development Program.

Fisher, R.J. (1989). *Indigenous Systems of Common Property Forest Management in Nepal*. Working Paper No. 18, Honolulu: Environmental and Policy Institute, East-West Center.

———. (2000). 'Decentralization and Devolution of Forest Management: A Conceptual Overview'. In T. Enters, P.B. Durst, and M. Victor (eds), *Decentralization and Devolution of Forest Management in Asia and the Pacific*. Regional Community Forestry Training Center (RECOFTC) Report No. 18 and Food and Agricultural Organization Regional Office for Asia and the Pacific (RAP) Publication 2000/1. Bangkok: RECOFTC and FAO RAP.

Gautam, A.P. (2002). *Forest Land Use Dynamics and Community-based Institutions in a Mountain Watershed in Nepal: Implications for Forest Governance and Management*. Doctoral dissertation, Asian Institute of Technology, Thailand.

Gautam, A.P., Shivakoti, G.P., and Webb, E.L. (2004). 'A Review of Forest Policies, Institutions, and Changes in the Resource Condition in Nepal'. *International Forestry Review*, 6(2), 136–148.

Gautam, A.P. and Webb, E.L. (2001). 'Species Diversity and Forest Structure of Pine Plantations in the Middle Hills of Nepal'. *Banko Jankari*, 11(2), 13–21.

Gautam, A.P., Webb, E.L., and Eiumnoh, A. (2002a). 'GIS Assessment of Land Use-Land Cover Changes Associated with Community Forestry Implementation in the Middle Hills of Nepal'. *Mountain Research and Development*, 22(1), 63–69.

Gautam, A.P, Webb, E.L., and Shivakoti, G.P. (2002b). 'Local Participants' Perceptions about Socio-economic and Environmental Impacts of Community Forestry in the Middle Hills of Nepal'. *Asia Pacific Journal of Rural Development*, 12(2), 60–81.

His Majesty's Government of Nepal (HMGN). (1992). *The Eighth Plan (1992–1997; Unofficial Translation)*. Kathmandu: HMGN, National Planning Commission.

———. (2000). *Revised Forestry Sector Policy*. Kathmandu: HMGN, Ministry of Forests and Soil Conservation.

HMGN/ADB/FINNIDA. (1989). *Master Plan for the Forestry Sector, Nepal: Forestry Sector Policy*. Kathmandu: HMGN, Ministry of Forests and Soil Conservation.

International Forestry Resources and Institutions (IFRI). (2001). *IFRI Research Program Field Manual Version 10.0*. Indiana University: Center for the Study of Institutions, Population, and Environmental Change.

Jackson, W.J., Nurse, M.C., and Chhetri, R.B. (1993). 'High Altitude Forests in the Middle Hills: Can They be Managed as Community Forests?'. *Banko Janakari*, 4(1), 20–23.

Jackson, W.J., Tamrakar, R.M., Hunt, S., and Shepherd, K.R. (1998). 'Land-use Changes in Two Middle Hill Districts of Nepal'. *Mountain Research and Development*, 18(3), 193–212.

Joint Technical Review of Community Forestry (JTRCF). (2001). *JTRCF: Report of the Joint Technical Review Committee*. Kathmandu: Ministry of Forest and Soil Conservation.

Kanel, K.R. (1997). 'Community Forestry: Implications for Watershed Management'. In C. Khenmark, B. Thaiuts, L. Puangchit, and S. Thammincha (eds), *Proceedings of the FORTROP'96: Tropical Forestry in the 21st Century, 25–28 November 1996*. Bangkok: Kasetsart University.

Messerschmidt, D.A. (1993). 'Linking Indigenous Knowledge to Create Co-management in Community Forest Development Policy'. In K. Warner and H. Wood (eds), *Policy and Legislation in Community Forestry. Proceedings of a Workshop held in Bangkok, Jan 27–29*. Bangkok: Regional Community Forestry Training Center.

Pokharel, B.K. (1997). *Foresters and Villagers in Contention and Compact*. Doctoral dissertation, University of East Anglia, Norwich.

Shrestha, K.B. (1996). *Community Forestry in Nepal: An Overview of Conflicts*. Nepal Madhyasthata Samuha. Discussion Paper Series No. MNR 96/2, Kathmandu: ICIMOD.

Sterk, A. (1998). *Leasing Degraded Forest Land: An Innovative Way to Integrate Forest and Livestock Development in Nepal*. Bangkok: Food and Agriculture Organization of the United Nations, Regional Office for Asia and the Pacific.

Virgo, K.J. and Subba, K.J. (1994). 'Land-use Change between 1978 and 1990 in Dhankuta District, Koshi Hills, Eastern Nepal'. *Mountain Research and Development, 14*, 159–170.

Webb, E.L. and Gautam, A.P. (2001). 'Effects of Community Forest Management on the Structure and Diversity of a Successional Broadleaf Forest in Nepal'. *International Forestry Review, 3*(2), 146–157.

Webb, E.L. and Khurshid, M. (2000). 'Divergent Destinies among Pine Forests in Northern Pakistan: Linking Ecosystem Characteristics with Community Self-governance and Local Institutions'. *International Journal of Sustainable Development and World Ecology, 7*, 44–45.

7 | IMPLICATIONS OF LEASEHOLD AND COMMUNITY FORESTRY FOR POVERTY ALLEVIATION

MUKUNDA KARMACHARYA, BIRENDRA KARNA and ELINOR OSTROM

COMMUNITY AND LEASEHOLD FORESTRY IN NEPAL

A Short History

Nepal has experimented with diverse forms of community forests for more than three decades.[1] Community forestry was first initiated in 1978 under the Forest Act, 1961, with subsequent amendments in 1976 and 1978 as Panchayat Forest and Panchayat Protected Forests. Although community forestry was officially started in 1978, many local communities had organized themselves unofficially to use and manage some forested areas in earlier times (Arnold and Campbell, 1986). The first 'official' community forestry development project was initiated in 1980, with the establishment of the Community Forestry Development and Training Project funded by the World Bank and the technical assistance provided by the Food and Agriculture Organization (FAO) of the United Nations. His Majesty's Government of Nepal (HMGN) passed the Forest Act in 1993, and then later, the Forest Regulations in 1995, in order to provide stronger regulations defining the rights and responsibilities of forest users and forest officials. Many international agencies and foreign governments have been involved in the community forestry development process in Nepal (see Appendix 7.1).

In 1989, a second type of 'community forestry program' was created by adding an amendment to the Forest Regulations to create a leasehold forestry program that intended to focus on the presumed needs of poor families. This program was first initiated in 1993 through establishment of the Hills Leasehold Forestry and Fodder Development Project (HLFFDP). The HLFFDP was financially supported with a loan from the International Fund for Agricultural Development and a grant from the Government of the Netherlands through the FAO. The project was jointly implemented by the Department of Forest, the Livestock Division of the Department of Agricultural Development, the Agricultural Development Bank of Nepal and the Nepal Agricultural Research Council. Initially, the project was implemented in 10 districts. The third phase of the project was extended up to July 2003 with a 90 percent loan from the International Fund for Agricultural Development (IFAD) and a 10 percent contribution of HMGN. At present, the leasehold forestry program is launched altogether in 37 districts, with IFAD's extended loan and grant assistance for 22 districts, as government's program in 11 districts and with other international donor assistance in four districts.

In 1989, the Master Plan for Forestry Sector recognized five types of forests: (*a*) national forests/government forests, (*b*) private forests, (*c*) religious forests, (*d*) community forests and (*e*) leasehold forests. A substantial proportion of government-owned forestry land has been turned over to forest user groups. So far, community forests comprise 0.8 million hectares (14.3 percent of the forested land in Nepal) managed by nearly 11,000 user groups involving over 1.2 million households.[2] Leasehold forests account for slightly over 7,000 hectares (0.1 percent) managed by 1,655 leasehold user groups composed of 11,253 households.[3] The efforts to develop an effective community forestry policy in Nepal have been generally evaluated as among the more successful efforts in Asia (Bartlett, 1992; JTRCF, 2001).

The level of conflict that has been observed in some leasehold forests, however, leads one to raise questions whether this program, which is specifically targeted at poor families, is designed in a manner that is likely to achieve its overall goal. In Baramchi village of Sindhupalchok district, for example, the other residents living in and near to forests that had been designated as leasehold forests, refused to stop using these forests (NFRI, 1998). As described later in this chapter, fights have broken out between the Forest User Groups (FUGs) authorized to use the leasehold forests and their neighbors. In one instance, a large group of neighbors mobilized and invaded a leasehold forest and harvested most of the grasses planted by the lessee households. The conflict has escalated into a more general set of disputes among local residents, including the destruction of pipelines carrying drinking water from a local reservoir. Noticing conflict of this nature in most of the leasehold forests observed by our research team led us to want to explore more fully a potential explanation for these costly events.

Basic Objectives of Community and Leasehold Forestry Approaches

Community forestry and leasehold forestry are two approaches that HMGN has practiced under its focus on community forestry systems. The concept of an FUG is an integral organizational form of importance for both programs. The management of both community and leasehold forests is handed over to FUGs. Members of FUGs are provided rights to the use of the forest land and are responsible for maintaining the sustainability of the forest. The FUGs are authorized to make rules for the implementation of an operational plan for a particular forest and/or to provide incentives to member households. The FUG can raise funds as fees, donations and fix sale prices of forest products as well as distributing forest products according to these plans. It can spend its income in social development and public welfare activities after spending one-fourth of its fund for the protection and development of the forest that has been handed over to it. The ownership of the forestland, however, remains under the ownership of HMGN for both arrangements.

The basic objectives of community forestry and leasehold forestry are to allow local communities, who are the traditional and/or legitimate forest users, to manage, develop and use forested areas in a sustainable way. Leasehold forestry has two additional objectives of reducing poverty and restoring the degraded forest area. Thus, in leasehold forestry, only the poor (economical criteria) households are supposed to be selected and small groups of them are formed before a degraded forest is handed over to them.

The formation of Community Forest User Groups (CFUGs) and Leasehold Forest User Groups (LFUGs) are provisioned and guided by the Forest Act, 1993 and the Forest Regulations, 1995. One aspect of these two forest regimes is similar. Both programs hand over some aspects of forest management to groups of forest users, which are defined and organized as FUGs. A community forest consists of a larger group of users as members while a leasehold forest consists of smaller groups of users, 5–12 families in a group. A member household is normally provided use rights for 1 hectare of forest land in leasehold forestry, whereas no limitation of the number of member households or the size of the forest is mentioned in the relevant regulations for a community forest.

While considerable similarity exists in the objective of the two programs, our research teams conducting past field studies observed considerable conflict in the effort to establish and sustain leasehold forests (see Kanel *et al.*, 1999; NFRI, 1998). A similar level of conflict was not observed in the early stages of establishing community forests. In the sites studied, the creation of leasehold forests itself appeared to cause increased conflicts. Households excluded from the leasehold groups refused to respect the rights of leasehold members and sabotaged forest management. In two leasehold sites, conflicts were reduced by expanding membership to households that were not originally considered to be within the target population. In two other leasehold sites, social conflict continues to fester as a result of the exclusion of members from the program. This conflict challenges the viability of forest management in these forests.

Research Question

The HMGN has been conducting community forestry and leasehold forestry programs side-by-side in order to develop forest resources and use the forest in a sustainable way. Since the concepts of both types of forest regimes are similar—with a small difference in the objective of the leasehold forestry—there is need for studying the rules and incentives provided and reactions of participants to the incentives. This chapter tries to examine these rules and incentives of the community forestry and leasehold forestry in an effort to provide an explanation for these findings from our past field studies.

Given the similarities in objectives and the differences in structure between the leasehold and community forest program in Nepal, the core research question to be addressed in this chapter is:

Why is it that the rules created by LFUGs, which are especially designed for poor households, tend not to be accepted by other residents of a community, while rules created or incentives provided by some CFUGs for the poor households in their groups appear to be accepted to a greater degree by other residents of the community?

To address this question, we will first address how user groups are formed for both types of forests. Then, we will examine the challenges that both types of user groups face in accomplishing their objectives. In the last part of the chapter, we will provide evidence obtained as part of the research program of the Nepal Forestry Resources and Institutions (NFRI) research program in Nepal.

THE USER GROUP FORMATION PROCESS

Community Forests

The District Forest Officer (DFO) is empowered to handover any part of the government forests to a CFUG as a community forest to develop, manage and use the forest. The CFUG has to submit an application, together with an operational plan, for the forest and a constitution of the FUG. The operational plan specifies the boundary of the forest and the identification of included forest users and also describes the schedules of forest management and utilization activities for the forest. The district forest officials provide technical assistance for the preparation of the operational plan. The constitution is the basic rule by which the group would be organized. The constitution will specify the rights and responsibilities of the chairman and other officials as well as those of the general members.

The boundaries of the villages, towns, districts and forest do not affect the handing over of a forest area as a community forest. In other words, the size of the community forest and the number of members can be of almost any magnitude depending on the consensus of local forest users. The community forest is handed over for a period of three to five years. This time frame can be extended. Basically, a CFUG is formed keeping in view accessibility of users and forest, traditional use rights and willingness to manage the forest as a community forest. The CFUG should receive a Certificate of Hand Over of the management. The DFO of the concerned district is required to monitor and evaluate the condition of the handed-over community forest.

Leasehold Forests

The leasehold forestry program is especially designed for poor households who are officially below the poverty line. It targets marginal farmers and landless or near landless farmers. The two eligibility criteria are: (*a*) owning less than 0.5 hectare of land and (*b*) a per capita annual income of Rs 3,035 (US$ 110 at 1985/86 prices). Thus, other residents of the same community traditionally using the forest (before converting it to be a leasehold forest), who are not categorized as poor, are not eligible to be members of an LFUG or, thus, to use this forest thereafter. The eligible households and the degraded forest patches are identified and listed down by the staffs of the Small Farmer Development Project of the Agricultural Development Bank and the DFO. The DFO issues a notice about the formation of a leasehold FUG and asks for any objection that may be present in the community about the process. The DFO is charged with the responsibility of obtaining a consensus (*Sahamati Patra*, meaning 'an agreement') from the community to form a leasehold FUG. Then, patches of degraded forest land are leased to the group for a maximum of 40 years, which authorizes the right to use the forest. A second term of 40 years can be granted after the first term has expired. Any part of the national forest, however, that is suitable for handing over as a community forest to a larger and more diverse user group is not supposed to be handed over as a leasehold forest (Section 30, Forest Act, 1993). In other words, so far as the community members are willing to manage the forest as a community forest, the forest should not be converted to a leasehold forest.

Once a leasehold group is formed, together with the formulation of an operational plan and a constitution, a leasehold contract is made that is signed by the chairperson of the group and the DFO. Staffs of the DFO and the HLFFDP provide technical assistance in the preparation of an operational plan. In addition, the technical assistance unit established within the department of forests/DFO provides research and extension, input supply in the form of forage seeds and seedlings for plantation and monitoring and evaluation. The operational plan is prepared for five years, even if the official handover of management is for 40 years. If the management and utilization of the leasehold forest are not found to be consistent with the operational plan for the forest, management of the forest can be taken back by the DFO from the leasehold FUG.

CHALLENGES IN ACCOMPLISHING OBJECTIVES

Community Forestry

In addition to the problems involved in deciding on the management and conservation strategies that will be undertaken, a major problem that community forests face relates to the identification of forest users in relation to a patch of forest and the development of a set of rules and practices that are agreed upon and followed by the members of the group. Many contemporary community forests do draw on the rough boundaries of traditionally used forest patches. While determining boundaries is always a challenge, since most users living in the surrounding areas are eligible to use a community forest, the challenge of drawing boundaries is not overwhelming. Since over 11,000 CFUGs have been formed during the past several decades, district foresters working with groups interested in creating a community forest have considerable experience. On the other hand, the vast number of CFUGs formed in recent times raises serious questions about whether district foresters are routinely following a blueprint when turning over forests to locally formed groups (Varughese, 1999). Given the wide diversity of ecological conditions in Nepal and the variety of historical experiences of local leaders and groups, a blueprint approach is unlikely to generate successful governance designs in the long run.

A major challenge facing CFUGs, once formed, is devising rules that will be followed by members of the group and will help to increase the productivity and sustainability of the forest under protection. Not all CFUGs have successfully accomplished this task.

In some locations, the local elite have exercised substantial leadership in forming the CFUG and in designing policies that protect their interests without protecting the interests of the poorer members of the community (Ojha, 2002). The program also appears to have been more successfully implemented in the middle hills of Nepal than in the *terai* (Paudel and Pokharel, 2001). In other locations where the local group has invested substantial time and effort in designing rules well tailored to the ecology and needs of their members, they have designed institutions that have a high likelihood of providing a set of incentives for users leading toward sustainable development over time (Varughese, 1999). Nothing is automatic about creating an FUG—either through the community forestry program or the leasehold forestry program—that guarantees success and sustainability.

Leasehold Forestry

The first difficulty in setting up a leasehold forestry project is to identify the degraded forest patches that need to be converted into leasehold forests. The word 'degraded' does not have a well-established method for identification, and, sometimes users help make a forest degraded. (In the leasehold forestry area of Shaktikhor, Chitwan, for example, users told our team that some standing trees were cut by local users in order to qualify the forest as degraded.) Then, the DFO should obtain a consensus from the residents of the community. For this, the DFO issues an official notification in the community that informs the residents of the community that if they would like to register the forest as a community forest, they should proceed to form a CFUG. Otherwise, the forest patch will be converted to a leasehold forest.

The second difficulty is that the poor households, which are the central focus of the program, have to wait several years for the degraded forest to produce adequate output. This comes after putting in substantial hard work in the degraded forest, which they are expected to do without any short-term reward. A third difficulty found in the leasehold forestry is that if the leasehold groups reorganize to add new members, the added members are not officially accepted. They lack legal protection even if the reorganization had the consensus of the entire community. Training programs, distribution of forage seeds, seedlings and other inputs as well as other development activities run by the DFO and the HLFFDP are provided on the basis of officially-accepted member households.

AN OVERVIEW OF THE RESEARCH SITES IN NEPAL

The International Forestry Resources and Institutions (IFRI) Research Program in Nepal

The NFRI center was among the very first Collaborative Research Centers (CRCs) of the IFRI research program. NFRI was established in 1993. The first four sites studied by NFRI in October 1993 were located in the central and western hills and were considered to be 'baseline' studies for leasehold projects. NFRI was then asked to conduct several studies of the initial leasehold forests established and four leasehold sites were first studied in the spring and fall of 1994. Many of these first sites have been revisited once (see Appendix 7.2 for a complete list of NFRI sites). A fifth leasehold forest was visited in April 1995 followed by another three leasehold forests in the same year. A set of revisits to HLFFDP sites in 1998 (two sites) and 2000 (two sites) were undertaken with a specific objective of assessing the impact of the project. As described later, the revisit studies found that leasehold groups achieved some levels of success only after other residents of the community accepted the leasehold project and were included in the leasehold group as a means of resolving the conflicts between leasehold members and nonmembers.

In early 1997, the first four community forest sites were revisited as well as four new community forest sites from eastern Nepal as part of the dissertation research of a then PhD student from Indiana University (Varughese, 1999). In 1998, the Parks and People Project of the United Nations Development Programme supported an impact assessment of their project in four national parks/wildlife reserve areas. For this, three national parks and one wildlife reserve area were selected. In order to assess achievements of the project, in-depth information about the benefits and outcomes of the project's investment and activities were obtained from the user groups formed by the project. A study in three community forests was carried out in eastern mountain and Siwalik area in 1999 with a grant received from the MacArthur Foundation to support research in eastern Nepal. In 2000, the Food and Agriculture Organization of the United Nations supported NFRI to conduct a study of the costs and benefits of community forests. For this purpose, two sites from the hills and two sites from the *terai* area were selected. As a continuing support of the MacArthur Foundation, a study on four community forest sites—two from the *terai* and two from the hills area—was conducted in 2001. Thus, all in all, the NFRI teams have studied 36 sites, of which eight have been revisited.

NFRI SITES CHOSEN TO ADDRESS THE
RESEARCH QUESTION OF THIS CHAPTER

We have chosen all five of the leasehold forest sites that have been studied by our team and are in the NFRI database. We were asked to study these sites by the HLFFDP and thus did not select the sites in the first place ourselves. They were selected by the leasehold project as more or less typical sites where they wanted to obtain information about the early processes of formation and what was happening after several years. Substantial conflict was noted in four of these sites. Only one of the sites appeared to be operating without conflict between members and nonmembers. The conflict has taken various forms but a common theme is a refusal to recognize and accept the very existence of the rights of the leasehold FUG itself. In some sites, this has led to violent confrontations. In other sites, the conflict has led to an unauthorized expansion of the leasehold FUG to include wealthier families as unofficial members of the leasehold FUG. In other sites, the leasehold FUG cannot function at all.

In addition to the five leasehold sites that will be described first, we will also describe three community forest sites (out of the 18 in the NFRI database) where our site teams were told about very specific policies and rules developed for the poor households who are members of a community FUG. These three sites illustrate the ability of a CFUG to develop policies and rules that are specifically focused on redistributing benefits to the poor families who are members of their group. We do not wish to argue that all CFUGs have made such special efforts to protect the interests of the poorest members of their groups. On the other hand, what is important to recognize is that some of the CFUGs have adopted policies that do substantially enhance the economic position of their poorer members. Given the substantial conflict among members of the leasehold groups and the wealthier families living in nearby communities but excluded from the leasehold forests, it is worth exploring whether there is a better mechanism for distributing forest benefits to poor families than one that generates a very substantial level of conflict and a lack of conformance with the rules that are officially established.

LEASEHOLD FORESTS

Social Conflicts in the Leasehold Forest Regimes

Baramchi Site
The site is located in Ward no. 4 of Baramchi Village Development Committee of Sindhupalchok district. The elevation of the site varies from 1,420 to 2,180 m. There are 10 leasehold groups in the site. Of these, eight leasehold groups were selected for the study. The site consists of six settlements with 78 households having a population of 427. The group size ranges from five/ten households. Each leasehold group is assigned to a leasehold forest varying from 2.5 to 9.0 hectares, making a total of 46.2 hectares. Tamang (61 percent) is the dominant ethnic group followed by Newar (30 percent) and Biswakarma (9 percent). However, each leasehold group consists of households from a single ethnicity. All the ethnic groups are included in at least one of the leasehold groups (see Table 7.1).

There were 72 households in these eight groups at the time of group formation in 1994. That number dropped to 67 households by 1998 due to migration and shifting to other leasehold groups. The vegetation is mainly sub-tropical hardwood type. The major forest product harvested from the leasehold forests is ground grass. Out of eight groups, ground grass was harvested by six groups. Fuelwood, timber (small poles) and leaf litter were harvested by one group each. The reason for not harvesting these products by other groups is the unavailability of the product in their forest. On an average, the leasehold forest supplies around

TABLE 7.1

Socio-economic Characteristics of Leasehold Forest Sites in the Middle Hills Region of Nepal

Site	Total Household (HH)	HHs in Leasehold Group	No. of Ethnic Groups Settlement	No. of Ethnic Groups LF Group	Dependency on Forest LF	Dependency on Forest CF	Dependency on Forest NF	Main Products Harvested from LF
Baramchi	78	78	Three	Single	Medium	–	High	Grass
Bhagawatisthan	90	80	Four	Single	High	–	Very low	Grass, leaf litter, fuelwood
Riyale	101	89	Two	Single	Very low	Low	High	Grass, fuelwood
Thulosirubari	105	34	Three	Single	Medium	Medium	–	Grass, leaf litter, fuelwood

Notes: LF: Leasehold forest, CF: Community forest, NF: National forest.

35 percent of their fodder requirement. Other forest product requirements (ground grass, fuelwood, tree fodder, leaf litter and small poles) are mainly fulfilled from national forest patches. The products from the leasehold forest were harvested collectively and divided equally, whereas products from national forests were harvested in an open access basis individually.

In the process of formation of leasehold groups, one forest, Eprepakha Forest, was given to two leasehold groups: to Eprepakha (Lama group) and to Eprepakha (Shrestha group). The other forest patch, Salmarang, was given to the Salmarang LFUG. But these forests had also been used by the residents living in Ward nos. 2, 3, 6 and 7 before they were converted to leasehold forests. People of these wards refused to give up their use rights over the forests and sacrifice forest products that they were obtaining from the time of their forefathers. As a result, Eprepakha and Salmarang leasehold groups had to fight with the nonmember residents for harvesting ground grass from Eprepakha leasehold forests and timber (small poles) and leaf litter from Salmarang leasehold forest. In addition, a third leasehold group, Dumsighari, had conflicts with residents of Ward no. 5 for harvesting forest products, because they also used to harvest from this forest traditionally.

The residents of Ward no. 3 came in a large group and harvested most of the ground grass (exotic breeds planted by the lessee households and giving very good production) from the leasehold forests. This has, of course, raised the important question about the viability of the official use rights provided by the government for 25 years to the LFUGs. The NFRI research team was also informed that livestock owned by nonmembers were grazed in the leasehold forests and planted seedlings were taken away by the nonmembers.

The combination of these various incidents has led to substantial social conflict among the communities surrounding the set of leasehold forests. After the initial incidents, the drinking water supply from a reservoir constructed in Ward no. 4 to Ward no. 3 was disrupted with destruction of pipelines going to Ward no. 3 by the residents of Ward no. 4. Later, this drinking water scheme serving the communities of both the wards was hampered and stopped due to the conflict between the residents of Ward no. 3 and Ward no. 4.

Bhagawatisthan Site

The site is located in Ward no. 9 of Sathighar Bhagawatisthan Village Development Committee (VDC) and Ward no. 1 of Kharelthok VDC of Kavrepalanchok district. The elevation of the site varies from 1,000 to 1,410 m. The site is comprised of five settlements with 90 households and 600 individuals. The size of the leasehold forest varies from 4.6 to 12.5 hectares, making a total of 78.1 hectares managed by eight LFUGs. Newar (70 percent) is the dominant ethnic group followed by Brahmin (23 percent), whereas Tamang (2 percent) and Pahari (5 percent) are the minorities. However, almost all of the leasehold groups are comprised of the single ethnicity of Newar except one group that has four ethnicities mentioned.

During the formation of leasehold groups in 1994, 49 households were included in these eight leasehold groups from a total of 70 households living in three settlements (Chandeni, Charpiple and Sathighar). As determined by the eligibility criteria of leasehold forestry, other residents were barred from membership in these user groups. People of Barbandi and Bhotekhola settlements claimed that they were offended by the formation of leasehold groups to use forests that they had also been using and they also wanted memberships in the groups at that time.

The type of vegetation in the site is subtropical deciduous. All of the groups have harvested ground grass and fuelwood from the leasehold forests. Leaf litter and tree fodder are harvested by four and three groups, respectively. On an average, 50 percent of fodder and leaf litter requirements are fulfilled from leasehold forests and the rest from private land. Leasehold Forests supply about 33 percent of the fuelwood requirement and the rest comes from private land. The user groups harvest forest products collectively and share equally. The timber requirement is fulfilled from private land and community forests located outside the site (managed by residents of other settlements). However, a small portion of fodder and fuelwood is collected from the national forest that is informally managed by the residents of the site.

The LFUGs could not carry out forestry development activities and utilization of the forest successfully because other nonmember households in the community have refused to recognize the use rights given to the LFUGs. This refusal has created an interruption in the functioning of the leasehold groups and disturbance in the management and development of the leasehold forests. It happened that the nonmembers allow their livestock to graze in the plantation area of leasehold forests and they also uprooted the planted seedlings and harvested forest products from the leasehold forests, violating the leasehold user groups' sole right for using the forest given by the government under the leasehold forestry program. This sort of conflict and functioning problem existed for four years.

These user groups finally achieved some success in the management and development of the forest, when their social conflict was resolved by accepting other residents of the community into the LFUGs irrespective of the criteria of the leasehold forestry project. Even though the forests are designated and handed over as leasehold forests, all the residents now have an equal right to use the leasehold forests and harvest forest products from the leasehold forests upon equal participation in the development of the forests and as long as they have an interest in joining the group. LFUG members went to 80 member households out of a total of 90 households in the site. Ten households have not joined the group on their own will.

The number of households varies from 7 to 22 in a group. The member households work together and divide all the forest products equally. Now, there are no differences between leasehold forests and community forests in this area. After this consensus, rules have been followed very strictly, grazing of livestock in the leasehold forest plantation area is fully controlled and the survival rate of planted seedlings and productivity of ground grass has increased.

Riyale Site

The site is located in Ward no. 4 of Riyale VDC of Kavrepalanchowk district. The elevation ranges from 1,620 to 2,235 m and the site has a cool temperate climate. There are four settlements inhabited by 605 people living in 101 households. Among 101 households, 89 households are associated with leasehold forestry. In this site, seven leasehold groups with 55 households were included in the NFRI study. A total of 42 hectares of forest is leased to these seven groups. The size of the leasehold forest ranges from 4 hectares to 8 hectares with group size varying from six/ten households.

Almost all the residents belong to Tamang (92 percent) ethnic group followed by Brahmin (8 percent). However, leasehold groups have only Tamangs as members, except in one group. One Brahmin family has been included in the leasehold group, because his house is adjoined to the leasehold forest. There is also a community forest of 29 hectares, officially handed over, managed by the residents of the site with 95 households as members. All the leasehold group members have membership in the community forest.

Ten households have been added in these seven groups after the formation of the group in 1993/94 in order to equalize use rights of the forest irrespective of the criteria of the leasehold forestry. The member households have been accepted in the groups' unanimous decision on the basis of their traditional use rights for the forest in order to avoid conflict in the society.

Fodder and fuelwood were harvested from the leasehold forest by only two groups each. The leasehold forest fulfilled 6 percent of the fodder and 2 percent of the fuelwood requirements for the group. The community forest supplied 1 percent of fodder and 10 percent of the leaf litter requirement. Private land fulfilled 40 percent of fodder and 26 percent of fuelwood requirements. The remainder of forest product requirements for the leasehold households was harvested from national forests. Both the leasehold and community forest groups have established rules for collective action for management and utilization of the forests. In practice, however, leasehold groups have not been successful in carrying out collective action effectively, partly because the leasehold forests are very bushy and thorny in this area.

Lack of coordination and lack of group interest and group action among the LFUG members in forest development activities (such as shrub removing and pruning) were observed due to members leaving one user group and joining other groups. Also, new members joined the leasehold groups. Some members do not feel any sense of ownership of the leasehold forests. They mentioned in discussions that they think that once the trees are grown, say 12–15 years time, the government would change the policy and take back the forest. The lack of group action, combined with the rule of 'zero-harvest' in the leasehold forests, has a direct negative impact upon the forestry and vegetation in the national forests which are in the immediate reach of the settlements. There is heavy and ever-increasing human and animal pressure on the national forests of the surrounding area in the site.

Thulosirubari Site

The site is located in Ward no. 8 of Thulosirubari VDC of Sindhupalchok district. Elevation of the site varies from 920 to 1,170 m. The site consists of three settlements with 105 households and a population of 843. Tamang (87 percent) is the main ethnic group followed by Newar (11 percent) and Chhetri (2 percent). There are 34 households in five leasehold groups assigned a total area of 14.1 hectares. One group was formed in 1995 and the others in 1996. Since the NFRI study was carried out in 1995 when there was only one group, it focused on that one leasehold group. The studied leasehold group is comprised of nine households and authorized to manage and use a forest of 5 hectares. The leasehold group under study comprises people from a single ethnicity (Tamang). The residents of the site have access to two community forests of 8 hectares each.

The site has tropical and subtropical deciduous forest vegetation. Grass, leaf litter, fallen deadwood, and branches/twigs for fuelwood are the main products harvested from the leasehold forest and community forests. Forest products are harvested individually and collective action is not practiced in either of the forest regimes here. A seasonal restriction is, however, applied to fuelwood collection from the community forests.

When degraded national forest patches were converted to leasehold forests and use rights were given to one leasehold group in 1995 and four leasehold groups in 1996, the lessee members did not anticipate that social conflict might arise at the time of harvesting even the minor forest product like ground grass from the leasehold forests. The residents of the community who were not included in the LFUGs also harvested ground grass. When the lessee members tried to stop them from harvesting, there was a social clash and a big fight. Since that time, the residents of the community are experiencing an unusual situation. They continue to feel ill-at-ease in the community. The nonmembers cannot sacrifice the harvesting of forest products from the leasehold forests. The chairman of the community forest and member of the Dhadeni LFUG expressed their opinion that the government had given a poisonous snake to them in the form of a leasehold forest.

A Leasehold Site without Social Conflict

Chitrepani

The site is located in Churiamai VDC and Hetauda Municipality of Makawanpur district. It is approximately 8 km southeast of Hetauda, the district headquarters and is accessible by an all-weather road. There are four settlements in the site.

There is one community forest, one leasehold forest and one national forest in the site. The size of the community forest is 146 hectares, the leasehold forest is 9 hectares and the national forest is 125 hectares. The CFUG, formed in 1991 to look after the plantation area in the forest, consists of 484 members. The leasehold group was formed in April 1994 and consists of nine members. Among the nine members of the leasehold forest, two members are from Brahmin and Biswakarma families and the rest are from Tamang family. These leasehold members are also members in the community forest as well. The number of member households in the leasehold forest has not changed since formation.

The total population of the four settlements is 3,161 living in 491 households, with an average household size of 6.44 persons. The settlement populations are heterogeneous, composed of Brahmin, Newar, Tamang, Rai, Chhetri, Bishwakarma, Magar and Gurung. Among these ethnic groups, Brahmins account for 52.1 percent of the total population. Other relatively large ethnic groups are Tamang (23 percent) and Chhetri (14 percent). Newar, Gurung, Rai, Bishwakarma and Magar are all in the minority.

The community forest is managed collectively by the group, whereas the leasehold forest is managed individually. The leasehold forest is allocated to nine members with 1 hectare of forest-land to each member. Firewood, fodder, leaf litter, bamboo and timber are the main products harvested from the community forest. The leasehold forest supplies grass and small poles. Leasehold members derive income from the sales of grass and grass seeds, as the productivity of the grass is good. The DFO has provided seeds of exotic grass species in connection with the leasehold forestry program.

Although there was no conflict between leasehold members and nonmembers at the time of the study, some nonmembers in the community were beginning to show an interest in becoming members in the group. These community members started to question the inclusion of only nine members in the leasehold group, because leasehold members have membership in the community forest also.

DISCUSSION

The process of achieving community consensus for converting forests to leasehold forests by issuing a notification in the community is uncertain and complex. The legal criteria do not specify a limitation of the boundary of the communities that could be included in a leasehold forest as contrasted to a community forest. Simply specifying that the forested area should be degraded is not sufficient to clarify which forests that have been used by an entire community at an earlier junction should now be turned over for exclusive use by a smaller—albeit poorer—community. The HLFFDP has experienced serious problems in obtaining community consensus for leasehold forest establishment. Once the technicalities of both leasehold and community forestry are well understood by the local people, the big farmers, who cannot be included in the leasehold groups, tend to start pressing for community forestry as they do not want to give up the use of the land in question no matter how degraded it is (Sterk, 1996). During community discussions, the better-off people generally stand against allocation of forest land exclusively to poor families (Singh and Sterk, 1996).

In the leasehold forests, diverse types of conflict (listed in Table 7.2) appear to be a common social phenomenon. They are observed chiefly during the process of trying to obtain community consensus. In some cases, conflict erupts after the completion of the leasing process, i.e., handing over lease certificates to the leasehold groups of poor families (Singh, 1996). It is found that the residents of the community who have not responded to the notification issued by the DFO have opposed the formation of the LFUGs and challenged the use right prescribed to lessee members. The leasehold groups (Eprepakha and Salmarang) of Baramchi site were disturbed by the residents of other settlements rather than the

TABLE 7.2
Causes and Effects of Conflict in Leasehold Forests of the Middle Hills Region of Nepal

Cause	Effects
Lack of recognition of use right	Product harvesting by nonmembers.
	Stealing/removing of planted seedlings.
	Interruption in the functioning of the group.
	Disturbance in the management and development of the forest.
	Social conflict between communities.
	Acceptance of nonmember households in the group (offer membership to all).
Lack of adherence to rules	Grazing of livestock in the forest.
	Violation of rules.
Social conflict	Interruption in community development activities, for example, disruption of water supply in Baramchi.
	Social environment and social feeling are adversely affected, for example, in Thulosirubari.

TABLE 7.3

Socio-economic Characteristics of the Three Community Forest Sites in the Middle Hills Region of Nepal

Site	Total Households (HH)	HHs in CF Group/s	No. of Ethnic Groups		Dependency on Forest		Main Products Harvested from CF
			Settlement	CF Group	CF	NF	
Khareha	107	104	Seven	Seven	High	–	Fodder, fuelwood, timber
Gumbadanda	210	210	Nine	Nine	Medium	–	Fodder, leaf litter, timber
Thoplebiran	362	347	Seven	Seven	High	–	Fuelwood, fodder, timber

Notes: CF: Community forest, NF: National forest.

residents of their own settlements. In Thulosirubari site, the leasehold group had conflict with their own neighbors.

Enforcement of rules became successful in Bhagawatisthan site only after the inclusion of all interested residents being accepted as leasehold members. As a result, grazing was controlled and group functioning ran well and an increase in grass productivity was reported. But the receipt per household was not increased to the poor targeted group as they had to share among the new leasehold members. On the other hand, in the Riyale site, even after accepting interested residents to join the groups, the leasehold groups have not been successful in assembling the expanded group members to conduct collective action in the forest. Out of seven leasehold groups, one group has collected fodder and a second group has performed shrub clearing and pruning.

Whether the leasehold forestry project has achieved the objectives of improving the condition of degraded forests while alleviating poverty with participation of the poor households is also questionable. The priority of poor farmers is to cultivate grain to feed their families. According to the forestry regulations, however, cereals cannot be cultivated on leasehold forest land. The permitted uses include cultivation of improved breeds of grass, fruit and medicinal herbs. These permitted uses do not solve the immediate problems of food deficiency that face poor families. In a true sense, poor people below the poverty line do not take advantage of this program (Chaudhary, 2000). Even the objectives of leasehold forestry seem contradictory to some observers. For example, Chapagain et al. (1999) have argued that community forestry should be utilized to fulfill subsistence needs while leasehold forestry should be used primarily for commercial purposes.

The conflicts and problems in the leasehold forestry program have been found in four sites (three revisited sites and one other site during the data validation and observation visit). The scope of violation of the rules and conflicts in the leasehold forestry sites is abundant. In Chitrepani site, the only revisited site that has not yet had substantial conflict, nonmember households have begun to question the authorities as to why they were not included in the leasehold group. Thus, there are early signs that they might create conflict in the future.

RULES AND INCENTIVES FOR THE
POOR HOUSEHOLDS IN SOME COMMUNITY FORESTS

Since an avowed reason for creating the leasehold forestry program was to reach the poor residents located near national forests, it is relevant to ask whether any efforts to reach the poorer households have been initiated in community forests. Of the 18 community forestry sites included in the NFRI sample, three community forests have taken particular efforts to ensure that poor households obtain sufficient forest products and make other efforts to uplift the poorer households through community forestry development. Let us take a brief look at these three sites.

Khareha Site

The site is located in Ward no. 1 of Siwalaya VDC of Parbat district. Elevation of the site varies from 840 to 1,200 m. The site consists of one settlement with 107 households and 613 persons. A complex ethnicity is found with high caste groups (Brahmin, Chhetri and Giri), tribal groups (Newar and Magar) and occupational groups (Kami and Damai), which comes to 62, 29 and 9 percent, respectively. The CFUG has a membership of 104 households with 57.5 hectares. One household has taken membership in another community forest located outside the site, whereas two households have not joined the community forest group voluntarily (see Table 7.2). The residents of the settlement were informally organized and started conservation of the forest in 1978. They imposed a complete restriction on harvesting of any type of forest product until 1993. The residents were officially recognized as a formal CFUG in May 1993.

The major forest products harvested are grass, fuelwood, leaf litter and timber. Grass harvesting is allowed only to selected needy households. Fuelwood is harvested in two methods: (*a*) fallen dry wood (sticks/twigs) is allowed seasonally for five days and (*b*) group harvesting at the time of pruning and thinning, which is distributed equally to participating households. There is no restriction of time period for leaf litter collection. The harvesting of timber is strictly limited to ten trees in a year. An executive committee of the group examines the actual requirement of the household and makes an allotment based on this assessment.

The rules used for grass allocation by this CFUG are particularly focused on ensuring that poorer households do obtain sufficient grass. The potential ground grass area in the community forest is divided into 34 small blocks. Out of 104 member households, 34 households are authorized to harvest ground grass from one block each and every year. The first priority in assigning rights to ground grass harvesting is provided to those households who do not have land for fodder production. As such, out of 34 blocks, 17 blocks are provided to poor households and they are allowed ground grass harvesting rights permanently each year. The remaining 17 households will be decided each year depending upon the need of the household. The decision is taken at the user group's general assembly. This provision was made because fodder availability enhances cash income through goat farming even to the poor households.

Gumbadanda Site

The site is located in Ward numbers 7, 8 and 9 of Ilam Municipality and Ward no. 1 of Barbote VDC of Ilam district. It has five settlements with 210 households and 1,146 persons. Elevation varies from 1,085 to 1,360 m. The vegetation falls under subtropical deciduous forest. Ethnicity is composed of high-caste groups (Brahmin and Chhetri), tribal groups (Newar, Rai, Tamang, Gurung and Magar) and occupational groups (Kami and Damai), which comes to 27, 63 and 10 percent, respectively. The site has two community forests, formally handed over to two user groups. About 56 percent of the households are members in the Gumbadanda community forest, whereas 44 percent have membership in the Odarebhaludhunga community forest. Besides, 65 percent of members of the Gumbadanda community forest have membership in two other community forests located outside the site.

Community forests provide about 40 percent of fodder, bedding material for livestock, and timber requirements. Sixty percent of fodder and bedding material and 70 percent of fuelwood come from private forest and farmland. Grass and bedding material are allowed to harvest individually year round. Fuelwood is harvested collectively during pruning and thinning processes.

The CFUG has devised several mechanisms to ensure financial support for the poor households in their group. The user group has provided financial assistance for purchasing mother goats for poor and disadvantaged households. In this connection, four goats were purchased from the user group's fund and distributed to four households, one goat for one household. Twenty percent of the profit was to put in the user group's fund and a mother goat was transferred to the next household after milking stage. This incentive was provided to ten such households in 1999. The decision to provide this incentive was driven by the suggestion and inspiration given by the CFUG of Kaski district, which came to this site for an observation study tour.

On a different front, the user group has also provided scholarships of Rs 200 per year to three intelligent primary school students of poor and disadvantaged households. This decision was the outcome of the suggestion of the officials of the DFO during the training session conducted for strengthening the CFUG.

Thoplebiran Site

The site is located in Ward numbers 4, 5 and 6 of Mechi Municipality of Jhapa district. The site consists of five settlements with 362 households and 2,090 persons. Ethnicity is composed of high-caste groups (Brahmin and Chhetri—50 percent), tribal groups (Tamang, Magar, Rai and Danuwar—40 percent) and occupational groups (Biswakarma—10 percent). The CFUG has a membership of 347 households. The site falls under tropical zone and is situated in the flat *terai* area at 195 m above sea level. The community forest was formally handed over to the user group in 1997. After handing over the forest, the user group started plantations of fodder, timber and some income-generating plants like bamboo and medicinal herbs. Grazing of livestock is partially restricted.

The user group members have the right to harvest fodder (grasses and tree fodder), foliage (branch cutting from shrubs and trees) for bedding material to livestock and fallen wood/twigs for fuelwood. Timber, small poles for agricultural and fuelwood from logged trees are harvested by the user group and distributed to the members of the group. Fodder and foliage are allowed for harvesting seasonally with payment of Re 1 per bhari (20–30 kg).

The user group allows members to obtain fuelwood in three ways: (a) during the time of thinning and pruning operations carried out in the forest and distributed equally among the participating member households free of charge; (b) the member households are authorized to collect dry and fallen wood/twigs every Saturday seasonally with a payment of Re 1 for 1 bhari (15–20 kg) and (c) the user group harvests fuelwood from dead, diseased and old trees seasonally and distributes it at a selling price of Rs 35 for one quintal (100 kg) to the user group members and at Rs 75 for one quintal to nonmembers (secondary members) as provisioned. Timber is distributed on the basis of actual requirement. The requirement of timber claimed by the member is examined and allocated by the executive committee of the group. Sale price varies from Rs 50 to Rs 160 per cft for user group members and Rs 100 to Rs 270 per cft for nonmembers. The product is mainly harvested from dead, diseased, and old trees three months a year. The forest is open for nonconsumptive uses such as recreational purposes and picnics.

Members of the user group have devised several ways of providing financial support for the poor members of their group. For example, one bedstead (furniture for bedding) per family was provided free of cost in 1999 to 11 poor and disadvantaged families (Danuwar, Limbu, Kami) who did not obtain fuelwood and timber sold by the user group. This incentive was provided because every member of the user group contributed an equal amount of labor for the maintenance and conservation of the forest resources. These households were not able to pay money for fuelwood and timber harvested from the community forest that was sold to members at the price determined by the user group. The households that were provided furniture did harvest fuelwood from two options: (a) during the time of thinning and pruning operation which is distributed equally among the participating member households free of change and (b) the member households are allowed to collect dry and fallen wood/twigs on every Saturday seasonally with a payment of Re 1 for 1 bhari (15–20 kg) but were not able to purchase fuelwood distributed at a selling price of Rs 35 for one quintal (100 kg) and timber sale price at Rs 50 to Rs 160 per cubic feet.

The CFUG has also provided scholarships of Rs 500 per annum for 10 intelligent high-school level students coming from poor households. This decision was passed by the general assembly of the User Group. The actual number of households receiving scholarships has to be decided by the executive committee of the group. The decision to provide scholarship was taken to help reduce poverty by increasing the opportunity available to students from poor households.

CONCLUSION

While there are challenges in implementing community forestry in Nepal, it would appear that the problems of implementing at least some of the leasehold forestry sites have been substantially greater. By its very definition, leasehold forestry limits the right of using a forest to a targeted group of people. It restricts the *de facto* rights of other people living in the same community who have used (and overused) this forest in the past. In practice, the excluded households are not eager to give up their *de facto* rights and not ready to recognize the formal use rights provided to lessee households due to an unwillingness to sacrifice the benefits that they had been obtaining from the use of the forest.

Therefore, the rules created by the LFUG may not be accepted by other residents of the community, creating social conflicts resulting in many types of obstacles in forest development and management activities, including the functioning of the User Group itself. The conflict raised in relation to the establishment of the leasehold forestry is likely to have adverse effects upon other community development activities too. Leasehold forestry appears to create problems in keeping a balance between right holders and duty holders in the sense that leasehold members are right holders and nonleasehold members are duty holders to recognize the right provided to lessee households. Thus, some of the leasehold forestry projects have become a 'tragedy of the poor' because they failed to secure property rights to the targeted group.

Sustainable use of the forest resources is impossible without durable institutional arrangements to regulate the harvest and distribution of forest products (Varughese, 1999). Although various scholars and practitioners may add other conditions they see as important, most agree that some form of these three—locals' valuation, ownership, and institutions—are central to successful natural resource management (Gibson and Becker, 2000). In addition to government-enforced rules, the recognition of indigenous rights to forest resources management is essential for the achievement of successful management practices (Banana and Gombya-Ssembajjwe, 2000).

While some community forestry groups may not pay much attention to the problems of the poor, they do not in general face the level of conflict found in relation to the leasehold forests. Further, the rules and incentives provided to poor households in some community forests—as illustrated by the example earlier—do tend to be accepted by all the residents, because they have been passed by the general assembly of the User Group with a general consensus. Rules made in community forestry favoring the poor households were accepted by the community as a whole, but leasehold groups were unable to enforce the rules created by them because the use rights given to lessee members were not recognized by other households of the community. We observed that community forestry possesses many advantages over the leasehold forestry practices. The incentives provided to poor households by CFUGs have been very successful in maintaining equity issues from the point of view of equal participation in developing and maintaining forest resources from the poor households.

Finally, we argue that the most serious problem in the leasehold forestry program is that if the use right provided to a group is not accepted and recognized by other groups in the community, the whole objective of the program is paralyzed. Rules overtly created for the purpose of helping the poor are of no use to the poor or to anyone else when they lack acceptance by a large proportion of those affected. If a leasehold group that has been formed strictly within the legal criteria of this program cannot operate as formed and has to accept other residents as members irrespective of the legal criteria, there is little meaning to launching a specific program for helping the poor exclusively. A community-based approach is considered by many to be the best strategy for the management of forests in Nepal, aiming to benefit many rather than to benefit a few (Chaudhary, 2000). Whether to adapt a community forestry or a leasehold forestry system creates a puzzle—whether to facilitate the organization of a larger group or a smaller group. Unless great care is taken in the development of an LFUG, dysfunctional conflict is easily created.

Community forests have made efforts to ensure forest use sustainability as well as provide benefits to uplift the poorer households. Given the evidence we have found related to the willingness of some CFUGs to provide special incentives to the poor, a worthwhile government program would be to share information about such programs and encourage other CFUGs to adopt similar programs.

APPENDIX 7.1

Community Forestry Programs in Nepal

Donor Agencies	Name of the Project	Number of Districts
Denmark (DANIDA)	Natural Resource Management Sector Assistance Program (NARMSAP)	38
UK (DFID)	Livelihoods and Forestry Program (LFP)	10
USA (USAID)	Environment and Forest Enterprises Activities Program (EFEAP)	8
Australia (AusAID)	Nepal Australia Community Resource Management Project (NACRMP)	2
Switzerland (SDC)	Nepal Swiss Community Forest Development Project (NSCFDP)	3
Germany (GTZ)	Churia Community Forestry Project (ChCFP)	3
The Netherlands (SNV)	Biodiversity Sector Programme for Siwalik and Terai (BISEP–ST)	8

Source: *Hamro Ban*, 2059 B.S. HMG. Ministry of Forests and Soil Conservation, Department of Forests, Kathmandu, Nepal.

APPENDIX 7.2

Nepal IFRI Sites

Site No/Date	Site Name	District	Study Focus on Forest Type	Eco. Zone
001-01/97	Raniswara (Revisit)	Gorkha	CF	Hills
001-10/93	Raniswara	"	"	"
002-10/97	Chhoprak (Revisit)	"	"	"
002-10/93	Chhoprak	"	"	"

(Appendix 7.2 continued)

(*Appendix 7.2 continued*)

Site No/Date	Site Name	District	Study Focus on Forest Type	Eco. Zone
003-02/97	Bandipur (Revisit)	Tanahu	CF	Hills
003-10/93	Bandipur	"	"	"
004-10/93	Chhimkeswari	"	NF	"
004-12/96	Chhimkeswari (Revisit)	"	"	"
005-03/2000	Chitrepani (Revisit)	Makawanpur	LF	Siwalik
005-03/94	Chitrepani	"	"	"
006-01/98	Baramchi (Revisit)	Sindhupalchok	"	Hills
006-05/94	Baramchi	"	"	"
007-02/98	Riyale (Revisit)	Kavrepalanchok	"	"
007-05/94	Riyale	"	"	"
008-06/94	Bijulikot	Ramechhap	"	"
009-09/94	Shaktikhor	Chitwan	NF	Siwalik
010-11/94	Shaktikhor Ward 1	"	"	"
011-04/95	Thulosirubari	Sindhupalchok	LF	Hills
012-05/95	Doramba	Ramechhap	"	"
013-09/95	Choubas	Makawanpur	"	"
014-06/95	Bhagawatisthan	Kavrepalanchok	"	"
014-12/99	Bhagawatisthan (Revisit)	"	"	"
015-04/96	Barandabhar Ban Devi	Chitwan	CF	Terai
016-06/96	Shivapuri-Manichur	Kathmandu	WR	Hills
017-09/96	Shivapuri-Sunkhani	Nuwakot	"	"
018-05/97	Barbote	Ilam	CF	"
019-05/97	Shantipur	"	NF	Siwalik
020-06/97	Chungmang	Dhankuta	"	Hills
021-06/97	Bhedetar	"	CF	"
022-04/98	Shivapur	Bardia	NP	Terai
023-05/98	Pipariya	Kanchanpur	WR	"
024-06/98	Pashim Kusaha	Sunsari	"	"
025-06/98	Jagatpur	Chitwan	NP	"
026-04/99	Sanuwa Sukanahi	Udayapur	CF	Siwalik
027-05/99	Num	Sankhuwasabha	"	Mountain
028-06/99	Hati Kharka Sanya	"	"	"
029-08/2000	Khareha	Parbat	"	Hills
030-10/2000	Danapur	Rupandehi	"	Terai
031-11/2000	Chandraban	Palpa	"	Hills
032-11/2000	Gijara	Banke	"	Terai
033-05/01	Balankhola	Siraha	"	"
034-09/01	Chuliban Deurali	Dhankuta	"	Hills
035-09/01	Gumbadanda	Ilam	"	"
036-11/01	Thoplebiran	Jhapa	"	Terai

Notes: CF: Community forest, NF: National forest, LF: Leasehold forest, NP: National park, WR: Wildlife reserve.

ACKNOWLEDGMENTS

The authors gratefully acknowledge the financial support provided by the MacArthur Foundation. The authors would like to thank Amy Poteete, George Varughese, Arun Agrawal, Harini Nagendra, Keshav Kanel, Clark Gibson, Charles Schweik, Ganesh Shivakoti and Edward Webb for their valuable comments and Patty Lezotte and David Price for their editing. Last, but not the least, the authors are grateful for the logistical support provided by the Workshop in Political Theory and Policy Analysis, Indiana University, USA.

NOTES

1. The 20th century saw several major changes of ownership and management practices in regard to forestry. After centuries of decentralized ownership and control of forests, all forests in Nepal were nationalized in 1957. Due to the lack of resource for effective monitoring and the loss of incentives for management by local users, heavy deforestation took place during the 1960s and 1970s (see Arnold and Campbell, 1986).
2. FUG Database Record (April 2002). Community and Private Forestry Division, Department of Forests, Kathmandu, Nepal.
3. Hills Leasehold Forestry and Forage Development Project, Project Completion Report, National Forest Division, Department of Forest, Kathmandu, September 2001.

REFERENCES

Arnold, J.E.M. and Campbell, J. Gabriel. (1986). 'Collective Management of Hill Forests in Nepal: The Community Forestry Development Project'. In *Proceedings of the Conference on Common Property Resource Management* (pp. 425–454). Washington, DC: National Academy Press.

Banana, A.Y. and Gombya-Ssembajjwe, W. (2000). 'Successful Forest Management: The Importance of Security of Tenure and Rule Enforcement in Ugandan Forests'. In C. Gibson, M. McKean, and E. Ostrom (eds), *People and Forests: Communities, Institutions and Governance* (pp. 67–78). Cambridge, MA: The MIT Press.

Bartlett, A.G. (1992). 'A Review of Community Forestry Advances in Nepal'. *Commonwealth Forestry Review*, 71(2), 95–100.

Chapagain, D.P., Kanel, K.R. and Regmi, D.C. (1999). *Current Policy and Legal Context of the Forestry Sector with Reference to the Community Forestry Programme in Nepal*. Working Overview. Nepal–UK Community Forestry Project, Kathmandu.

Chaudhary, R.P. (2000). 'Forest Conservation and Environmental Management in Nepal: A Review'. *Biodiversity and Conservation*, 9, 1235–1260.

Gibson, C.C. and Becker, C.D. (2000). 'A Lack of Institutional Demand: Why a Strong Local Community in Western Ecuador Fails to Protect Its Forest'. In

Clark Gibson, Margaret McKean and Elinor Ostrom (eds), *People and Forests: Communities, Institutions, and Governance* (pp. 117–135). Cambridge, MA: The MIT Press.

Joint Technical Review of Community Forestry (JTRCF). (2001). *JTRCF: Report of the Joint Technical Review Committee*. Kathmandu: Ministry of Forest and Soil Conservation.

Kanel, K.R., Karmacharya, M.B. and Karna, B.K. (1999). *Leasing Public Land to Poor and Marginal Families: An Initial Assessment of Baramchi Site*. Kathmandu: Hills Leasehold Forestry and Forage Development Project/Food and Agriculture Organization.

Nepal Forestry Resources and Institutions (NFRI). (1998). 'Field Reports of Baramchi and Riyale Sites submitted to the Hills Leasehold Forestry and Fodder Development Project, Kathmandu during Impact Assessment Study'. Kathmandu.

Ojha, H.R. (2002). 'Current Issues in Community Forestry in Nepal and Implications for Research'. Paper presented at the ODI meeting on October 11.

Paudel, S.K. and Pokharel, B.K. (2001). 'Looking at the Prospects of Community Forestry in the Terai Region of Nepal'. *Banko Janakari, 11*(2), 27–33.

Singh, B.K. (1996). 'Recognition of Customary Use Rights: A Medium to Avoid/Prevent Conflicts in Group Leasehold Forestry'. Project Working Paper No. 31. Hills Leasehold Forestry and Forage Development Project, Kathmandu.

Singh, B.K. and Sterk, A. (1996). 'Conflict Management in Group Leasehold Forestry'. Hills Leasehold Forestry and Forage Development Project, Kathmandu.

Sterk, A. (1996). 'Marrying NGOs and Government: A Desirable Partnership or a Foolish Fashion'. Project Working Paper No. 32. Hills Leasehold Forestry and Forage Development Project, Kathmandu.

Varughese, G. (1999). 'Villagers, Bureaucrats, and Forests in Nepal: Designing Governance for a Complex Resource'. Doctoral dissertation, Indiana University, Indiana.

DISENTANGLING A COMPLEX WEB: FORESTS, PEOPLE AND DECENTRALIZATION IN NEPAL

HARINI NAGENDRA, MUKUNDA KARMACHARYA and BIRENDRA KARNA

INTRODUCTION

The past two decades have witnessed increasing interest in alternative, decentralized methods of forest management in several countries across the world. This can be traced to increasing concerns about escalation of forest degradation, especially in developing tropical regions. In comparison to the heavily top-down state-centered systems of management that were extensively promoted in the 1950s, the trend has increasingly shifted towards encouraging decentralized, local and participatory forms of governance, now being promoted on paper with great enthusiasm as panaceas for developing countries (Agrawal et al., 1999; Agrawal and Ostrom, 2001). However, in practice most of these efforts at decentralization lead either to privatization or deconcentration of power from central to state or district governments and only rarely result in the strengthening of local institutions (Agrawal and Ostrom, 2001; Ribot, 2002, 2004a, 2004b). Programs that apparently aim at decentralization tend to emanate from state initiatives and/or pressure by external aid agencies. Such programs tend to be implemented by official machinery in a manner that results in the delegation of responsibilities and liabilities, while keeping most of the benefits and the power firmly vested in the hands of the state and without any real downward accountability (Poffenberger and McGean, 1996; Sundar, 2000; Ribot, 2002; 2004a, 2004b, but see Bray et al., 2003 for a very interesting discussion of highly successful, exceptional 'bottom-up' initiatives in Mexico).

In the South/Southeast Asia region, Nepal has taken a lead in initiating innovative policies of community forestry (Agrawal *et al.*, 1999; Agrawal and Ostrom, 2001). The emphasis has been to decentralize and deregulate previously top-down policies, strengthen local institutions and ensure greater economic equity (Agrawal *et al.*, 1999). In practice, however, the rhetoric seems to be louder than the actual levels of devolution of power (Nagendra, 2002). Major changes in Nepalese forest policy and the initiation of efforts towards decentralization can be traced to the early 1970s. Since then, these programs have gone through a variety of transformations, including the establishment of large protected area networks and the initiation of community forestry, leasehold forestry and park buffer zone management programs in the mid-1990s (Agrawal *et al.*, 1999). In this variable environment of constantly shifting policies, careful empirical studies are necessary to evaluate the impact of these changes on local communities and the forests that they are supposed to protect.

Several studies indicate that community forestry has succeeded in several instances in improving the conditions of the people and forests in the Nepal middle hills (Gautam *et al.*, 2002; also as summarized in Chakraborty, 2001). However, not all community forestry groups are able to successfully overcome problems of collective action and some of the reasons for success can be explained by the rules they have been able to craft to fit local circumstance (Varughese and Ostrom, 2001). In contrast to the middle hills, strong reservations have been expressed about the feasibility of community forestry in the plains of the Nepal *terai* (Brown, 1998; Chakraborty, 2001). While the middle hills of Nepal have supported local populations for centuries (Messerschmidt, 1987), the *terai* was thinly populated prior to the 1960s, due to a high incidence of malaria. Extensive migration from the middle hills has taken place since malaria was eradicated by a massive DDT spraying program carried out in the 1960s, resulting in increased deforestation in recent years (Schweik *et al.*, 1997; Brown, 1998; Matthews *et al.*, 2000). As a result, the challenge for community forestry in the Nepal *terai* is to support the creation of new institutions of community forest management (Chakraborty, 2001).

Considerable difference of opinion has been expressed about the outcome of decentralized forestry programs in the Nepal *terai* in terms of their impact on institutional and social issues, as well as forest condition (Chaudhary, 2000; Poudel, 2000, 2001). Unlike the middle hills, where the initiation and expansion of community forestry has been largely driven by local communities, in the *terai* these initiatives are government driven to a larger extent. Further, the decisions and performance of the management committees tends to be upwardly accountable to government officials rather than downwardly accountable to the local communities themselves. Empirical evaluations using primary data are needed to investigate this controversial issue (Heinen and Mehta, 2000; Nagendra, 2002).

Issues of human involvement are complex and cannot be studied using a single axis of evaluation. The factors impacting forest cover change need to be examined at multiple scales for an integrated understanding (Nagendra and Gadgil, 1999). It is essential to broaden the spatial extent of single case studies, in order to arrive at a complete understanding of the effect of tenure on forests not just within a single forest patch, but on the entire region. Remote sensing and other spatial analysis techniques allow us to locate research questions within a spatio-temporally explicit framework of analysis that is very useful to provide landscape-level under-standings of such complex issues (Nagendra *et al.*, 2004; Gautam *et al.*, 2002, 2003; Schweik *et al.*, 2003). A two-pronged approach using a combination of fine-scale field-researched case studies and field surveys with broad-scale remote sensing techniques is useful for researchers wishing to address multi-scale problems of this nature (Nagendra *et al.*, 1999, 2004).

This research used information from a range of research methods, including satellite remote sensing to Geographical Infor-mation Systems (GIS) analyses and interviews with forest user groups, to examine the conditions within which common property management regimes function, in developing countries and in par-ticular within Nepal. We analyzed changes in the forests around the Royal Chitwan National Park (RCNP), Nepal's oldest protected area. These changes were related to implementation of the com-munity forestry and buffer zone management programs, two pre-dominant recent initiatives towards co-management of forests in the Nepal *terai* (Schweik *et al.*, 2003). We analyzed the impact of these two different management regimes in terms of multiple factors including forest conservation, income generation and local decision-making capacities.

Study Area

Located along the Nepal–India border, the *terai* region of Nepal constitutes the foothills and valleys below the Himalayan mountains. During the last 40 years government-sponsored resettlement and spontaneous land occupation by migrants from the middle hills of Nepal have converted large parts of this once thickly-forested land to a densely-populated mix of agriculture and forests (Mathews *et al.*, 2000). The study area was located primarily within the eastern section of Chitwan district, with a small portion extending into the neighboring district of Makwanpur (Map 8.1). The Chitwan district of southern Nepal is an inner valley *terai* district, located between the middle hills to the north and the Siwalik ranges to the south. The climatic regime is tropical monsoon, with rainy summers and almost dry winters. Semi-deciduous forests constitute the climax vegetation in this region (Schweik *et al.*, 1997). In addition, tropical deciduous riverine forest patches are found along the banks of rivers and streams, along with patches of grassland, bamboo and swampy vegetation in these areas (Stainton, 1972; Negi, 1998).

Chitwan provides a major entry to the capital city, Kathmandu, through a network of roads. The first planned national resettlement scheme by the Nepal government was carried out in Chitwan, in the 1950s. The district now contains a complex mix of ethnicities, with people from all over the country.

The RCNP is the first national park of Nepal and was established in Chitwan in 1973. Most agriculture is carried out by small, subsistence farmers. The pressure on forests is high, with as much as 75 percent of the population actively harvesting products from the surrounding forests (Matthews *et al.*, 2000).

Decentralization Programs

This research on the effect of decentralization policies on forests was conducted through a comparative analysis of the two predominant categories of user-managed forests in the Chitwan: community forests and buffer zone forests in the lowland *terai* region of Nepal. Both are policies designed to decentralize decision-making

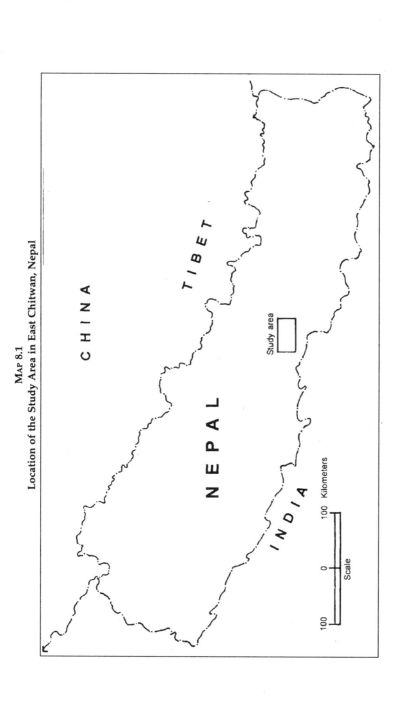

MAP 8.1
Location of the Study Area in East Chitwan, Nepal

authority to the local level and are the most prevalent of the current approaches to community involvement with forest management in the *terai*.

Community Forestry

The National Forest Act of 1976 and its subsequent Amendments of 1977 and 1978 attempted to address the limitations of nationalization of forests and return some degree of ownership and control over forest resources to the people. However, this attempt at decentralization was formally linked to centrally defined local government structures, was not really decentralized in practice and did not achieve notable success (Shrestha, 1998; Thapa and Weber, 1995). Awareness of these limitations, a growing appreciation for the capacity of local communities to manage common property institutions (Ostrom, 1990) and increasing donor pressure led to the introduction of the Community Forestry Act in 1993 (Thapa and Weber, 1995; Varughese, 1999). Most community forests are located in the mountains, where community forestry is generally believed to be successful (Gautam, 2002; Webb and Gautam, 2001). In contrast, only 17 percent of all area under community forests is located in the *terai* (Hobley, 1996 in Chakraborty, 2001).

Buffer Zone Management

A sizable portion of the available flat terrain in the Chitwan is now cleared for agriculture or other development (e.g., settlements), with the notable exception of the park land in the south. The Fourth Amendment to the National Parks and Wildlife Conservation Act, passed in 1993, provided the Department of National Parks and Wildlife Conservation (DNPWC) with the legal power to establish buffer zones in forested areas surrounding parks where forest resources are used on a regular basis by locals (Heinen and Mehta, 2000).The DNPWC began implementing the parks and people program in the Chitwan and in other protected areas of Nepal in early 1995 to fulfill two primary objectives, socio-economic well-being of the buffer zone communities and biodiversity conservation of the parks and their surrounding forests (Maskey *et al.*, 1999). This program receives financial and technical assistance from the

United Nations Development Program (UNDP) and was later rechristened the Participatory Conservation Project.

Following the initiation of the buffer zone program, buffer zone forests were delineated by wardens and handed over to user group committees with the authority to manage these forests in accordance with the Buffer Zone Management Guidelines (HMG, 1999). Several of the communities appear to earn significant income from ecotourism (Schweik *et al.*, 2003; Bookbinder *et al.*, 1998). The buffer zone regulations and guidelines allow committees to maintain their own accounts. User groups must spend 40 percent of their income on conservation, followed by 30 percent on community development, 20 percent on income generation and skill development, and 10 percent on administration (HMG, 1999; Heinen and Mehta, 2000). The warden retains the power at all times to stop projects and acts as the secretary of the committee overseeing expenditures (Heinen and Mehta, 2000). Although some of these user groups earn substantial incomes from tourism, the financial impact is believed to be limited on a per-household basis and mostly limited to the user groups near the main entrance of the park in Sauraha (Bookbinder *et al.*, 1998). Thus the real impact of the program in terms of improving participation and forest conservation is questionable and needs further investigation.

Although buffer zone and community forestry programs were only initiated in 1993, with most formal notifications taking place after 1996, some of the forests under study have been under community protection as far back as 1986 (Table 8.1).

METHODS

Forest Change Data

Three data sets were used for this study. The first set of data came from US Landsat Thematic Mapper (TM) images. This satellite data set allowed us to provide an explicitly temporal perspective and examine the forests in Chitwan before and after initiation of community programs of management. Satellite images provide a spatial synoptic and through-time view of forests and biodiversity (Nagendra and Gadgil, 1999; Nagendra, 2001). The temporal perspective afforded by the analysis of multi-date satellite images is

TABLE 8.1
Description of Study Forests in East Chitwan, Nepal

Management Regime	Total Area (ha)	Deforested (%) (1989–2000)	Regrowth (%) (1989–2000)	User Group Size	User/ Forest Ratio (per ha)	Annual Income (NRS)	Year of Beginning Protection
BZ	95.9	4.60	56.43	450	4.69	14,000	1995
BZ	182.0	2.32	21.86	1,880	10.33	7,500	1992
BZ	76.3	2.71	76.18	1,100	14.42	75,000	1996
BZ	192.8	68.95	2.29	2,100	10.89	50,000	1995
BZ	327.2	15.05	13.07	1,866	5.70	600,000	1996
BZ	375.6	0.48	58.66	8,000	21.30	2,400,000	1986
BZ	32.9	4.92	10.66	917	27.87	30,000	1995
BZ	85.6	15.14	2.52	1,519	17.74	70,000	1995
BZ	47.7	0.94	42.26	5,000	104.82	400,000	1991
BZ	85.5	4.74	24.21	1,100	12.87	80,000	1992
BZ	64.5	38.49	3.77	1,750	27.12	120,000	1995
BZ	130.3	56.42	3.18	6,000	46.05	80,000	1996
BZ	195.9	0.46	39.00	4,570	23.33	5,100,000	1989
BZ	150.7	62.66	4.96	1,280	8.49	103,000	1996
CF	62.9	65.95	0.00	1,235	19.63	150,000	1989
CF	199.7	37.40	0.14	3,525	17.65	15,000	1998
CF	138.2	38.80	0.00	2,444	17.68	80,000	1993
CF	129.5	18.21	0.00	1,512	11.68	58,000	1993
CF	1,272.2	28.78	0.31	3,500	2.75	10,000	1989
CF	72.9	36.42	0.00	790	10.84	150,000	1994
CF	359.2	51.57	0.03	2,690	7.49	10,000	1989
CF	166.7	17.87	0.00	1,080	6.48	16,000	1994
CF	265.9	18.82	0.07	1,300	4.89	25,000	1993

Notes: For management figure, BZ is buffer zone and CF is community forest.

essential in order to place the changes seen in the forests in their proper context and to follow the impact of changes in formal institutional arrangements on forest cover over time. Landsat images cover a broad spatial extent (approximately 185 × 185 kilometers) and there are seven sensors that enable us to distinguish and identify broad types of land cover such as forest, agriculture, soil and water. The spatial resolution is relatively fine, with a pixel size of 28.5 meters, allowing the detection of changes in forest cover on a fairly detailed scale (Schweik et al., 2003).

Two nearly cloud-free Landsat TM images: January 24, 1989 and March 27, 2000 were selected to analyze changes in forest cover between 1989 and 2000. Both images were taken during the pre-monsoon season, where the distinction between fallow agriculture and tree cover is marked and easy to distinguish. This analysis allowed us to evaluate efforts towards community forestry in the *terai* over the last decade, during which community-based programs have seen the most activity in the *terai*. The 1989 image was geo-referenced using 1:25,000 scale topographic maps and the 2000 image geo-referenced to the 1989 image with an RMS error of less than 0.5 pixels. This enabled us to overlay information from different images within a GIS to evaluate forest change. Radiometric calibration, atmospheric correction and radiometric rectification procedures were used to ensure image comparability (Jensen, 2000). Without such calibration, change detection analysis may evaluate differences at the sensor level rather than changes at the earth's surface.

A Normalized Difference Vegetation Index (NDVI) (ibid.) was computed for the calibrated images. This index can range from −1 to +1, and has been shown to have a positive correlation with the amount of green biomass and vegetation cover on ground (ibid.). Between February and May 2000, field training data were collected on the distribution of forest cover in the Chitwan. These data were used to identify thresholds of NDVI values that correspond to cleared areas, open tree cover (less than 40 percent canopy cover) and dense tree cover (more than 40 percent canopy cover), respectively. These thresholds were used to classify the NDVI images for 1989 and 2000 into the above three categories using ERDAS IMAGINE™ software.

Individual land cover images for 1989 and 2000 were recoded to provide a single image that identified change trajectories (i.e., sequences of land cover classes across observation dates, Petit *et al.*, 2001). The output was a categorical 'change image', where each pixel now includes information on land cover for both dates. Areas of no change indicated pixels that remained in the same land cover category across both dates, while areas of deforestation had experienced a decrease in forest cover and areas of regrowth had experienced an increase in forest cover (Figure 8.1). The regrowth, or increase in tree cover, can be due to replanting of saplings, or due to natural regeneration. In most forests, the communities utilize both of these approaches for encouraging regrowth. As it was not possible to distinguish between replantation and 'natural'

FIGURE 8.1

Change Classification for East Chitwan (1989–2000) Overlaid with Buffer Zone and Community Forests Boundaries

Legend

■ Deforested
■ No change
■ Reforested

■ Buffer zone
■ Community forest

Scale

5   0   5
Kilometers

reforestation through remote sensing and the scale of variation in these management practices is too detailed to map in the field, we treated both of these as instances of regrowth. By incorporating information from images of both dates, change trajectories high-lighted the dynamic character of the land cover within the study region (Mertens and Lambin, 2000). We utilized ARC/INFO™ GRID software, a raster-based program, for this procedure.

Institutional Information

Spatial information on institutional boundaries was collected during the months of March and April 2002. An initial checklist was prepared, identifying a total of nine formally-registered and handed-over community forests and 14 formally-registered buffer zone forests located in the study area. The spatial boundary of each of these forest patches was collected by using a Geographical Positioning System (GPS) unit to walk around the perimeter of the forest and by using information from local forest users and forest officials to locate the boundary on a 1:25,000 scale survey topographic map with reference to major landmarks.

These spatial boundaries were converted to digital form and overlaid onto the change trajectory satellite image. Using ArcInfo GRID, for each of these forest patches we calculated the percentage of total forest area that remained stable, experienced deforest-ation and experienced regrowth. Then, these pixels were classified according to the institutional regime (community forest or buffer zone forest). In addition, for each of these institutions, a user-group survey was conducted based upon the survey forms developed by the International Forestry Resources and Institutions Program (Ostrom, 1998). These forms provided us with information on vari-ables thought to affect the effectiveness of local institutions, in-cluding total area, user group size, number of livestock and cattle, income derived from the user group, monitoring activities and ability to modify the rules. For each delineated forest patch, we then related these variables to the satellite information on forest cover change within the boundary of that patch and to the institu-tional tenure type for that patch.

Given our focus towards understanding the impact of policy changes on forest condition, our independent variable was formal policy intervention, or the formal property rights regime: specified here as a binary variable, buffer zone vs community forest. We recognize that this is a broad classification and at this level, by lumping all community forests into one category and all buffer zone forests into another, we are ignoring the variation that is known to exist within these categories and which may potentially influence their impact on forest regeneration. Nevertheless, given that this binary classification is precisely the way in which most policy interventions are defined and implemented (in a 'one-size-fits-all manner') and that user rights to timber and other forest resources are severely constrained by the *de jure* management regime in practice, it is important to first investigate differences at this level. Crucially, we supplement our discussion of statistical analyses at this binary level of classification with qualitative explorations of intra-type variation.

Forest conservation is a major objective of the community forestry and buffer zone management programs (Chaudhary, 2000). We consider deforestation to be an indicator of lack of effective conservation and regrowth of tree cover as an indicator of effective forest management and conservation. Thus, the two dependent variables we consider in this analysis are percentage regrowth and percentage deforestation (together), as an indication of forest conservation. We had asked the forest user groups to indicate whether they or the government officials were responsible for creating the forest association rules, and further, whether there were any constraints placed on their capacity to modify the rules of the forest association. Their ability to influence the development and modification of forest management rules was taken as an indicator of the amount of local control within these two largely government-influenced management regimes.

Finally, we examine whether there are significant differences between buffer zone and community forests in terms of the distribution of moderator variables that are associated with these regimes. Given the long list of potential variables that are known to influence institutional management of natural resources (Agrawal, 2001), we have chosen to limit ourselves to a study of a smaller set of variables that we believe important in this system. Moderator variables are factors that are not part of the initial policy design, and out of the control of short-run policy interventions, but which may influence the outcome (Stern *et al.*, 2000). For instance, user group income is one of the moderator variables we consider. While this is not a criteria for deciding whether a forest is to be assigned to buffer zone management or to community management, the differences in the location of these two types of forests (with buffer zone forests closer to the RCNP, and hence having better potential for ecotourism) may give rise to differences in user-group income. While it is difficult to formulate short-term policy interventions to deal with these types of differences (Stern *et al.*, 2000), these constitute important factors that need to be taken into account while thinking of long-term policy changes. We consider four potential moderator variables: forest size, user-group size, user/forest ratio and annual income of the user group.

RESULTS

Table 8.1 describes the nine community forests and 14 buffer zone forests in the study area and provides information on their size, percentage of area that has experienced regrowth and deforestation between 1989 and 1991, user-group size, annual income and year in which forest protection was initiated. For purposes of confidentiality, the names of the settlements and forests are not provided here.

On an average, buffer zone forests demonstrated a net increase in forest cover over time, while community forests showed a net decrease in forest cover over time. A non-parametric Mann Whitney U test revealed that the percentage of deforestation was significantly lower and the percentage of regrowth significantly higher in buffer zone forests as compared to community forests ($p < 0.05$). There was no significant difference between buffer zone forests and community forests in terms of size (Figure 8.1, Table 8.1), or in terms of user-group size (Table 8.1), but the user/forest ratio was significantly higher in buffer zone forests ($p < 0.05$). Finally, the buffer zone user groups indicated that the major income earned by them was from tourism, supplemented by smaller income from annual user fees and sale of firewood and other forest products. In contrast, community forests were not able to access income from tourism and their major sources of earning were from annual user fees, sale of firewood, medicinal plants, timber and other forest products.

FIGURE 8.2
Scatter plot, Date of Initiation of Forest Protection vs Percentage of Deforestation (A) and Regrowth (B)

(A)

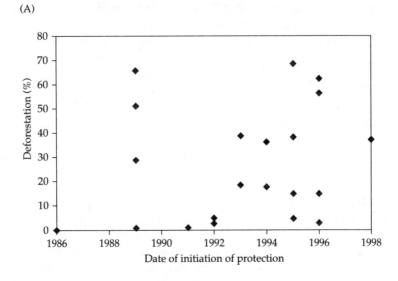

(B)

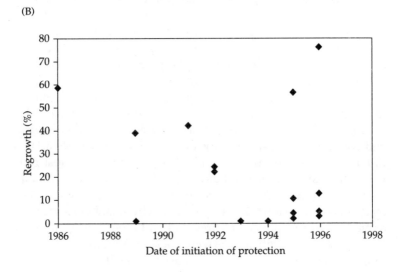

Finally, there was no significant correlation between the age of initiation of forest protection and the percentage deforestation (Spearman's R = 0.313, p > 0.05) or between age of initiation and percentage regrowth (Spearman's R = 0.434, p > 0.05, Figure 8.2).

Discussion

As with the study of several other complex systems, studying common-pool resource management necessitates multivariate analysis of complex, path-dependent phenomena. Given the complex interactions between human and ecological systems that influence the dynamics of forest cover change, developing a nuanced understanding requires the integration of theories and methods from the social and natural sciences and the use of a comparative approach involving multiple case studies (Stern et al., 2000). Applications of remote sensing techniques to analyze social incentives and actions and explore environmental and social change have been increasingly explored over the past few years (Liverman et al., 1998; Fox et al., 2003). Recent research has used these methodologies to good effect for studies of the human factors impacting land cover change in Nepal (Millette et al., 1995; Gautam et al., 2002, 2003; Schweik et al., 2003; Nagendra and Schweik, 2004). This research utilized information from remote sensing, Geographical Systems analysis and interviews with forest user groups to analyze the impact of Nepalese initiatives towards decentralization on forests and institutions in the terai.

Although there is much current controversy on the effectiveness of community forestry in the Nepal terai, there are few empirical investigations of this issue (Nagendra, 2002; Schweik et al., 2003). We find that the forests within the purview of buffer zone management are in noticeably better condition compared to the community forests located at a distance from the park. This is no surprise, given the financial and technical resources input into the buffer zone area by several international and national NGOs, most significantly the UNDP (Maskey et al., 1999), but also including Biodiversity Conservation Network, World Wildlife Fund and the King Mahendra Trust for Nature Conservation (Bookbinder et al., 1998; Heinen and Mehta, 2002; Schweik et al., 2003). The user groups in these forests tend to receive larger incomes through ecotourism and are thus able to afford and pay for better monitoring through hiring more guards and through forest fencing. Unlike community forestry user groups, who pay a royalty to the government on proceeds from the sale of timber to non-users, buffer zone groups are exempted from paying this royalty, thus enabling them to earn potentially greater incomes from the sale of timber. However, in-depth surveys indicate that the user groups have limited decision-making authority over creating or modifying forest management rules. Thus this management, although it may be effective in the short-term, is not very participatory, and this has negative implications for the degree of grassroots support for this program and for its sustainability over the long-term.

Two of the most 'successful' cases of buffer zone forestry (Baghmara and Kumrose forests), much touted success stories of this policy intervention (e.g., see Seidensticker, 2002), have received substantial support from the Biodiversity Conservation Network and the World Wildlife Fund (Bookbinder *et al.*, 1998). In contrast, the community forests have received only limited technical inputs, mostly from local NGOs and from the forest department. The extensive financial and technical inputs into managing the buffer zone forests can account for much of their 'success' in terms of forest regeneration. The point we are making here is that although the forested areas within the buffer zone management program appear to have higher levels of regeneration, non-institutional factors including the location of the forests and technical and financial assistance from international and local NGOs are likely to explain some of this regeneration.

A potentially confounding factor is the variation in the time period of forest protection. Although both programs were formally initiated in 1998, Table 8.1 indicates that some communities began protecting the forest as far back as in 1986 (as also often observed in the middle hills, see Gautam *et al.*, 2002, 2003). Several of the community and buffer zone forests actually began being protected and managed by local communities as early as 1986, with inputs from the King Mahendra Trust for Nature Conservation (Table 8.1). Most of these forests were formally constituted as buffer zone forests only after 1996. Our interviews also indicate that several communities began managing areas that are now formally notified as community forests as early as 1986, inspired by the implementation of the Community Forestry Act in the middle hills around that time. This trajectory of local community management initiatives followed by formalized notification is often encountered in Nepal (Gautam *et al.*, 2002, 2003). An alternative hypothesis could be that the forests that have been protected for longer periods of time are the areas with less deforestation and greater regrowth. A rank correlation analysis however showed that there was no significant correlation between the number of years the forest has been protected and the percentage of deforestation or regrowth.

Although there are no significant differences in terms of forest size or user-group size, the user group/forest ratio in buffer zones is significantly higher than in community forests. We also found that the extent of regrowth in buffer zones was significantly higher than in community forests. This agrees with findings by Agrawal (2000) in the Kumaon Himalayas of India, where up to a point, larger forest groups appear to be more successful at managing forests, due in large part to the fact that more people involved with management and monitoring are able to do a better job of forest management. This may be a factor influencing the relative success of buffer zone forests, with a higher number of users potentially available to participate in management and monitoring per unit forest area. We also find that buffer zone forests tend to have a larger annual income than community forests. In large part this is due to income from ecotourism which is more prevalent in the buffer zone forests near the RCNP. Our interviews indicate that the buffer zone user groups that possess higher incomes are able to utilize this increased income to pay more to hire a larger number of forest guards and to fence the forest boundaries, thus enabling them to enforce limitations on harvesting more easily than the less wealthy community forests and resulting in increased reforestation in the buffer zone.

While it is heartening to observe regeneration of forest cover in these areas, we also need to ask questions about the degree of control that community forest and buffer zone forest user groups have over determining, enforcing and modifying the rules of management. The flexibility to adapt according to circumstances and learn from previous experiences is crucial to the success of local management initiatives and their sustainability over the long-term (Ostrom, 2000; Varughese and Ostrom, 2001). Our interviews indicate that the forest association rules for the community forests and the buffer zone forests are based on the initial set of rules created by the forest department and park warden, based on the Buffer Zone Act and buffer zone management regulations. Our respondents state that they have very limited flexibility under both management regimes to adapt the management rules according to their local needs. In the community forests, they have more flexibility over the expenditure of income that is earned by the forest user group, although a new policy by the Nepalese government has recently stipulated that 40 percent of the income from the sale of timber be handed over to the government. In buffer zone areas, the expenditure of income is more strictly controlled. Expenditure is proportionally and mandatorily pre-assigned to defined categories and monitored by the park warden, who also functions as the secretary of the committee overseeing expenditures (HMG, 1999; Heinen and Mehta, 2000). This constraint is an important factor to recognize and raises questions for the future sustainability of the buffer zone program.

Unlike the community forestry user groups, the communities in the buffer zone have had to deal with more frequent shifts in policy regimes. Prior to the declaration of the buffer zone development area the forests that were located below the east-west highway were under the jurisdiction of the District Forest Office, as community forests. Since the buffer zone program was initiated, these forests have been shifted to the buffer zone and under the jurisdiction of the chief warden of the park. They now have to deal with an increased level of restrictions, which have led to conflicts. The primary source of conflict stems from the fact that during the course of demarcation of the buffer zone area, a number of households that used to harvest forest products from the identified forest patches have been excluded from the buffer zone user groups. In perhaps one of the most extreme instances of such exclusion, in the Barndhabar Forest, of the 1,180 user households that used to harvest products from this region, only 65 households have been officially recognized as belonging to the buffer zone user group. In other forests in our study area as well, between 5 and 25 percent of the forest user households have been excluded from the buffer zone program, not a small proportion by any account. The excluded households question the criteria that have been used to demarcate the buffer zone area and have approached the warden's office with repeated requests to be included in the buffer zone program, so far without success. This has obviously led to social conflicts between excluded households and the registered users who are able to benefit from the programs of the buffer zone development council.

Registered households have also had to deal with a greater set of restrictions under the buffer zone program. While under the Forest Act (under the DFO), the community forest user groups are autonomous and self-governing institutions, this is no longer the case after the development of the buffer zone program (Ghimire, 2004). Formerly, the forest constitution and work plan were developed by the community forestry user groups and then sanctioned from the DFO's office, but now they have to go through the buffer zone development user committee to the warden, which is a much longer process. Unlike before, when harvesting fuelwood, grass and dead fallen trees, the user groups have to take permission in advance from the warden: which they resent as 'undemocratic' interference with their management and protection activities. Further, although both the DFO and the warden retain the right to dissolve community forestry and buffer zone user groups respectively at any time, the community forestry user groups have the right to challenge such changes in court, while it is unclear as to what provisions, if any, exist for legal recourse in the case of the buffer zone user groups.

The user groups have managed to deal with some of these issues in innovative ways. For instance, specifications in the buffer zone regulations indicate that the power to punish individuals involved in illegal harvesting activities in the forest has shifted from the user committee (with whom such power vests in the community forests) to the warden. However, on ground, most user groups continue to monitor and sanction offenses themselves and have even written this into some of the user-group constitutions. However, in most part, they now have to deal with an even more restrictive set of forest policies that have excluded a large proportion of users from the program. Thus this management, although it may be effective in the short-term, is not very participatory and this has negative implications for the ability of this management regime to sustain itself through local empowerment into decision making over the long-term.

Externally implemented institutions do not make their way into a vacuum but are instead transplanted into a pre-existing social context of norms, customs and rules (Poffenberger and McGean, 1996;

Sundar, 2000; Prasad and Kant, 2003). As we observe, upwardly accountable and externally enforced rules tend to be relatively inflexible and unable to adapt to changing social or biophysical conditions that require changes in appropriate management practices (Berkes *et al.*, 1998). At a time when the Nepalese government is considering expansion of this program to cover several other national parks in Nepal, this calls into doubt the long-term sustainability of these programs. The high degree of external financial and technical input provided by governmental and international aid agencies and their limited role in actual local empowerment raises questions regarding the capability of these communities to continue with successful management policies after conclusion of the project and termination or reduction of external support.

ACKNOWLEDGMENTS

This chapter draws substantially on data presented in H. Nagendra, M. Karmacharya and B. Karna (2005). 'Cutting across space and time: Examining forest co-management in Nepal'. *Ecology and Society* 10(1): 24. [online] URL: http://www. ecologyandsociety.org/vol10/iss1/art24/. We gratefully acknowledge financial support from the National Science Foundation (NSF) (SBR-9521918) as part of the ongoing research at the Center for the Study of Institutions, Population, and Environmental Change (CIPEC) at Indiana University and from the Society in Science: Branco Weiss Fellowship to Harini Nagendra. We thank Kanchan Thapa for assistance with field research, Dr Charles Schweik, Dr Ganesh P. Shivakoti and Dr George Varughese for helpful discussions and Dr Edward L. Webb and Dr Elinor Ostrom for invaluable feedback on earlier drafts of this chapter.

REFERENCES

Agrawal, A. (2000). 'Small is Beautiful, but is Larger Better? Forest-management Institutions in the Kumaon Himalaya, India'. In C. Gibson, M. McKean, and E. Ostrom (eds), *People and Forests: Communities, Institutions, and Governance.* Cambridge, MA: The MIT Press.

———. (2001) 'Common Property Institutions and Sustainable Governance of Resources'. *World Development, 29,* 1949–1672.

Agrawal, A., Britt, C. and Kanel, K. (1999). *Decentralization in Nepal: A Comparative Analysis.* Oakland, CA: ICS Press.

Agrawal, A. and Ostrom, E. (2001). 'Collective Action, Property Rights, and Decentralisation in Resource Use in India and Nepal'. *Politics and Society, 29,* 485–514.

Berkes, F., Folke, C. and Colding, J. (eds). (1998) *Linking Social and Ecological Systems: Management Practices and Social Mechanisms for Building Resilience*. Cambridge: Cambridge University Press.

Bookbinder, M.P., Dinerstein, E., Rijal, A., Cauley, H. and Rajouria A. (1998). 'Ecotourism's Support of Biodiversity Conservation'. *Conservation Biology*, *12*, 1399–1404.

Bray, D.B., Merino-Pérez, L., Negreros-Castillo, P., Segura-Warnholtz, G., Torres-Rojo, P.M. and Vester, H.F.M. (2003). 'Mexico's Community Managed Forests as a Global Model for Sustainable Landscapes'. *Conservation Biology*, *17*, 672–677.

Brown, K. (1998). 'The Political Ecology of Biodiversity, Conservation and Development in Nepal's Terai: Confused Meanings, Means and Ends'. *Ecological Economics*, *24*, 73–87.

Chakraborty, R.N. (2001). 'Stability and Outcomes of Common Property Institutions in Forestry: Evidence from the Terai Region of Nepal'. *Ecological Economics*, *36*, 341–353.

Chaudhary, R.P. (2000). 'Forest Conservation and Environmental Management in Nepal: A Review'. *Biodiversity and Conservation*, *9*, 1235–1260.

Fox, J., Rindfuss, R.R., Walsh, S.J. and Mishra, V. (2003). *People and the Environment: Approaches for Linking Household and Community Surveys to Remote Sensing and GIS*. Boston: Kluwer Academic Publishers.

Gautam, A.P., Webb, E.L. and Eiumnoh, A. (2002). 'GIS Assessment of Land Use/Land Cover Changes Associated with Community Forestry Implementation in the Middle Hills of Nepal'. *Mountain Research and Development*, *22*, 63–69.

Gautam, A.P., Webb, E.L., Shivakoti, G.P. and Zoebisch, M.A. (2003). 'Land Use Dynamics and Landscape Change Pattern in a Mountain Watershed in Nepal'. *Agriculture, Ecosystems and Environment*, *99*, 83–96.

Ghimire, S. (2004). 'Buffer Zone Management: A Challenge'. *Hamaro Ban Sampada, Forest Action*, *2*, 13–16 (in Nepali).

Heinen, J.T. and Mehta, J.N. (2000). 'Emerging Issues in Legal and Procedural Aspects of Buffer Zone Management with Case Studies from Nepal'. *Journal of Environment and Development*, *9*, 45–67.

His Majesty's Government of Nepal (HMG). (1999). *Buffer Zone Management Guidelines*. Kathmandu: His Majesty's Government, Ministry of Forests and Soil Conservation and Department of National Parks and Wildlife Conservation.

Jensen, J.R. (2000). *Remote Sensing of the Environment: An Earth Resource Perspective*. Upper Saddle River, NJ: Prentice-Hall.

Liverman, D., Moran, E.F., Rindfuss, R.R. and Stern, P.C. (eds). (1998). *People and Pixels: Linking Remote Sensing and Social Science*. Washington, DC: National Academy Press.

Maskey, T.M., Bajimaya, S., Dhamala, B.R., Joshi, B.K.L. and Budhathoki, P. (1999). *Park People Programme: 1999 The Year in Review*. Kathmandu: Department of National Parks and Wildlife Conservation Parks People Program and United Nations Development Program.

Matthews, S.A., Shivakoti, G.P. and Chhetri, N. (2000). 'Population Forces and Environmental Change: Observations from Western Chitwan, Nepal'. *Society and Natural Resources*, *13*, 763–775.

Mertens, B. and Lambin, E.F. (1997). 'Spatial Modelling of Deforestation in Southern Cameroon'. *Applied Geography, 17,* 143–162.

————. (2000). 'Land-cover-change Trajectories in Southern Cameroon'. *Annals of the Association of American Geographers, 90,* 467–494.

Messerschmidt, D.A. (1987). 'Conservation and Society in Nepal: Traditional Forest Management and Innovative Development'. In P.D. Little and M.M. Horowitz with A.E. Nyerges (eds), *Land at Risk in the Third World: Local Level Perspectives* (pp. 373–397). Boulder, CO: Westview Press.

Millette, T.L., Tuladhar, A.R., Kasperson, R.E. and Turner, B.L. III. (1995). 'The Use and Limits of Remote Sensing for Analyzing Environmental and Social Change in the Himalayan Middle Mountains of Nepal'. *Global Environmental Change, 5,* 367–380.

Nagendra, H. (2001). 'Using Remote Sensing to Assess Biodiversity'. *International Journal of Remote Sensing, 22,* 2377–2400.

————. (2002). 'Tenure and Forest Conditions: Community Forestry in the Nepal Terai'. *Environmental Conservation, 29,* 530–539.

Nagendra, H. and Gadgil, M. (1999). 'Biodiversity Assessment at Multiple Scales: Linking Remotely Sensed Data with Field Information'. *Proceedings of the National Academy of Sciences USA, 96,* 9154–9158.

Nagendra, H., Munroe, D. and Southworth, J. (2004). 'Introduction to the Special Issue. From Pattern to Process: Landscape Fragmentation and the Analysis of Land Use/Land Cover Change'. *Agriculture, Ecosystems and Environment, 101* (2–3), 111–115.

Nagendra, H. and Schweik, C.M. (2004). 'Forests and Management: A Case Study in Nepal Using Remote Sensing and GIS'. In B. Warf, K. Hansen, and D. Janelle (eds), *100 Geographic Solutions to Saving Planet Earth: Association of American Geographers Centennial Volume* (pp. 391–396). Boston: Kluwer Academic Publishers.

Negi, S.S. (1998). *Forests and Forestry in Nepal.* New Delhi: Ashish Publishing House.

Ostrom, E. (1990). *Governing the Commons: The Evolution of Institutions for Collective Action.* New York: Cambridge University Press.

————. (1998). 'The International Forestry Resources and Institutions Program: A Methodology for Relating Human Incentives and Actions on Forest Cover and Biodiversity'. In F. Dallmeier and J.A. Comisker (eds), *Forest Biodiversity in North, Central and South America, and the Caribbean: Research and Monitoring, Man and the Biosphere Series* (vol. 1, pp. 1–28). Paris: UNESCO; New York: Parthenon.

————. (2000). 'Reformulating the Commons'. *Swiss Political Science Review, 6,* 29–52.

Petit, C., Scudder, T. and Lambin, E. (2001). 'Quantifying Processes of Land-cover Change by Remote Sensing: Resettlement and Rapid Land-cover Changes in South-eastern Zambia'. *International Journal of Remote Sensing, 22,* 3435–3456.

Poffenberger, M. and McGean, B. (eds). (1996). *Village Voices, Forest Choices: Joint Forest Management in India.* New Delhi: Oxford University Press.

Poudel, K. (2000). 'Community Forestry: Government vs. Community'. *Nepalnews.com: News from Nepal as it Happens, 19*(47): June 9–15 (online URL: http://www.nepalnews.com/contents/englishweekly/spotlight/2000/jun/jun09/coverstory.html).

Poudel, K. (2001). 'Community Forestry: Under Threat'. *Nepalnews.com: News from Nepal as it Happens, 20*(34): March 9–15 (online URL: http://www.nepalnews. com/contents/englishweekly/spotlight/2001/mar/mar09/national3.html).

Prasad, R. and Kant, S. (2003). 'Institutions, Forest Management and Sustainable Development: Experiences from India'. *Environment, Development and Sustainability, 5,* 353–367.

Ribot, J.C. (2002). *Democratic Decentralization of Natural Resources: Institutionalizing Popular Participation.* Washington, DC: World Resources Institute.

———. (2004a). *Decentralization of Natural Resource Management: Encountering and Countering Resistance.* Washington, DC: World Resources Institute.

———. (2004b). *Waiting for Democracy: The Politics of Choice in Natural Resource Management.* Washington, DC: World Resources Institute.

Schweik, C.M., Adhikari, K. and Pandit, K.N. (1997). 'Land-cover Change and Forest Institutions: A Comparison of Two Sub-basins in the Southern Siwalik Hills of Nepal'. *Mountain Research and Development, 17,* 99–116.

Schweik, C., Nagendra, H. and Sinha, D.R. (2003). 'Using Satellites to Search for Forest Management Innovations in Nepal'. *Ambio, 32,* 312–319.

Seidensticker, J. (2002). 'Tiger Tracks'. *Smithsonian, 32,* 62–69.

Shrestha, B. (1998). 'Changing Forest Policies and Institutional Innovations: User Group Approach in Community Forestry of Nepal'. In *Proceedings of the International Workshop on Community-Based Natural Resource Management (CBNRM),* May 10–14, Washington, DC.

Stainton, J.D.A. (1972). *Forests of Nepal.* London: John Murray Publishers.

Stern, P.C., Dietz, T., Dolsak, N., Ostrom, E. and Stonich, S. (2000). 'Knowledge and Questions after 15 Years of Research'. In M. McKean Gibson and E. Ostrom (eds), *People and Forests: Communities, Institutions, and Governance.* Cambridge, MA: The MIT Press.

Sundar, N. (2000). 'Unpacking the 'Joint' in Joint Forest Management'. *Development and Change, 31,* 255–279.

Thapa, G.B. and Weber, K.W. (1995). 'Natural Resource Degradation in a Small Watershed in Nepal: Complex Causes and Remedial Measures'. *Natural Resources Forum, 19,* 285–296.

Varughese, G. (2000). *Villagers, Bureacrats, and Forests in Nepal: Designing Governance for a Complex Resource.* Doctoral thesis, Workshop in Political Theory and Policy Analysis. Bloomington, IN: Indiana University.

Varughese, G. and Ostrom, E. (2001). 'The Contested Role of Heterogeneity in Collective Action: Some Evidence from Community Forestry in Nepal'. *World Development, 29,* 747–765.

Webb, E.L. and Gautam, A.P. (2001). 'Effects of Community Forest Management on the Structure and Diversity of a Successional Broadleaf Forest in Nepal'. *International Forestry Review, 3,* 146–157.

9

Evolution of Community-Based Management and Forest Health in Northern Thailand: Case Study of Nahai and Huai-muang Villages in Sopsai Watershed, Thawangpa District, Nan Province

NITAYA KIJTEWACHAKUL, GANESH P. SHIVAKOTI and
EDWARD L. WEBB

Introduction

Thailand is similar to many developing Asian countries in that it has adopted a model of forest conservation that excludes local communities from protected areas. These protected areas include national parks, wildlife sanctuaries and legal head-watershed areas (designated watershed Class 1 and 2). Despite having a policy emphasizing forest protection by exclusion, many communities in northern region traditionally manage their forests according to their spiritual beliefs, uses, and biophysical and cultural circumstances (Ganjanapan and Kaosa-ard, 1995). Local forest management practices have not been formally recognized by the Thai state (Ganjanapan, 1992) and traditional practices have deteriorated in part because of the state's centralized control over forests (i.e., the Royal Forest Department [RFD]) and its awarding of timber concessions prior to 1989 (Ramitanondh, 1989). The concessions and centralized policies have resulted in numerous and often wide-spread conflicts between local people and the state (Duanglamyai, 2001). The negative impact of these state policies on local communities has in turn driven communities to initiate social resistance

(Narintarangkul Na Ayuthaya, 1996; Wittayapak, 2002) and collective action for forest conservation (Ganjanapan and Kaosa-ard, 1995; Wittayapak and Dearden, 1999). Community-based forest management (CBFM) in Thailand has evolved through people's movements to gain power and decision-making control for forest resources in their locality (Gilmour and Fisher, 1998).

More recently, the Government of Thailand has begun to recognize the necessity of people's participation in forest conservation. This has come about as a result of both local movements and state-sponsored pilot projects such as the Sam-maun Highland Development Project and the People's Participation in Village Woodlot Project of the RFD (Apichatvullop, 1993; Pragtong, 1993; Tan-Kim-Yong, 1993). Although these developments are encouraging, we have observed that this implementation strategy is based on the application of state-driven rules on the community in order to achieve state objectives.

Entrenched within the governmental system is the belief that local communities are incapable of or unwilling to sustainably manage forests and conserve biodiversity. In this chapter, we have sought out the answer to the question, whether it is possible to maintain good forest health while making management decisions through community-collective management for community objectives, rather than by the communities under state-influenced objectives for state objectives (ostensibly, conservation). In an attempt to find an answer to this question, we surveyed the forests of two communities in northern Thailand, both of which divide their forests into zones according to two different strategies: conservation, which is influenced by state policy, and 'utilization', which is designed through community-collective behaviors. Forest health parameters were compared in order to address the question of whether forest management used to achieve community objectives could be consistent with state objectives for conservation. We also discuss the scope of management and institutional arrangement with special reference to recognition at the local level.

STUDY SITE

This study was undertaken in two villages in the Sopsai Watershed, Nan Province, northern Thailand (Map 9.1). Nahai is a lowland

Map 9.1
**Forests Managed by Nahai and Huai-muang Villages in the
Sopsai Watershed, Nan Province, Thailand**

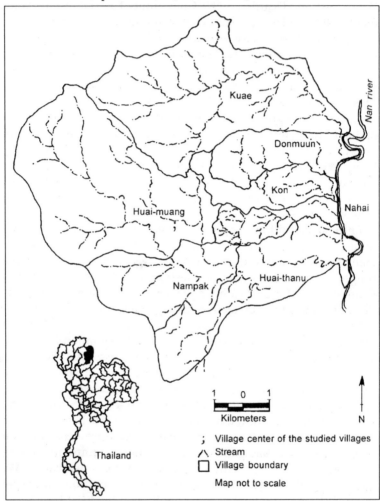

village located near the Nan river. Villagers use the flood plain
area for growing rice in the rainy season and vegetables and pea-
nuts in the dry season. Villagers irrigate their land with water
supplied from two small reservoirs above the settlement area.

To the west are low hills where regenerating swiddens can be found interspersed with permanent agricultural fields. At the time of this research (2001), only a few households (four-five) were continuing the practice of shifting cultivation. The overall land use pattern was a mosaic of regenerating forest and annual and perennial cropping areas (Map 9.2). Most Nahai villagers had access to agricultural areas in the lowland and near the road in the upland areas. There is a very good road to the district center and it takes about 45 minutes to get to the provincial center by vehicle.

Huai-muang is an upland village situated on relatively steep hills approximately 6 km to the west of Nahai. Access to the village is difficult because the road is not paved, making situations difficult for pedestrians during the rainy season. Huai-muang villagers grow paddy rice on limited irrigated land that does not permit dry-season cropping. They also practice extensive shifting cultivation with upland (dry) rice. Many households have changed from shifting cultivation to perennial cropping. The areas under different land uses in both villages are illustrated in Table 9.1.

The forests in Nahai village are dominated by bamboo and deciduous tree species with good coppicing ability. Locally, this forest type is known as *pa-pai* (directly translated as 'bamboo forest'). Forests in Huai-muang are at a slightly higher elevation and are dominated by deciduous species with fewer evergreen species in the understory. This forest is known as *pa-benjapan*. In general, these forests would be classified as 'mixed deciduous' according to most classification systems. A summary of biophysical conditions and a history of land and forests in both villages is given in Table 9.2.

DATA COLLECTION METHODS

In this study, the interdisciplinary framework of the International Forestry Resources and Institutions (IFRI) was used for data collection (Ostrom, 1999). Participatory mapping techniques using 1998 aerial photographs as a reference (scale 1:10,000) were used to identify the villages and the forests accessed by each village. In-depth interviews, group discussions and participant observations

MAP 9.2

Community Forest Management Overlapped with the Forest Restoration Schemes (Planted or Enrichment Forests) of Sopsai Watershed Management Unit (SWMU) and Agricultural Land Use in 2001

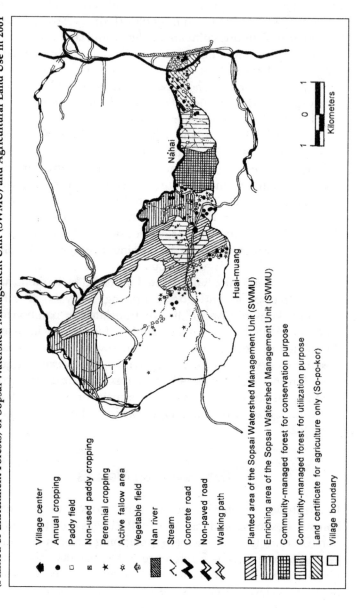

♠	Village center
●	Annual cropping
□	Paddy field
ış	Non-used paddy cropping
★	Perennial cropping
☆	Active fallow area
⚘	Vegetable field
	Nan river
	Stream
	Concrete road
	Non-paved road
	Walking path
	Planted area of the Sopsai Watershed Management Unit (SWMU)
	Enriching area of the Sopsai Watershed Management Unit (SWMU)
	Community-managed forest for conservation purpose
	Community-managed forest for utilization purpose
	Land certificate for agriculture only (So-po-kor)
	Village boundary

Nahai

Huai-muang

Kilometers

Table 9.1
Areas under Different Non-forest Land Use in Nahai and Huai-muang Villages, Nan Province, Thailand

Village		Areas under Different Land Use (rai)			
	Lowland Paddy	Upland Paddy	Perennial Cropping	Annual Cropping (under Shifting Cultivation)	Fallow Land (under Shifting Cultivation)
Nahai (n = 73)	109.8 (1.5)	4.5 (0.1)	194.3 (2.7)	43.6 (0.6)	316 (4.4)
Huai-muang (n = 66)	–	94.8 (1.4)	313.0 (4.7)	52.5 (0.8)	396.5 (6.0)

Notes: Figures in italics are average areas claimed per household.

6.25 rai = 1 ha.

Data collected from village census (all existing households).

TABLE 9.2
Summary of Biophysical Conditions in Association with Land Use History in
Nahai and Huai-muang Villages, Nan Province, Thailand

Characteristics	Nahai Village		Huai-muang Village	
	Conservation Purpose	Utilization Purpose	Conservation Purpose	Utilization Purpose
Biophysical conditions	Elevation: 290–470 m msl Soil type: sandy clay loam Soil A depth: 4–12 cm Soil organic over: 95–100% PH of soil A: 5–6 Crown cover: 35–95%	Elevation: 300–470 m msl Soil type: sandy clay loam Soil A depth: 3–7 cm Soil organic over: 95–100% PH of soil A: 3–7 Crown cover: 45–80%	Elevation: 380–420 m msl Soil type: sandy clay loam Soil A depth: 5–9 cm Soil organic over: 90–100% PH of soil A: 5–6 Crown cover: 30–85%	Elevation: 250–510 m msl Soil type: sandy clay loam Soil A depth: 3–15 cm Soil organic over: 80–100% PH of soil A: 4–6 Crown cover: 30–90%
Local classified forest type	'Pa-pai'—bamboo forest	'Pa-pai'—bamboo forest	'Pa-dong' or 'Pa-dip'—dense forest	'Pa-dong' or 'Pa-dip'—dense forest
Forest ecosystem type	Dry deciduous forest	Dry deciduous forest	Moist deciduous forest	Moist deciduous forest
History of land use	Under shifting cultivation Then lay in fallow for 15–20 years	Under shifting cultivation Then lay in fallow for 15–20 years	Under shifting cultivation Used for People Volunteer Self-Defense Camp (UVSDC) against the Communist Party of Thailand (CPT)	Under shifting cultivation Taken by the Sopsai Watershed Management Unit for tree planting

were used to collect information on use and management practices by the communities, rules and institutions governing the use, silvicultural manipulation, monitoring and protection. Particular emphasis was placed on how the communities divided the forest into management units with separate objectives, namely state-driven conservation or community-designed utilization objectives (hereafter, conservation and utilization, respectively).

After the forest management zones were mapped, a random sampling method was used to establish nested circular plots to survey forest conditions using IFRI research protocols. To ensure botanical accuracy, a botanical reference collection was made. A performance curve using the mean stem density per plot was used to determine the statistically appropriate number of sampling plots per management unit. Topographic and physical data such as location, soil depth, color, drainage and texture were also recorded. The inventory was carried out between January and April 2001 (the dry season).

Forest health was compared by using the following parameters: (a) height-class distribution of trees and saplings; (b) dbh-class distribution of trees and saplings; (c) density of trees and bamboo and (d) basal area. Before we discuss the findings on the forest health, we discuss the evolution and features of CBFM in the study area.

Pattern and Evolution of Forest Resource Management

Community initiatives in forest resource management are found only at the village level, not as collaborative activities among the villages in the research area. The community-initiated forest management can be divided into three main categories:

1. *Sacred forest.* This type of traditional forest was established soon after the settlement of a community to express their relationship and respect to nature sprits and ancestors. Generally, sacred forests were established near the settlements. The area was very limited, not exceeding 10 *rai*[1] in the villages studied. The forests were initially conserved by villagers themselves

for a long period of time. Because of dense vegetation and high moisture content, the forest provided benefits in fire-protection in addition to the original objective of being a site for cremations or other ritual ceremonies.

2. *Collective forest for headwater protection or fire prevention.* This type of forest is referred to as community forest for conservation. After the period of extensive shifting cultivation, the upland villagers integrated conservation forest with the major objective of restoring and maintaining good forest condition to ensure regular water flow in streams. The management strategies through rule setting have evolved over-time and these forests were established near the settlement and the head-watershed of some main streams. In collective forest for conservation, collection of non-timber forest products (NTFPs) and dead wood is allowed. But, due to its topography, use of this type of forest is limited.

3. *Collective forest for direct resource use.* Such categories of community forest are meant for utilization and are either private or commonly owned, depending on the property rights regimes recognized in the locality. Under a common property rights regime, the members of each upland village reached a mutual agreement to maintain and restore secondary forest for common utilization objectives and benefit sharing. An example would be to allow village members to collect products within the village forest boundary and ask the village committee for permission before harvesting wildlife or timber for subsistence. In Huai-muang village, the collective forest for utilization was allocated from the areas which used to be under the reforestation scheme of the local government implementing agency, the Sopsai Watershed Management Unit (SWMU). In addition, small areas of forests along the streams are also classified as commons. Some of these forests are not clearly demarcated but cover a large area of over a thousand rai in Huai-muang village.

In Nahai village, a second type of community forest for utilization is seen in active old-fallow forest that has been claimed under private property but that holders have 'collectively maintained', promoting natural regeneration and allowing villagers to use non-cropped resources without degrading the landscape and ecosystems. Under collective maintenance, individual landholders can gain benefits from valued products, especially timber and firewood. These utilization forests are very important for food security and generating income.

The sacred forest and community forest for conservation are managed under a common property rights regime or village property. Village members have rights to manage the resources (setting rules and excluding non-authorized users) within the village boundaries. Sacred forests have been traditionally developed in both villages while the community forests for conservation exist only in the upland village. In general, the sacred forests are densely covered with trees and are situated near roads.

In the Sopsai Watershed, community forest for conservation has evolved only during the last few decades. Initially, the upland communities managed their forest areas around the settlement for conservation after an incident of forest-fire in Huai-kwang village that destroyed the forest substantially; that village does not exist any more. Huai-kwang and another nearby community, Hai village, decided to move to the more secure and accessible settlement adjacent to the main road. Instead of moving the settlement to the more secure areas, Huai-muang has set the rules and developed collective-action mechanisms to protect the houses from forest-fire and to ensure an adequate water supply. Most villagers in Huai-muang felt that without collective action they would be more prone than the people in the lowland to the rapid flooding in the rainy season and face drought in the dry season.

In Huai-muang village, written rules for forest conservation have been enforced since 1985. These rules were set due to the external social and political pressure and established by the state officials. But, these rules may not address the collective behavior of existing resource uses and availability. The conservation rules established by Huai-muang leaders under external pressure for conservation must match with their willingness to conserve the forests. In Huai-muang, however, controlling logging and immigration have been the prime objectives of both the villagers and the project officials. Yet another characteristic of the community forest in the upland villages is that the decisions about conservation rules were mostly made by only few village leaders, not developed through the adaptive norms of most village members in maintaining the long-term benefits to the communities.

The village leaders also set rules and made decisions to limit the amount of allowable harvest of timber in an attempt to disprove the (urban) perception that villagers' use of forest resources is indiscriminant and destructive. The logging ban of 1990 and the state's strict 'forest conservation' policy meant that the forest officers and other government officers were very concerned about illegal cutting of timber, particularly by Huai-muang. These attitudes of administrative officials, forest officers and urban people have put pressure on the village to implement a self-controlled timber harvesting practice at the local level. Therefore, in this case, the harvesting of timber is not much influenced by market-driven factors, but is under a community-controlled mechanism that governs and regulates forest-use, particularly of trees for house constructions by members of Huai-muang.

However, it should be noted that the amount of timber harvested is also limited due to its inaccessibility (i.e., distance and geographical conditions). And although the communities have initiated rules for forest management, collective action remains limited to forest areas where degradation of the resources could possibly cause negative impacts on livelihood security (e.g., forest adjacent to the settlement areas and headwater forests supplying water for households' consumption). These are rather small when compared to the whole watershed area or forest areas that are accessible for utilization such as NTFP collection.

Some areas under extensive shifting cultivation around the head watershed utilized by Huai-muang have evolved into conservation areas, with an increasing priority on indirect uses of resources (headwater and fire protection). At the same time, multiple direct uses of forest resources in many conservation areas near the settlements are allowed after these forests have sufficiently regenerated. In effect, these new utilization forests are the product of collective behaviors of forest and land resource use that maintain and restore the landscape and ecosystems. This reflects the livelihood dynamics of Huai-muang village. Many areas around the settlement have changed from shifting cultivation to perennial cropping which require protection from fire and adequate water supply in the dry season. Therefore, the villagers prefer to have forests as a buffer zone for fire and as the sources for firewood and edible products for consumption.

Although Nahai village did not initiate the conservation areas, their rights to use and manage uplands have been recognized by the local right systems for more than a decade and are another system of community forest for utilization. Many of these upland areas have been collectively maintained forest areas that have regenerated and major forest products (i.e., firewood, timber) are managed and controlled by individual land-holders. These tenurial arrangements by individuals within the lowland villages have been recognized by local government officers. The upland areas of Nahai village thus have less external pressure on their use and management of uplands compared to Huai-muang village.

In principle, community initiatives for managing a forest should include the maintenance and appropriate uses of forest products through the development of local institutions in response to the needs of the community now and in the future. The initiatives of the upland village like Huai-muang in forest management are the result of biophysical conditions and external social relationships. Thus, the upland community has adapted their responses to these changing conditions and relationships by positioning themselves within the image of coexistence between people and the forest. This, in turn, has influenced the positive change towards creation of rules and the evolution of collective actions which have been institutionalized. The summary of the existing community initiative in forest management and external recognition is presented in Table 9.3.

As summarized in Table 9.3, sacred forest is a traditional form of community forest which generally has a widely-recognized community right over its management regime. With or without legal recognition, this type of community forest is often well maintained in rural society. However, the areas of the sacred forests are of rather limited significance, contributing ecological benefit at a landscape scale or in the management of a watershed in comparison to other recently-evolved community forests.

TABLE 9.3

Summary of the Existing Community Initiatives in Forest Management and External Recognition across Upland and Lowland Villages, Nan Province, Thailand

Village Group	Sacred Forest		Community Forest for Conservation		Community Forest for Utilization	
	Existing Management	Key Issues	Existing Management	Key Issues	Existing Management	Key Issues
Upland villages	Yes	High recognition by external agencies of community capacity and rights Small area (only a few rai)	Yes	Low recognition by external agencies of community capacity and rights Cover an area of a few hundreds to a thousand rai	Yes	Evolved from CBF for conservation Low recognition by external agencies of community capacity and rights The community-managed areas are similar to the area for conservation. But more resource extraction by the communities
Lowland village (both type 1 and type 2)	Yes	High recognition by external agencies of community capacity and rights Small area (only a few rai)	No	–	Yes	High recognition by external agencies of community capacity and rights Collectively-maintained inactive fallow under private property regime

Community forestry for conservation in the upland village has evolved from the externally-defined objectives of community-based systems in order to conserve and derive limited benefits of specific nature of the products in a specific time from the forest. The extent of local recognition depends on the local power, ability to bargain or negotiate and the legal classification of forests. For example, people face uncertainty when a national park decides to include 'forest land' conserved or farmed by local people or when the SWMU wants to carry out reforestation programs on people's fallow lands. Under such uncertain situations, people feel no long-term security of the rights to manage the forests and as a result limit their investment (including labor and time provision) for forest protection and conservation.

LEGAL RIGHTS VS LOCALLY-RECOGNIZED RIGHTS

While government officers and the Sub-district Administrative Organizations (SAOs) implement laws and government policies, they also recognize that (to various degrees) local systems affect land and resource use. A state program that provides formal documentation of land rights to individual landholders also influences many decisions about land use and the local property rights system at the individual and village level.

In a study of land security in the northern region, Ganjanapan (2000) found that, for people in the highlands, tenure insecurity had a negative influence on land improvement. However, in the lowland communities at Chom Thong district, many farmers did not perceive the benefits of title deeds in terms of increasing security of property rights, but for increasing credit access and land value (Ganjanapan, 1994). According to Ganjanapan (ibid.), under the existing situation of expansion of business and marketization, the issuance of title deeds neither provided benefits equally to the farmers nor access to credit, but did increase the risk of indebtedness and loss of land.

In the Sopsai watershed, different legal land titles exist in various communities (see Table 9.4). *De jure* land documents (e.g., *Nor-sor 3*) have been issued only in the lowland areas although the issuance

TABLE 9.4

Landholding Documents under Statutory Laws
(Title Deeds, Nor-sor 3, Sor-por-kor) for Land Uses, Nan Province, Thailand

Land Use	Upland Villages			Lowland Village Type 1	Lowland Villages Type 2		
	Huai-muang	Numpak	Huai-thanu	Kuae	Donmuun	Kon	Nahai
Lowland paddy field (eastern side of settlement area)	—	—	—	Mostly Nor-sor 3 Title deeds	Some Nor-sor 3	Some Nor-sor 3	Some Nor-sor 3
Upland paddy field	Mostly none	Some Sor-por-kor	Some Sor-por-kor	Some Sor-por-kor	None	Sor-por-kor	Some Sor-por-kor
Upland perennial cropping	Mostly none	Mostly none	Some Sor-por-kor	Mostly Sor-por-kor	Mostly Sor-por-kor	Mostly Sor-por-kor	Mostly Sor-por-kor
Upland annual cropping (many under shifting cultivation)	None	None	Mostly none	Some Sor-por-kor	None	Some Sor-por-kor	Some Sor-por-kor

Source: Focus group meetings, 2001.

Notes: Land titles for private land (under the Land Code 1954) have been issued with land documents *Nor-sor 4* (equal to title deeds) and other lower levels of rights (i.e., *Nor-sor 3, Nor-sor 3 Kor, Nor-sor 2*). *Sor-por-kor*, land rights documents for agricultural uses only, is generally a land document issued by the Agricultural Land Reform Office.

process has been criticized by many lowland people for its double standards. There are many households that do not have legal land documents (e.g., *Nor-sor 3*), although most lands have been cultivated for many generations. In some part of the upland areas extending approximately two kilometers to the west of the main road, most lands have formal land documents—*Sor-por-kor*. Under land reform law, areas under *Sor-por-kor* are not allowed to be sold, but are allowed for agricultural use only, although in reality those lands have been bought and sold by village members. Beyond the two kilometer zone, no legal land title documents have been issued to landholders. These land areas include some upland areas of the lowland villages, including Nahai, and most areas of the upland villages, including Huai-muang.

Regardless of whether individuals possess the legal land documents, people have recognized their individual rights (from use to sale) in ownership of both lowland and upland paddy rice fields. As indicated in Table 9.4, the *de jure* rights to lands that are consistently cultivated in the lowlands and uplands of Sopsai are well recognized in the locality regardless of the possession of legal land rights documents (e.g., *Sor-por-kor* or *Nor-sor 3*). However, land for which legal documents have been granted by the state can be used as collateral for loans and other financial transactions. But it is clear that in the Sopsai watershed, long-term investment and land improvement are not determined by the issuance of *Sor-por-kor* or other legal land documents.

However, the legal rights have begun to reduce the authority of village committee in controlling negative impacts to the village to only act as a body to deal with the conflicts between legal land-rights holders and the impacted parties. In addition, the past practice of shifting cultivation is based on usufruct rights-based system while the existing system becomes more claiming of individual ownership. Therefore, the pattern and evolution of community forestry and ultimately the land use and management are apparently influenced by changes in legal rights and recognition and integration of local customary rights. In the following section we present chronology of implementation strategies of community-based forestry system and how these new management regimes affected the forest health with measured biological condition of the forest in the two communities in northern Thailand.

GOALS AND OPERATIONAL STRATEGIES IN COMMUNITY-BASED FOREST MANAGEMENT

Nahai village has been settled for more than 200 years in its present area. In the past, villagers were dependent not only on paddy fields for lowland rice cultivation, but they also practiced shifting cultivation nearby their settlement area. The production of the area was low, unreliable and often insufficient. Until the 1960s, most Nahai villagers as well as people from other nearby villages were encroaching further into the higher altitude areas (upland and highland) on the west for shifting cultivation. In the 1970s, some households started to permanently resettle in that area and it was named Huai-muang village. Therefore, both Nahai and Huai-muang communities have similar backgrounds as lowlanders traditionally depending on shifting cultivation in higher altitudes to supplement their lowland paddy cultivation. At present, Nahai and Huai-muang generally have similar income and population (Table 9.5). Nahai, however, is more accessible to public resource facilities and information than Huai-muang village.

TABLE 9.5
Number of Households and Population in Nahai and Huai-muang Villages, Nan Province, Thailand

Village	Household Income (baht)*	No. of Households	Population (Persons)		
			Male	Female	Total
Nahai	10,143	77	137	154	291
Huai-muang	11,093	67	136	129	265

Note: * During the study period the exchange rate was approximately US$ 1 = THB 37.

The Conservation Forest of Huai-muang Village

After permanent settlement in the present area, Huai-muang villagers started to protect the forest in order to prevent the risk of fire encroachment. After the termination of the Station of the People's

Volunteer for National Security (Ministry of Defense) group in 1974, the ex-village headman of Huai-muang initiated the process to keep the area as commons. This area is the nearest head-watershed of the Huai-muang village, which supplied water for daily use by the villagers. The area has been protected and the forest has been restored. At present, this is known as community forest for conservation purposes of Huai-muang. By the time the conservation community forest was established, Huai-muang and many villages in the upland and highland forest areas in the northern region were being pressured by the state as illegal settlers or forest encroachers. Therefore, setting up a community forest was an adaptation mechanism to gain legitimacy in the face of negative attitudes of external agencies. Besides protection of head-watershed degradation, in the conservation forest of Huai-muang, the direct uses of forest resources are very limited. Regular maintenance and guarding of firebreak lines has been carried out. Although the institution of the conservation forest in Huai-muang was only partly due to the concern for watershed function, the villagers have increased their willingness to protect well-regenerating forest as a result of the perceived changes for the better in the water supply after a decade of protection.

It should be noted that there are many head-watershed forests that provide a water supply, and the Huai-muang villagers have shown their interest in conserving these areas. However, the state and local state agencies are not as accepting because many of these areas are targeted for their reforestation programs.

The Utilization Forest of Huai-muang Village

In 1977, the SWMU, under the Watershed Conservation Section of the Royal Forest Department (RFD), was established in Huai-muang village. The SWMU asked people to stop shifting cultivation and work with the unit as temporary labor workers. Then, in the following year after a negotiation with a few ex-leaders of Huai-muang, the SWMU opened the areas around the settlement to plant tree seedlings under a watershed restoration scheme. In the mid 1980s, the SWMU office moved from the village to a higher altitude (far from Huai-muang). The tree-planted areas around the settlement started to regenerate naturally through the protection of the Huai-muang villagers. Huai-muang villagers have claimed these replanting areas as their *de facto* community forest for the purpose of a fire invasion buffer. After the forest was restored, the villagers used them for forest resources, household consumption and income generation. This community-utilization forest is an important source of firewood, timber and various NTFPs for all villagers of Huai-muang, especially disadvantaged groups who are not able to access other sources of income. Therefore, the utilization forest of Huai-muang has evolved through the needs of people to maintain their livelihood in the upland environment.

In order to achieve the long-term goal of having abundant volumes and growth of preferred species in this utilization forest, many collective rules were developed to control timber selling and to maintain forest resources by making firebreak lines. The CBFM of Huai-muang effectively excludes access to their forest area from outsiders. The establishment of community-managed forests, especially in the utilization zones, is not appreciated by the SWMU, which is regarded as the most related local state agency in the area. This is because the chief believes that the forest cannot be maintained without compromising local needs.

The Conservation Forest of Nahai Village

Nahai dwellers did not set up their community forests until 1997 when the Upper Nan Watershed Management Project (UNWMP) was supported. The forest area of Nahai has regenerated for the last 15–20 years due to individual villagers' willingness to stop shifting cultivation and to leave the area under inactive old-fallow.

The UNWMP which was implemented by the SWMU has proposed to promote people's 'participation' in watershed restoration through forest protection. The UNWMP staff is aware that the regenerating forest area has been traditionally claimed by many individuals of the Nahai village. Many forums were organized for negotiations among the villagers of Nahai and the staff of the UNWMP. The staff claimed that the state through SWMU had legal rights to control and manage the forest land and much of the area could possibly be declared a national park. If the declaration would become official, people would lose their rights to control or even access minor products from the forest. After a long discussion, people decided to 'participate' in forest conservation by adopting rules of forest resource use and maintenance. By establishing conservation community forests, people expected to maintain the community rights over the land and forest resources at a negotiable level and hoped it would be better than to lose control of the resources under the National Park Act. The National Park Act is said to be the strictest forest law established to prohibit local community access. Therefore, the initial stage of conservation community forest was driven by the need to maintain collective rights over the land and resources and to respond to the state purpose of forest protection and community. After only four years of establishing the conservation forest of Nahai, people increasingly recognized the need to maintain good forests for the purpose of watershed protection. This new recognition was influenced by the improvement of water reservoirs in the conservation forest, which in turn ensures the Nahai people better access to the water supply from the watershed. Nahai's village committee has managed the conservation forest by establishing rules with effective enforcement and monitoring. In addition, individual households in Nahai have been more recognized in the collective decision making and management than the Huai-muang villagers.

The Utilization Forest of Nahai Village

During the process of establishing the conservation forest in Nahai, the villagers also negotiated to set up the utilization zone. The Nahai people were aware that they needed to access forest resources in the short-term and to receive important long-term benefits such as protection of the head watershed. Within the utilization zone of Nahai, regenerating forest is interspersed with agricultural land uses such as rotational and sedentary cropping systems. The utilization forest, much like the conservation forest, has been kept for 15–20 years under inactive fallow at the size of approximately 1–2 hectares. The establishment of the utilization zone ensured the Nahai people their right to access land and resources under the recognition of local state agencies.

In the utilization forest of Nahai, they have established long-term management goals to ensure the supply of firewood and timber for individual households. This clear goal influences their operational strategies such as selective cutting of firewood and maintaining some good stands of the preferred species for timber. Making a fire-break prior to shifting cultivation is just one rule that has been developed and adopted by village committee.

The summary of collective behaviors, management purposes and operational strategies of each forest is illustrated in Table 9.6.

COMPARISON OF FOREST HEALTH MEASUREMENTS

Diameter at 1.30 m (dbh) and Height–Class Distribution

A (diameter) dbh-class distribution indicates maturity and succession of a forest unit. Figures 9.1 and 9.2 illustrate the dbh-class distribution of Nahai and Huai-muang villages, which can roughly be divided into three zones. Trees with a dbh over 30 cm have probably been retained during shifting cultivation. There is a minor difference in the dbh-class distribution of 10–30 cm within these two villages. Forests in Huai-muang where it has taken a longer time to establish *de facto* community forests, have a greater number of trees at each dbh-class distribution of 10–30 cm than those in Nahai.

However, a vast difference between forest areas has occurred in the number of individual trees with a dbh less than 10 cm (saplings), which implies a significant change during the last few years. In both Nahai and Huai-muang, more stems were found in the utilization zones than in the conservation zones. The highest density of saplings is found in the utilization zone of Nahai. This may reflect the effective management of utilization in Nahai even though the collective decision to set up community forests was made only 3–4 years ago.

Forest succession usually results in an increase in average tree height. As shown in Figures 9.3 and 9.4, more than half of trees

TABLE 9.6

Collective Behaviors, Management Purposes and Initiation of Community-based Forest Management in Nahai and Huai-muang Villages, Nan Province, Thailand

Characteristics	Nahai Village		Huai-muang Village	
	Conservation Purpose	*Utilization Purpose*	*Conservation Purpose*	*Utilization Purpose*
Indirect/direct uses (timber firewood)	*Direct uses* Collect dead standing or fallen broken wood for household use. Timber harvesting for public uses only. Collect NTFPs. *Indirect uses* Head-watershed protection	*Direct uses* Timber or firewood harvesting for household use in individual old-fallow only. Collect NTFPs. Open for agriculture under permission of the village committee	Head-watershed protection	*Direct uses* Timber harvesting for household use under permission of the village committee. Timber harvesting for public uses. Firewood collection for household use only. Collect NTFPs. *Indirect uses* Buffering fire invasion to the settlement
Maintenance	Forest guarding against non-authorized users and possible harm to the forests. Making firebreak lines	Maintenance by individual households that claim old-fallow areas, i.e., selective harvesting, making firebreak lines	Forest guarding against non-authorized users and possible harm to the forests. Making firebreak lines	Forest guarding against non-authorized users and possible harm to the forests. Making firebreak lines (some part)

(Table 9.6 continued)

(Table 9.6 continued)

	Nahai Village		Huai-muang Village	
Characteristics	*Conservation Purpose*	*Utilization Purpose*	*Conservation Purpose*	*Utilization Purpose*
CBFM initiatives and driven factors	Project intervention through discussion of the significance as head watershed of the stream going to their lowland farms Public awareness of the CBFM of the forest at the local, provincial and national levels	Community uses the negotiation forum for establishing and classifying conservation and utilization zones Less interest in shifting cultivation in the upland areas	Community initiative by an ex-village headman with agreement of the members The area which was the stream supplying water for household consumption was abandoned for the UVSDC, so no individual claimed External pressure on the upland settlement	Tree planting plots under the Sopsai Watershed Management Unit (but very little planted trees found) Community adaptation for their intermediate benefits by developing collective behaviors and rules for use and maintenance of forest resources
Management purposes of the community	Maintain good forest for head-watershed protection and sources of forest resources for public uses	Multipurpose of direct uses to maintain livelihood security	Maintain good forest for head-watershed protection	Multipurpose of direct and indirect uses to livelihood improvement

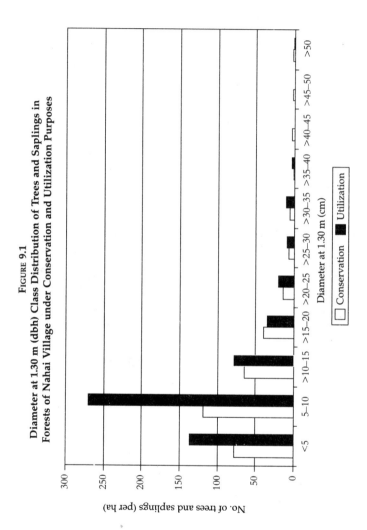

FIGURE 9.1

Diameter at 1.30 m (dbh) Class Distribution of Trees and Saplings in
Forests of Nahai Village under Conservation and Utilization Purposes

FIGURE 9.2
Diameter at 1.30 m (dbh) Class Distribution of Trees and Saplings in
Forests of Huai-Muang Village under Conservation and Utilization Purposes

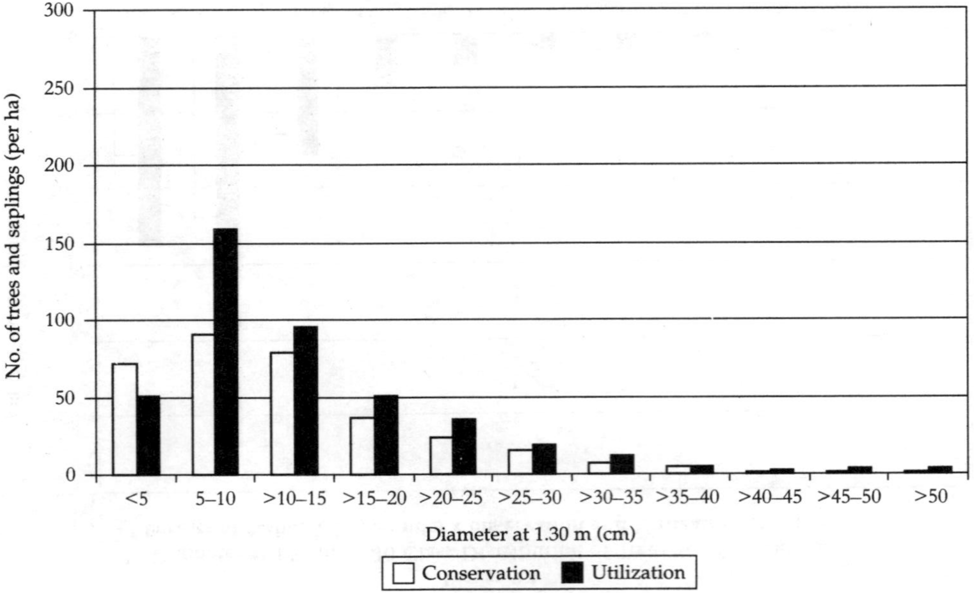

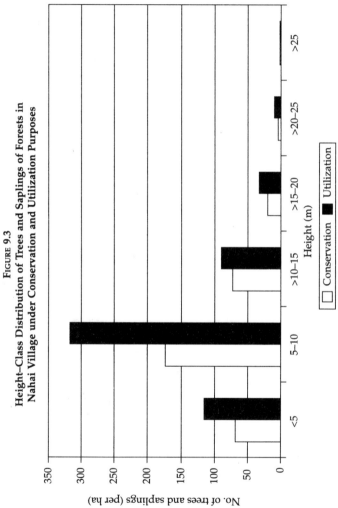

FIGURE 9.3
Height–Class Distribution of Trees and Saplings of Forests in
Nahai Village under Conservation and Utilization Purposes

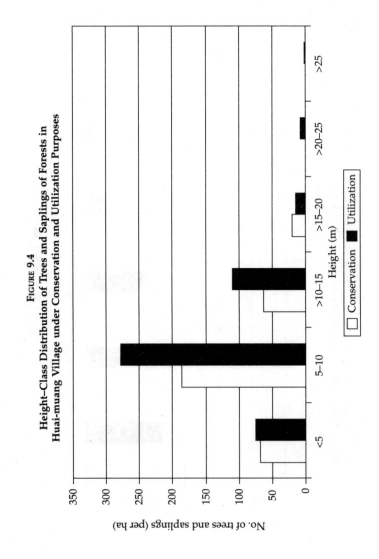

FIGURE 9.4

Height-Class Distribution of Trees and Saplings of Forests in Huai-muang Village under Conservation and Utilization Purposes

and saplings are between 5 and 10 m tall. Thus, their height-distribution is similar under different management practices. In this case, there is not much difference in forest health between the forest area under conservation and the forest area under utilization when considering height–class distribution only.

Density, Basal Area and Regeneration

Basal area is correlated with forest biomass and wood volume, which respond to both the protection objectives and the local need for wood products. As seen in Table 9.7, the total basal area in the utilization zone of Huai-muang is approximately two times higher than in the conservation zone of the same village. For Nahai, the total basal area of the conservation (9.27 m²/hectare) and the utilization forest (9.08 m²/hectare) areas are similar. See Appendix 9.1 for a list of preferred species for timber and fire-wood. It is important to note that the basal area or preferred species is much higher in utilization forests than in the conservation forests of both villages (Table 9.7). Therefore, CBFM for utilization, responding to local need of direct resource uses, can return forest biomass as good as the forest with high protection. Under the utilization practice, people in Nahai have carried out some silvi-cultural treatments such as selective cutting and prioritizing tree species so the more valued tree for timber would be conserved and the optimum size of firewood would be selected for the long-term benefits.

TABLE 9.7

Basal Area of Tree and Bamboo Species in Forests of Nahai and
Huai-muang Villages under Conservation and Utilization Purposes

Village	Purpose of Management	Total Basal Area of Tree and Bamboo (m²/ha)	Basal Area of Preferred Species of the Villagers (m²/ha)	
			Timber	Firewood
Nahai	Conservation	9.27	2.22	2.31
	Utilization	9.08	3.07	2.76
Huai-muang	Conservation	7.52	1.55	2.91
	Utilization	14.55	5.54	4.53

Similar trends in the density of tree species (including tree, sapling and seedling) were recorded in Table 9.8, with higher trends in Huai-muang than in Nahai. Within a village, the utilization zone had a higher tree density than in the conservation zone. The highest tree density was found in the utilization forest of Huai-muang, but the highest sapling and seedling densities were found in the utilization forest of Nahai.

FOREST HEALTH AND COMMUNITY-BASED FOREST MANAGEMENT: THE IMPLICATIONS

Establishment of CBFM and Forest Health

As seen from the public hearing events on the Community Forest Act (CFA) of Thailand, the right to establish community forest has been an issue for discussion. Most people and state agencies have recognized the rights of the old settling communities, particularly the ones who have traditionally conserved the forest and have tried to establish a community forest legally (Community Forest Section, 1994). The study by Chamarik and Santasombat (1993) has shown that community forests have traditionally existed in Thailand for many purposes such as responding to the needs of local communities for utilization, grazing areas, environmental protection and spiritual values. However, it becomes a controversial issue when the people-oriented group proposes to support communities that are able to show their capability to manage the forest in their nearby communities. The wilderness-oriented group and many urban societies have not agreed upon the rights to establish a community forest of new-settling communities in the upland and highland areas (Punthasain, 1999, 2002; Wittayapak, 2002). The group, as well as the state and the urban people believe that most people in the upland and highland communities are forest encroachers and illegal settlers. Therefore, this group felt it unfair to give rights to the new-settling communities to establish community forests (Ganjanapan, 1998). Whether it is a new or old settlement under traditional or recent management, the

TABLE 9.8

Number of Total Tree Species and Distribution in the Forests of Nahai and
Huai-muang Villages under Conservation (C) and Utilization (U) Management Purposes

Village	Management Purpose	No. of Tree Species (in all size)	Tree Size (≥10 cm dbh)	No. of Tree Species in Different Sizes					
				Sapling Size (2.5–9.9 cm dbh)		Seedling (<2.5 cm dbh)			
				Total	Found in Tree Size	Total	Found in Tree/Sapling Size		
Nahai	C	103	48 (47%[a])	49 (48%, 100%)	19 (18%, 39%)	54 (52%, 100%)	25 (24%, 58%)		
Nahai	U	71	35 (49%)	51 (72%, 100%)	31 (44%, 61%)	43 (61%, 100%)	27 (38%, 50%)		
Huai-muang	C	50	28 (56%)	26 (52%, 100%)	10 (20%, 38%)	24 (48%, 100%)	6 (12%, 25%)		
Huai-muang	U	158	90 (57%)	96 (61%, 100%)	61 (39%, 64%)	69 (44%, 100%)	31 (20%, 45%)		

Notes: [a] Percentage of species number found in particular sizes compared to total species.

communities that intend to be legally recognized (the community forests) need to go through procedures and mechanisms of checks-and-balances to ensure their capability to manage forest resources, as many academics have explained (Ganjanapan, 2000; Makarabhirom, 1999; Punthasain, 1999, 2002). Using Nepal as an example of one of the most progressive countries in community forest development, it has been shown that through process-oriented support and facilitation, forests can be managed well by local people themselves (Gilmour, 1995; Blockhus *et al.*, 1997).

It is interesting to note that a recent-settling community like Huai-muang has a longer established community forest in comparison to an old-settling community like Nahai. The longer established community forests of Huai-muang have the higher dbh-class distribution and total tree density in comparison to the recently established forests of Nahai. In addition, the external support and facilitation led to the establishment of the community forest in Nahai. The institutional features include: collective behaviors of individuals to reduce shifting cultivation, maintaining natural regeneration of their inactive fallow areas and the exclusion of non-authorized users to access land and wood products.

COMMUNITY-BASED FOREST MANAGEMENT FOR WHOSE BENEFIT? DIRECT RESOURCE UTILIZATION AND CONSERVATION IN HEAD-WATERSHED AREAS

Nahai and Huai-muang villagers perceive that the forests under community-based management have better health because of the observed rapid natural regeneration. In the period prior to community-based management, the villagers experienced water shortages.

In the views of the state and urban people, the forest under conservation or less intensity of uses should reflect standard health parameters of forest management. The utilization forests show similar height-class distribution and total basal area to the conservation forests. Therefore, community management for utilization can be a strategy of forest and biodiversity conservation.

It was quite difficult to directly compare forest health under different management practices in the Huai-muang village since the forests have different land-use histories. The comparisons of forest health were made between forest areas under different collective behaviors and management practices in the Nahai villages only due to their similarity in biophysical and land-use background. After the classification for conservation and utilization, the collective behaviors in use and maintenance were different in both forests responding to their evolved intermediate and long-term expectations of benefits.

In response to the people's purposes in the forest health parameter, the utilization forest of Nahai shows significantly higher total density (especially sapling and seedling), basal area and density of preferred species than the conservation forests. This is confirmed by the more productive management of the utilization forest of Nahai than the conservation forest. This implies that utilization of the forest areas at a certain level of intensity can benefit the forest conditions including biodiversity. Similar results have been reported in the studies carried out by Habeak (1968) and Peet (1978). The forest under utilization, therefore, is not only able to support conservation, but also increase productivity in the forest. Since the plant community is dynamic and an intermediate disturbance can lead to an increase in biodiversity, Sukwong (2002) has suggested that an intermediate disturbance can be managed through appropriate size, intensity and frequent use of resources.

Through the classification of management purposes and implementing the operational strategies responding to the purposes, communities themselves can gain benefits from their collective action. At the same time, the state objective can also be achieved. However, no one can guarantee future success. People need to be trusted to manage their forest resources. Ekachai (1997), a senior journalist who follows the debate over CFA and discussion on community-based forest management, challenged her readers by suggesting encouragement of local people participation in CFA rather than blaming them.

Without neglecting roles and concerns of various groups in Thai society, it has been proposed by many academics to have an external monitoring system, where outsiders can participate together with local communities to monitor or develop other check-and-balance mechanisms to ensure proper management by communities (Makarabhirom, 1999; Punthasain, 2002; Wittayapak, 2002).

Conclusions

In several of Asian countries including Thailand, forest conservation by restricting human activities in natural forests have caused conflicts between local communities and the state and in turn has led to further degradation. Natural resources such as water and forests are not only the socio-economic buffer of the poor people, but they are also important basics for the livelihood development of rural communities. Therefore, it is necessary to recognize the balance of ecological and sociocultural bases and roles of communities in forest resource management in response to their need for short-term and long-term benefits. Operational strategies of local communities are not static, but have evolved through pressure and internal needs under changing circumstances, as is evident from the findings in this chapter. The establishment of state-driven conservation forest for claiming rights on land and resources of a community has evolved toward the immediate and long-term benefits. In addition, if there is process-oriented support and formal recognition of local institutional arrangement, the recently established community forest also shows effective management as is evident by the high sapling and seedling density of Nahai's forests. Although most communities have classified their forests into conservation, utilization or for some other purpose (i.e., spirit forests), the people are aware of multiple functions and have gained multiple benefits from that. Under collective management for utilization, people have more access to resources and use silvicultural operations for improving productivity. The density and basal area of the locally-preferred species are higher than in the conservation forest without losing biodiversity and retarding natural restoration. CBFM is not only implemented for the benefits of the communities themselves, but may also be used to complement to state and public purposes of conservation. Therefore, in the forest areas under collective management or accessing by the communities nearby for maintaining their livelihood, the process-oriented support and formal recognition by the state agencies would be an effective strategy. Therefore, co-management mechanisms should be developed to ensure that they are managed by including many stakeholders' concerns as well as securing community rights to access the resources for improving livelihoods.

APPENDIX 9.1

Locally-preferred Species for Firewood and Timber in Nahai and Huai-Muang Villages, Nan Province, Thailand

Local Name (in Thai)	Scientific Name	Firewood	Timber
		Local Preferred Species	
'Tew'	*Cratoxylum sumatranum*	✓	
'Now-nai'	*Ilex umbellulata*	✓	
'Kab'		✓	
'Gai'	*Nephelium* sp.	✓	
'Ma-kok'	*Spondias pinnata*	✓	
'Tew-luang'	*Cratoxylum formosum*	✓	
'Odd-add'		✓	
'Ja-nga'		✓	✓
'Pradu'	*Pterocarpus macrocarpus*	✓	✓
'Ma-muan'	*Irvingia malayana*	✓	✓
'Teen-nok'	*Vitex limonifolia*	✓	✓
'Ngew'	*Bombax anceps*		✓
'Ton'	*Albizia procera*		✓
'Saw'	*Gmelina arborea*		✓
'Ma-geam'	*Albizia lebbekioides*		✓
'Ma-ha'	*Syzygium albiflorum*		✓
'Jam-pee-pa'	*Michelia baillonii*		✓
'Boo'	*Lagerstroemia tomentosa*		✓

ACKNOWLEDGMENTS

The authors would like to express their appreciation to the Integrated Watershed Development and Management Program at the Asian Institute of Technology assisted by DANIDA for supporting the study. Funding was also provided to the authors by the International Forestry Resources and Institutions (IFRI) program, Indiana University. We acknowledge with appreciation the editing assistance provided by Nicole Todd of Indiana University.

NOTE

1. One rai = 0.16 hectare (6.25 rai = 1 hectare).

REFERENCES

Apichatvullop, Y. (1993). 'Local Participation in Social Forest'. *Regional Development Dialogue, 14,* 34–42.

Blockhus, J., Ingles, A., Gilmour, D. and Mittelman, A. (1997). 'Supporting Income Generation from Community Forests: Some Policy and Practical Considerations'. In M. Victor (ed.), *Income Generation through Community Forests* (pp. 15–30). Proceedings of an International Seminar held in Bangkok, Thailand, October 18–20, 1996. RECOFTC Report 13. Bangkok: RECOFTC.

Chamarik, S. and Santasombat, Y. (eds). (1993). *Community Forestry in Thailand: Directions for Development* (vol. 1). Bangkok: Local Development Institute (in Thai).

Community Forest Section. (1994). *Guideline for Community Forest Development Project.* Royal Forest Department (RFD), Ministry of Agriculture and Cooperatives.

Duanglamyai, P. (2001). 'Centralized Power and Lack of Participation: Political Problems in Forest and Land Management'. In A. Rakyutitum (ed.), *Forest Land—Watershed Resource Management through People's Participation* (pp. 2–30). Proceeding of the Seminar on Administrative and Management of Natural Resources in Watershed Areas through People's Participation. Thailand: Chinag Mai (in Thai).

Ekachai, S. (1997). 'Forests Clearly Deserve Better' *Bangkok Post,* May 28.

Ganjanapan, A. (1992). 'Community Forestry in Northern Thailand: Learning from Local Practices'. In H. Wood and W.H.H. Mellink (eds), *Sustainable and Effective Management Systems for Community Forestry* (pp. 83–88). Proceedings of a Workshop held in Bangkok, January 15–17. Bangkok: The Regional Community Forestry Training Center (RECOFTC).

———. (1994). 'The Northern Thai Land Tenure System: Local Customs versus National Laws'. *Law and Society Review, 28*(3), 609–622.

Ganjanapan, A. (1998). 'The Politics of Conservation and the Complexity of Local Control of Forests in the Northern Thai Highlands'. *Mountain Research and Development, 18,* 71–82.

———. (2000). 'Local Control of Land and Forest: Cultural Dimensions of Resource Management in Northern Thailand'. Regional Center for Social Science and Sustainable Development (RCSD), Faculty of Social Science. Bangkok: Chiang Mai University.

Ganjanapan, A. and Kaosa-ard, M. (1995). *Evolution of Land Pioneering for Agriculture: A Case Study of the Upper Northern Region,* Research Monograph No. 13. Bangkok: Thailand Development Research Institute (TDRI) (in Thai).

Gilmour, D.A. (1995). 'Conservation and Development: Seeking the Linkages'. In H. Wood, M. McDaniel, and K. Warner (eds), *Community Development and Conservation of Forest Biodiversity through Community Forestry.* Proceedings of an International Seminar held in Bangkok, October 26–28, 1994. RECOFTC Report 12. Bangkok: RECOFTC.

Gilmour, D.A. and Fisher, R.J. (1998). 'Evolution in Community Forestry: Contesting Forest Resources'. In M. Victor, C. Lang, and J. Bornemeier (eds), *Community Forestry at a Crossroad: Reflections and Future Directions in the Development of Community Forestry.* Proceedings of an International Seminar, held in Bangkok, July 17–19. RECOFTC Report 6, Bangkok: RECOFTC.

Habeak, J.R. (1968). 'Forest Succession in the Glacier Park Cedar-Hemlock Forests'. *Ecology, 49,* 872–880.

Makarabhirom, P. (1999). 'How to Consider the Appropriate of the Community Forest Act'. *Forest and Community Newsletter, 6,* 38–39 (in Thai).

Narintarangkul Na Ayuthaya, P. (1996). 'Community forestry and Watershed Networks in Northern Thailand'. In P. Hirsch (ed.), *Seeing Forests for Trees: Environment and Environmentalism in Thailand* (pp. 116–146). Chiang Mai: Silkworm Books.

Ostrom, E. (1999). *International Forestry Resources and Institutions (IFRI) Research Program: Field Manual.* Indiana: Indiana University.

Peet, R.K. (1978). 'Forest Vegetation of the Colorado Front Range: Patterns of Species Diversity'. *Vegetatio, 37,* 65–78.

Pragtong, K. (1993). 'Social Forestry in Thailand: Policy Evolution and Institutional Arrangements'. *Regional Development Dialogue, 14,* 59–69.

Punthasain, A. (1999). *How to Restore Forest and Green Areas.* Bangkok: Thammasart University Publishing (in Thai).

———. (2002). 'The Sustainable Directions of Thai Society and Community Forests: Economics Perspectives'. In S. Wankaew (ed.), *The Sustainable Directions of Thai Society and Community Forests: Interdisciplinary Perspectives.* Center for Social Development Studies (CSDS), Faculty of Political Sciences. Thailand: Chulalongkorn University (in Thai).

Ramitanondh, S. (1989). 'Forests and Deforestation in Thailand: A Pan-disciplinary Approach. Culture and Environment in Thailand'. In a Symposium of the Siam Society. Bangkok: The Siam Society under Royal Patronage.

Sukwong, S. (2002). 'Theories of Biodiversity and Forest Resource Management'. *Forest and Community Newsletter, 9,* 18–29 (in Thai).

Tan-Kim-Yong, U. (1993). 'Participation Land-Use Planning as a Sociological Methodology for Natural Resource Management'. *Regional Development Dialogue, 14,* 70–83.

Wittayapak, C. (2002). 'Community as a Political Space for Struggles over Access to Natural Resources and Cultural Meaning'. In P. Dearden (ed.), *Environmental Protection and Rural Development in Thailand: Challenges and Opportunities.* Thailand: White Lotus Press.

Wittayapak, C. and Dearden, P. (1999). 'Decision-making Arrangements in Community-Based Watershed Management in Northern Thailand'. *Society and Natural Resources, 12,* 673–691.

10 Incentives of the Forest Land Allocation Process: Implications for Forest Management in Nam Dong District, Central Vietnam

NGO TRI DUNG and EDWARD L. WEBB

Introduction

Vietnam has conducted radical renovation in the forestry sector since 1990 by involving local people in forest management. Households and village communities have been increasingly recognized as important stakeholders in national forestry policies. Most of these policies have been towards allocating land and forests to households for forestry-related purposes. Allocation is the process by which a household or group of households receive 50-year-use and management rights over a specified area of barren land for reforestation (plantation), or natural forest for management and protection. The ownership rights are contained in an allocation document called the Red Book.

In the central Vietnamese province of Thua Thien Hue, forests have been under state control since the reunification of the country in 1975. State control and management of forests was executed through State Forest Enterprises (SFE), which logged forests and were charged with forest 'protection' from degradation, particularly unauthorized logging. Forest protection duties have also been shared with the Forest Protection Department (FPD).

Starting with Program 327 (1992), however, local households were involved with SFEs in joint-plantation programs that provided a benefit-sharing mechanism. Later, local people were allocated forestry land for long-term forestry purposes (forestry land include two sub-categories, land with forest and barren land for forestry purposes according to the government) under

Decree 02/CP (1994) which was replaced by Decree 163 (1999) afterwards. Also included in these decrees was the option to allocate existing natural forests to households; however, this did not occur until after 2001. Supporting these two decrees was Decision 178 (2001) which articulated the rights and duties of households and individuals participating in the forest allocation programs. Finally, the Land Law (2003) and the Forest Protection and Development Law (2004) added provisions for communities to be allocated forest land and natural forest. These forestry policies ostensibly were a result of the *doi moi* policy in the 1980s when the country embarked on economic renovation, where individuals and private corporations were given ever increasing opportunities for capital gains. This extended to forests, and through the forestry policies the government was trying to provide local people privileges and opportunities that were absent in the state forest management system before the 1990s.

In addition, from the government point of view forest destruction occurred mainly because of the 'open access' status of forests resulting from nationalization and low levels of protection by the SFEs. The government designed the forest allocation program to improve forest protection by local people, who would protect it as their own asset given appropriate long-term incentives. In this sense, the government intends to use 'ownership' as one of the incentives to local people for a long-term management strategy. As defined in Decrees 02/CP, 163 and Decision 178, the desired outcomes from forest allocation program include (*a*) better protection for natural forest, (*b*) procurement of land for agricultural production to reduce pressure on forest resources and (*c*) forest improvement in both quality and quantity, through long-term investment strategy resulting from secure land tenure.

Forests of Thua Thien Hue province are allocated by the district level government offices. There may be several stakeholders involved in the process of allocation, but there are only three main stakeholders upon which allocation is fully dependent. The SFE is the state-managed entity charged with forest exploitation, management and protection since 1975 and is now responsible for relinquishing land for allocation. The Forest Protection Unit (FPU) is the district arm of the FPD, which facilitates that forest allocation. Finally the villagers are the recipients of the allocated forest and receive the Red Book over the allocated forest tracts (Table 10.1).

TABLE 10.1
Key Actors and Required Duties in the Forest Allocation
Program of Nam Dong District, Central Vietnam

Stakeholder (Actor)	Required Duty
State Forest Enterprises	Allocate forest to local people
Forest Protection Department	Facilitate allocation procedures related to forest inventory and local meetings
Villagers	Group formation, forest inventory and boundary setting

The policy statements above define three main desired outcomes of forest allocation: improved forest protection, acquisition of agricultural land and forest improvement through long-term investment. Given the fact that allocation only began in the 1990s, it may be too soon to evaluate whether those outcomes have been achieved. Yet it is clear that in order to achieve those objectives, full *participation and compliance* of all actors in the allocation process must occur. By investigating whether participation and compliance are occurring, we can evaluate whether the allocation program is going in the right direction. Achieving the desired outcomes envisioned by national policy requires that all stakeholders engaged in the allocation process participate and comply fully with the policies.

However, measuring participation and compliance introduce their own complications that preclude immediate research, because this would require statistics on the number of households that did or did not participate in the program, as well as whether the rules were being followed (e.g., records of complaints). Since the allocation program is still underway, those statistics are not available or are not yet statistically robust. What we can do, however, is to analyze the *incentives* to the three actors in the allocation process, thereby determining if they rationally should participate and comply with the program, thereby leading to the desired policy outcomes. In this chapter, an incentive is 'both external stimulus and internal motivation' (Gibson *et al.*, 2005). An incentive analysis can be mixed with field data to triangulate the theoretical information, thereby completing the picture of whether the desired policy outcomes may be achievable. This is similar to the work done by Gibson *et al.* (ibid.) in their study of the incentives (or disincentives) leading to successful or failed outcomes of international development aid. Actors making decisions work on incentives, whether they are related to the delivery or implementation of aid funds or the allocation and management of forests.

The objective of this chapter is to evaluate the incentive structure presented to the three main actors involved in the forest allocation process in one district of Thua Thien Hue Province, central Vietnam. We then compare the incentive structure with some of the preliminary results we have obtained from field studies where we investigated whether the desired outcomes of the forest allocation policy were being achieved. We finally identify how the observed disincentives can be reduced, leading to a greater opportunity for participation and compliance of all actors in the forest allocation process.

STUDY AREA

We take Nam Dong district in southwestern Thua Thien Hue province as a case study. Nam Dong was selected because it is characterized by diverse forms of allocation in terms of stakeholders (government organizations, NGOs, local people), recipients of allocation (household, group of households) and nature of resources (barren land, plantation and natural forest). Of the total district area of 650.5 sq km, the majority of the area is forest land (degraded and natural forest, 64.5 percent) while agricultural land accounts for 5.3 percent.

The forest allocation program started in early 1990s. Since then, seven out of the 11 communes comprising Nam Dong have embarked on forest allocation to households and household groups. The forest allocation occurrs in different forms such as barren and degraded land allocation, plantation allocation, and natural forest allocation.

METHODS

This research utilized two approaches. First, we used the IAD framework (Ostrom *et al.*, 1994) to analyze the incentive structures presented to the three main actors in the allocation process:

the SFE, the FPU and the village recipients. Second, we used the IFRI (International Forestry Resources and Institutions) methodology as a core data collection tool to interview households and collect information on the outcomes of forest allocation.

As described in Chapter 1, the IAD framework recognizes that actors are engaged in the process of decision making in an action arena, which is modified by the characteristics of resources, community (or in this case, the household) and the rules-in-use (i.e., policy). The IAD framework can be used to define and then analyze the forest allocation scenario in Nam Dong.

Implicit in the IAD framework is that each decision made by the actors is only one of the several possible decisions available. The decision is ultimately made based on the foreseeable outcomes assessed by the actors and the incentives associated with each possible decision. An incentive can be represented as the ratio of the potential benefits to the potential costs. Although this ratio may not be a quantifiable entity, the point is that both the potential benefits and the potential costs are integrated into an actor's assessment of potential outcomes. Therefore, incentives are a central concept in analyzing why actors make certain decisions.

We constructed the theoretical incentive structure based on the provisions given in the policy, along with our observations of the field situation. At first, we reviewed all the policies related to forest and forest land allocation to find out what benefits and what costs local people would have when participating in allocation programs. Findings from this review helped to focus on specific questions in key informant interviews and discussions with local people. Because the allocation program is still on-going, we could not quantify actual benefits and costs for each stakeholder that participated in the allocation program.

The second methodology we used was interviewing households and key informants. The core data collection protocol was IFRI. This was supplemented with a separate household questionnaire on traditional forest management systems. In addition, key informants from SFEs, participating FPU, and relevant district offices in forest allocation were interviewed for information on the process of allocation.

The main information collected for use in this chapter was about households' and group of households' perceptions on their costs and benefits when participating in allocation programs. From IFRI field survey forms (Form V, Form I and Form U) we collected information on roles of each party participating in the allocation process.

Results

In the first part of the results, we will use the IAD framework to describe the actors and the contextual parameters of the action arena, in which decisions are made about whether to participate in and comply with the forest allocation policy. As described earlier, there are three main actors in the allocation process, the SFE, the FPU and the local villagers (Table 10.1).

The Actors

State Forest Enterprises
Until the early 1990s, all forests outside of protected areas in Vietnam were under the purview of the SFE system. In each province, these SFEs belong to the Department of Agriculture and Rural Development (DARD). The main tasks of the SFEs are to carry out silvicultural activities and operate annual timber harvests. Due to changes in the national forestry strategy, the SFE system was transformed to be either the Watershed Management Board (WMB) or the Forestry Business Company (FBC) following Decision 187/ 1999 by the prime minister in 1999. Forest areas, which were under management of SFEs, were reclassified to be either protection forest or production forest. These forest categories are managed by WMB and FBC. Besides, some areas of these forest categories are allocated to local people for protection and management.

In order to decide which forest areas were to be allocated, thorough land use planning was conducted by the Forestry Sub-Department (under DARD). At first, the forestry sub-department carried out a survey on total forestry land (forest and forest land) and associated management schemes in the province. Two classification systems of natural forest and barren land were then created. Natural forests were classified into three categories: special use forest, protection forest and production forest. Barren land was grouped into two types: land for production purpose and land for protection purpose. The forestry sub-department then conducted an analysis on management capability of each SFE in terms of their staff, total area of forestry land under the SFE's management, and their achievements of forest management during last several years. The results of this analysis were used to design a list of all newly-reformed SFEs with areas of forestry land assigned under their management. State forest enterprises that occupied large areas of forestry land without effective management were required to return the surplus areas to the district for allocation. The Provincial People's Committee (PPC) issued a decision that specified forest areas under SFE's management. The earliest result shows that there were 34,753 hectares of natural forest and about 36,000 hectares of forest land available for allocation to local people (Ho Hy, 2005).

Since the emergence of the forest allocation policy, the SFEs have been given the responsibility of relinquishing forest land and forests under their purview for allocation to households and communities. Thus, this actor is responsible for making the decision to allocate its land to local people.

Forest Protection Unit

The Forest Protection Unit (FPU) in Nam Dong is the district section of provincial forest protection sub-department. The main tasks of the FPU are to enforce the Forest Protection and Development Law. The FPU also carries out other outreach activities such as environmental education and forestry-related training for local people. Recently, the government decided to improve the relationship between local people and FPUs by sending all FPU staff to the local communes to obtain a better understanding of the local situation and to provide prompt solutions when conflict occurred. Because the FPU tended to have a better relationship with local people than the SFEs, this government entity was selected to facilitate forest allocation from the SFEs to the local people.

The FPU coordinates allocation at Nam Dong district through two mechanisms: by providing technical services and by facilitating local participation. Through technical support, the FPU collaborates with the Forest Inventory and Planning Section (under DARD) to conduct forest surveys and forest demarcation. The results of these activities are maps of different forest categories divided into coupes and blocks with estimated timber volumes. This is a pre-requisite for allocation because the future harvest scheme will be based on the increment of timber volume. The FPU also carried out several training courses on simple silvicultural practices and protection activities for local people in order to help them manage forest after allocation.

The FPU facilitates allocation by assisting in local meetings to establish user groups and get agreements on forest boundaries among user groups and villages. In each meeting, FPU staff members explain the rights and duties of the recipient, as well as the detailed structure of timber harvest as per Decision 178. All of the FPU activities related to allocation programs were funded by the Netherlands Development Organization (SNV) through the Project 'Strengthening Forest Management Capacity in Thua Thien Hue province' (2000–2004).

The Villagers

Two ethnic groups live in Nam Dong. About 41 percent of local people in this district are ethnic minority Katu, who were resettled into Nam Dong district from the forest immediately following reunification in 1975. Forest-based activities such as swidden agriculture, wildlife hunting and timber extraction form an important component of Katu livelihoods. The second ethnic group is the ethnic majority Kinh (the majority throughout Vietnam), who were resettled from the coastal areas to this district as part of the sedentarization program or new economic zone development program beginning in 1976. All villages rely on farming for principal livelihood support. Both ethnic groups are allowed to participate in the allocation program depending on their needs of land for permanent agriculture after the resettlement programs.

The Context of the Action Arena

The action arena, within which the actors are situated, is modified by the three contextual attributes: the characteristics of the resource, the characteristics of the community and the rules-in-use. This section briefly describes the possible contextual situations in the Nam Dong forest allocation process.

We classify the resources to be allocated to the local level into two forms—degraded forest land or natural forest. Degraded forest land is barren land that was claimed by the state in 1975 because it was not under permanent agriculture and no person had legal claim to it. The allocation process of this resource was to individual households beginning in the early 1990s for tree planting. In contrast, natural forest has only been allocated in Nam Dong district since the year 2003 (Nam Dong District Report, 2004).

In the context of the forest allocation program, the IAD term 'community' can be recast as 'recipient'. The essence of community for the IAD framework is a group of individuals making decisions about resource governance. However, both households and groups of households have been allocated forests through this program, and therefore it is necessary to differentiate the two subtypes of recipients. Moreover, those recipients have been temporally segregated: the initial allocation in the 1990s was to the household, whereas since 2002 the allocation has included groups of households. Therefore, we must view the incentives to both types of recipients as well.

Finally, the *de jure* rules-in-use of forest allocation generally do not vary across Nam Dong. The allocation program, regardless of recipient type, follows the same forestry policies including Decree 163, Decision 178, Program 327 and Program 661. Essentially the commune office must approve the application of the household or the group of households, at which point the approval is passed to the District People's Committee to issue the Red Book (Land Use Certificate).

In addition, the rules-in-use are enforced by the local authority through allocation procedures. For household allocation, each household has to register at the commune office the size, type of forest land (barren, with/without shrubs or plantation) and purpose of land being allocated. After considering the land resources available for the specific land use type as well as the household's labor status (i.e., the ability to actually perform the desired activities), the commune office approves the allocation and submits the approval to the district office for issuing the Red Book.

For group allocation, there are several additional steps before getting the Red Book from the district office. At first, local people must create a group of 10–20 members. The group submits the member names and the expected size, type and location of forest they would like to receive for management. During this meeting, the head of user group is selected and becomes the contact person afterwards. The commune office, with support from the FPU, considers the land resources availability to approve for each group. The district PC has the right to issue the Red Book for the group in which all members' names appear equally. Before getting the Red Book, all recipients are taken to the field by the FPU in order to receive forest or forest land with clear demarcation. From the date mentioned in the Red Book, each individual household or group of households can enforce their management practices and other legal status as specified in the Land Law.

Thus, the theoretically possible contexts for forest allocation is a 2 × 2 matrix (resource × recipient) with one distinct set of rules possible for each recipient type (which does not, therefore, add a third dimension to the context matrix). However, in reality there are only three possible contexts, because as will be discussed later, bare forest land was allocated first and only to households prior to the enactment of the Land Law (2003) and the Forest Protection and Development Law (2004) (Table 10.2).

TABLE 10.2
Theoretically Possible Contexts for Action Arenas during the Forest Allocation Program in Nam Dong, Thua Thien Hue Province, Central Vietnam

		Resource	
		Bare Forest Land (Plantation)	Natural Forest
Recipient	Household	X	X
	Community		X

Note: The overarching rules in use structure is consistent across all resource and recipient types and is stated in existing policy documents.

The Action Arenas and the Incentive (or Disincentive) Structures

The action arena consists of the three actors in a physical space (Nam Dong district) during a particular time (present day), modified by the possible permutations of the contextual factors above. We have identified three possible action arenas within which decisions are made by each actor. As we argued earlier, rational decisions will be made based on the incentives presented to the actors. Our analysis of incentive structures is simple and relies on a qualitative comparison of the perceived benefits and costs associated with full, compliant participation in the forest allocation program in that action arena.

Degraded Forest Land Allocation to Households

The first action arena is the allocation of degraded forest land for plantation activities under the Programs 327 and 661 (Table 10.3). This allocation only occurred for individual households that worked in an SFE or that previously praticed swidden agriculture. In this action arena there are only two main actors, namely Khe Tre SFE (Khe Tre town is the administrative center of Nam Dong) and the local household. The FPU was not involved in degraded forest land allocation for plantation purposes because FPU only deals with natural forest protection.

TABLE 10.3
Incentive Structure for Participation in Degraded Forest Land Allocation for Household Plantation Purposes in Nam Dong District, Central Vietnam

Stakeholders	Perceived Benefit(s) of Allocation	Perceived Cost(s) of Allocation
State Forest Enterprises	Reduced responsibility of areas covered by plantation Plantation products shared with local people when harvested Reduce management cost (protection, tending, etc.)	Reduced income from state plantation programs
Forest Protection Department	None	None
Villagers	Increased area of crop production Government subsidies Plantation products when harvested (trees) Collateral for bank loans	Labors

As shown in Table 10.3, the incentive structure in this action arena theoretically favors swift allocation and compliance with the regulations by both actors. By allocating degraded and barren land, the SFE could reduce its burden of maintaining low-quality plantations, while still being entitled to a benefit-sharing mechanism with local people after harvesting. The reduction in costs and responsibilities over low productivity plantations (when compared with high-yielding natural forests) made rapid allocation appealing to the SFE.

The incentives to local people to participate in degraded forest land allocation should also have been favorable because they could continue to intercrop between plantations for as long as possible. Moreover, the recipient household would receive subsidies such as tree seedlings, labor payment (for planting and tending forest afterwards) and trees when harvested. Third, the household would get the majority of the benefits from the plantation output when eventually harvested. Finally, the recipient could deposit their Red Book for bank loans to meet other urgent needs on cash (e.g., school fees for children, wedding parties for relatives, etc.). Thus, in this action arena both SFE and local households appeared to be presented with incentives to fully participate in and comply with allocation policy, thus achieving the first step towards the desired policy outcome.

Surprisingly, however, at the onset of the program the incentives of participating in and complying with the objectives of the allocation program (planting and maintenance of trees) were not very strong to the local people. This occurred for two reasons. First, the forest to be allocated for plantations was traditional swidden land. The reduction in swidden land as per Decree 327/CT was being fulfilled through the forest allocation program. In other words, policies to reduce swidden and increase plantation cover appeared to have been crafted hand-in-hand by the national government. Household participants had to sacrifice their swidden areas for the allocation program. Second, the plantations were generally low quality, with inappropriate species and low attention paid to tending. Thus, during the inception of the forest allocation program, only a small area of plantation was successful and the majority of barren land was covered by cassava or maize (Tiziano et al., 2000).

Since the introduction of high-yielding forestry tree species, however, the incentive for household participation began to increase to the point where benefits were significantly greater than costs (i.e., loss of swidden and labor input). New plantation species gave high yields within short-term period of growth, e.g., *Acacia mangium*, which has a rotational period of seven years. Moreover, with investment from Program 661, local people started planting other native tree species in their allocated land such as *Aquilaria crassna* (aloe wood) and *Hopea odorata*. All these species grow fast and appeared to be suitable with local conditions. Finally, the rubber tree (*Hevea brasiliensis*) was introduced in Nam Dong district in 1993 in several areas of Huong Son commune. Due to high demand from the market in recent years, the attractive sources of income from rubber latex have drawn local households to expand the area covered by this species under contract with the Nam Dong Rubber Company. Therefore, the incentives for participation were initially not exceptionally appealing due to low perceived benefits and high perceived costs. However, with the introduction of high yielding species, participation and compliance of recipients became highly profitable and tipped the scale in favor of participation in degraded forest land allocation.

Natural Forest Allocation to Individual Households

The second action arena is allocation of natural forest to individual households. Different from the first action arena, the incentives to the SFE are much lower, because it is required to bear higher costs than benefits when they allocate degraded forest land to individual households (Table 10.4). These costs are in the form of losses due to foregone timber extraction from natural forest, which had been under their management since 1975.

However, the FPU and individual households should participate in and comply with the allocation program with stronger incentives than the SFE. The FPU had high incentives to fulfill the allocation process due to two sources of benefits. First, the FPU could reduce its workload by transferring duties of forest protection to local households. After forest allocation, the FPU would only be involved with sanctions applied to violators of forest law, in forests monitored by the forest owner. Second, project investment (and direct payment) by SNV that facilitates the allocation process is an important benefit that FPU gains from the allocation program. This source of payment covers forest demarcation, forest inventory, local meetings and issuance of the Red Book.

Table 10.4
Incentive Structure for Participation in the Natural Forest Allocation
in Nam Dong District, Central Vietnam

Stakeholder	Allocation to	Perceived Benefit(s) of Allocation	Perceived Cost(s) of Allocation
State Forest Enterprises	Individual Group	Reduce forest protection duties	Less benefits from timber extraction
Forest Protection Unit (district level)	Individual	Reduced protection duties Direct payment from SNV	Less direct benefits from sanction High time and effort in allocation (forest inventory and demarcation)
	Group	Reduced protection duties Direct payment from the SNV	Effort in allocation (but lower than for household allocation)
Local People	Individual	Forest products Red Book for long-term investment and loan from bank Rationale for sanction Integrated other land uses (plantation, NTFPs)	Time and effort in management Protection cost higher if allocated patches are in remote area
	Group	Forest products Red Book for long-term investment and loan from bank Rationale for sanction Receive larger areas of natural forest	Transaction costs associated with penalty agreement, harvest approval Investment to generate incomes from degraded forest

Local households, too, should have high incentives for participation in the natural forest allocation through exclusive forest product rights and use of the Red Book as collateral for bank loans. More importantly, the allocation recipient could protect the resource and enforce sanctions to any violator in her/his allocated forest. With these strong incentives, the desired outcomes of allocation policy should be achieved through forest protection and helping local people with short-term income generation.

Results from interviews with the FPU, Khe Tre SFE and field observations have supported the theoretical incentive table.

The Khe Tre SFE, under requirement of DARD who expressed their previous initiative of developing community forestry in Phu Loc district, had returned natural forest to the Nam Dong district People's Committee in order to prepare for allocation of natural forest areas to households. In addition to provincial initiatives of allocation program, the prime minister signed Decision 264 on December 16, 2003 for a 'strategy of land management in state-forest enterprises'. This decision indirectly required all provincial authorities to re-arrange land resources managed by state forest enterprises. Forest and forest land, not in critical watersheds that could be used for agro-forestry production, should be allocated to local people to maximize land productivity. The Khe Tre SFE, therefore, had to follow these central and provincial regulations.

The FPU finished all forest inventory and forest demarcation by 2003. Most households in this commune practiced agro-forestry models in their allocated forest. Besides, they also cultivated some species of NTFPs such as rattan and bamboo. Some of them deposited the Red Book to get a loan from the Agribank for planting high-value tree species such as *Aquilaria crassna* (aloe wood). Local households in this commune practiced fruit tree gardens integrated in allocated forest. Most of these models have proved to be effective land-use strategies with positive initial results (Ogle *et al.*, 2004).

Natural Forest Allocation to Groups of Households

The third action arena is the allocation of natural forest to a group of households in Thuong Quang, Thuong Long and Huong Son communes of Nam Dong district. Natural forest in these communes is highly degraded and on steep slopes. The majority of local people in these two communes are the Katu, who have a long history of traditional, collective forest management by villages. Given these biophysical and social characteristics, the FPU has encouraged groups of households to receive natural forest. The major incentives for different actors in natural forest allocation to groups of households are presented in Table 10.4.

The allocation process can only happen when the Khe Tre SFE agrees to return certain areas of natural forest to make them available for allocation. Similar to allocation of natural forest to individual household, this SFE sustains high costs (i.e., foregone income) when participating in the allocation program.

For the district FPU, however, similar benefits are gotten from the direct payments of SNV and relinquishing protection duties to local groups of households. Thus, the FPU tries to efficiently and quickly carry out all allocation activities such as local meetings, group formation and forest boundary demarcation even though some areas of natural forest were not withdrawn from Khe Tre SFE at the time (e.g., forest areas in Huong Son and Thuong Long communes). In fact, the overall incentives to the FPD of participating in the group allocation should be higher than the household allocation, because the perceived costs of allocation are lower. The boundary demarcation costs should be much lower for a group than for the same number of individual households.

For the allocation recipient, local groups of households should receive more benefits than costs in allocation programs. Within allocated forests, a group of local households can harvest and maintain those NTFPs for their benefits. The only difference in benefits compared with individual household allocation is that the total forest allocated to groups of households is much larger than to individual households.

Moreover, we found that there could be high transaction costs associated with group management of an allocated forest. These transaction costs begin during the process of forest allocation, where group agreement must be achieved in all aspects of the application and demarcation process. Subsequently, agreement must be maintained in the group in terms of management, protection, sanctions to illegal logging or applying for approval of timber harvesting. Nevertheless, the incentive structure to groups of households may remain sufficiently high to encourage participation and compliance in the allocation program.

Field research results suggest that there is a substantial disincentive to the SFE during the implementation of natural forest allocation to groups. The Khe Tre SFE delayed to return certain areas of natural forests in which significant tracts of timber have provided long-term benefits to the enterprise and where future potential benefits remained. As pointed in the second action arena, the allocation of natural forest to individual households occurred in the early stage of land allocation programs. The allocation of forest to groups of households, however, happened later with two main differences from the allocation to individual households. First, forests allocated to individual households were of lower quality than forests allocated to groups of households. The SFE would always give up low quality forest first before handing over medium or good quality forest given the high opportunity cost they have to bear. Thus, the more they delay in handing over forests to local people, the higher the possibility that they can get forest products before transferring forest 'ownership'. Second, forest in Thua Thien Hue province was being re-classified before allocation program. This classification process took a long time due to large forest areas of the province. Because several forest areas remained unclassified, the SFE had good reason to postpone the releasing of good quality forest from their management. This resistance on the part of the SFE has resulted in two out of five communes in Nam Dong being unable to fulfill the allocation program even though all forest inventories and local meetings had been carried out. Both the FPU and all groups of households are now waiting for provincial decision to withdraw forests from Khe Tre SFE to continue the allocation process.

The delay of returning the forests by SFE has resulted in postponing the Red Book issuance to group recipients. This has created important negative impacts on both forest and local people. Villagers and people outside of groups tried to harvest the remaining big trees in forest that had not been allocated. Several cases of illegal logging were detected but local groups could not enforce sanctions because they lacked the Red Book over the area. The situation became frustrating in Thuong Quang commune when different people tried to make use of this unclear status of forest ownership by cutting trees in forest designated for allocation. Results from our IFRI survey showed that the majority of forest group recipients had heavy disincentives towards the allocation programs. They also expressed preference of breaking up forest allocated to groups into individual parcels in order to apply more effective management.

DISCUSSION

During the implementation of the allocation program, several 'side effects' have occurred far from the desired outcomes of the allocation policies. This section discusses those effects based on two types of resources allocated to local people—degraded land and natural forest.

Whereas, the incentives for the SFE and the FPD to allocate degraded forest land were high (reduction of costs [SFE and FPD] and responsibilities [FPD] while maintaining some benefits [SFE]), the initial incentives to local people were low due to the low perceived benefits for plantations. However, with the visible success of the *Acacia* and rubber plantations in Nam Dong, there emerged a race to register for land allocation. That high-land value has led to unintended consequences, in that some areas of regenerating natural forest had been cleared in order to increase the probability of fast allocation and subsequent plantation establishment. Other low-productivity agricultural lands have also been converted to rubber plantations. Even land with high slopes was used for rubber plantations without taking into consideration the difficulties of future latex harvest. While high subsidizations in cash (US$ 1,000–1,500/hectare) and planting materials are the main incentive for rubber plantations, a short-term harvesting period (approximately seven years/cycle) is the main reason for local people to plant *Acacia* tree species.

The results show two trends for natural forest allocation. First is that the incentives to the two government agencies in this action arena differ remarkably. The incentives to the FPD for allocation are in all cases positive. The FPD burden for protection is reduced (after the initial investment of time to demarcate and facilitate allocation) and meanwhile they accumulate benefits through the support of international NGOs that support allocation with funds (e.g., SNV). On the other hand, the incentive for the SFE to allocate high quality, timber-rich forest to communities is very low. Activity by the SFE to maximize short-term benefit by increasing the rate of timber extraction (legal or illegal) prior to allocation is the most rational response. Indeed, preliminary evidence from remote sensing and field research indicates that rates of timber extraction have been rapid since 2000, when allocation of natural forest was being planned and executed (Thiha *et al.*, 2007). Moreover, this has resulted in delays in forest allocation.

Thus far, most of the allocated natural forests appear to be of poor or medium quality, containing only a small amount of timber and NTFPs available to local needs (e.g., house construction, short-term income). This is not surprising because in other countries community forestry tends to preferentially hand over degraded forest to local communities, while keeping the forest with high timber volumes for state management (Nagendra, 2002). Allocating poor quality forest has two consequences in Nam Dong. First, local people perceived low short-term 'feasibility of improvement' (*sensu* Gibson *et al.*, 2000), which provided a low incentive for participation. Second, low resource availability in those allocated natural forests meant that people continued to rely on state forest for timber and NTFP extraction, e.g., *Rhapis laosensis* (for making conical hats), *Thysanolaena maxima* (for making brooms) and various species of rattan (Wetterwald *et al.*, 2003). Our field research in 2004 revealed that in Village 5 of Thuong Quang commune, all young men below 30 years of age entered the forest outside of their allocated forest for timber extraction or other NTFPs.

The second trend of natural forest allocation is that the incentives for the FPD to facilitate natural forest allocation are stronger towards group allocation than household allocation. With lower transaction costs to the FPD in terms of forest demarcation, meetings, and contractual preparation, combined with the interest of international agencies towards 'community-based forest management' (Sikor and Apel, 1998), we expect that the long-term trend will be towards group allocation.

However, groups of households have lower incentives for sustainable forest management than individual households. This may be due to both characteristics of the groups and characteristics of rules-in-use. Prior research has shown that Katu villages exhibited strong community-based institutions for forest management prior to 1975 (Thang, 2004). These institutions have been weakened since 1975, similar to the general situation in the whole country (Sikor and Apel, 1998). The present village administrative system follows the commune system, which although for group allocated forest requires 'community management', makes virtually no mention of supporting the locally-crafted, traditional institutional arrangements. Thus, despite the long history of communal forest management, particularly by Katu and other ethnic groups, those indigenous systems are not integrated into the contemporary allocation process. Hence, the households in the recipient groups are faced with new dilemmas and decide to work independently, rather than sustain the high transaction costs of new institutional adjustment. Groups did not create any regulations regarding access, withdrawal, or management of the forest. The only task done by the group was patrolling the forest once per month at the beginning of the allocation program. Later, however, the frequency of forest patrolling decreased and only the group head man continued this activity by the end of year 2004.

In terms of rules-in-use, there has been a lack of direct payment and delaying the provision of the Red Book, which also has led to disillusionment and erosion of collaborative spirit. As mentioned in the desired outcomes of allocation policy, secure tenure is a necessary condition for long-term investment to improve the quality and quantity of allocated forest. Lacking this, local people could not apply any improved measures for allocated forest (e.g., pruning, enrichment, facilitation of natural regeneration). The rules-in-use (i.e., land allocation policies) here are not properly implemented both in temporal aspects (i.e., long time of waiting for the Red Book) and spatial aspects (i.e., some communes received the Red Book before others even though the allocation programs were carried out at the same time).

Conclusions

Our analysis traced both the incentive structures and the responses of actors to those incentives within the action arena of forest allocation in Nam Dong district, central Vietnam. We have shown that substantial challenges remain for both the allocation process and the long-term sustainable management of both allocated and non-allocated forest.

Not only are there positive incentives for people to participate in household allocation of degraded forest land but also perverse incentives actually support increased conversion of natural forest so that the degraded or cleared patches can be replanted with *Acacia* or rubber and then allocated. Solving this dilemma will require action on two fronts. First, the potential costs to non-compliant behavior (natural forest clearing) need to be increased, to reduce this perverse incentive. This may be achieved by increased monitoring and enforcement by the FPD as well as the local village leaders. A second course of action would be to create multi-income generation models for plantations, so that local people could receive diverse benefits for both short-term and long-term demands. This might include domestication of several major NTFPs that are not presently available in allocated forest. Such plant species include medicinal herbs, rattan, fast-growing native tree species for timber (e.g., *Tarrietia javanica*) or multipurpose trees (e.g., *Scaphium lychnophorum* for both plywood and fruits). This type of model has been carried out in Ha An village in consultancy with a research center and the preliminary results are encouraging. While success with NTFP domestication may reduce the frequency of going to natural forest for products collection, or land clearing for exotic tree plantations, it still would require support from development organization in terms of training and finding markets for the products after production. Moreover, enforcement by the FPD with collaboration of local leaders would continue to be necessary. The central point of this idea is to maximize land productivity because land resources are increasingly scarce. Other models of land and forest productivity can be explored as well.

The procedures of allocating natural forest should be revised in both content and implementation. Findings from our survey revealed that ownership as expressed by the Red Book, although very important, was not the highest priority of local people for forest management. Their largest concern was what type of forest would be allocated to them and how to improve its quality. It seems clear that it is necessary to involve local people at the beginning of allocation process in order to establish an appropriate incentive. For example, local villagers should be invited for identification of forest types, uses and boundaries. By putting them in the context of the real 'owner', local people will have more confidence in deciding suitable measures for their particular forest. To apply this approach, information on their forests should be collected from and shared with them. This can be done through workshops in which local people are encouraged to express or show their knowledge on the forest they expect to manage by themselves. For example, they may discuss historical trends of wildlife or valuable tree species in that forest. By doing this analysis, local people would have more interest in finding solutions for specific challenges of a forest. The process of identifying current problems and proposing possible solutions is called 'future scenarios' analysis (Wollenberg *et al.*, 2000). These meetings would help them share knowledge and common understandings among group members and create motivation for all members. The next step would be facilitation for legal procedures. These steps would increase the probability of long-term investment in allocated forest by local people. Without this long-term ownership, local people will not try their best to improve forest quality or to apply other protection measures as expected to achieve the desired outcomes of the allocation programs.

To address the issue of high transaction costs to group recipients, the steps above will go a long way in reducing the transaction costs among members of an allocation group. Indeed, the costs to communities must be substantially borne by the entities implementing the policies. However, further steps should be taken. Policy flexibility should be incorporated whereby local rules and institutions are clearly accepted within the bounds of the larger state allocation objectives. Moreover, this may be applicable to the formation of user groups—user groups with longer histories are more likely to have better capacity to adapt their institutional arrangements to meet with the state requirements. Thus, ethnic homogeneity and groups with the highest level of social capital, shared norms and forest management objectives should be encouraged.

Finally, attention needs to be paid to the incentives of the SFE to delay forest allocation and maximize timber extraction in the short term. This is a very challenging and sensitive issue that needs to be addressed in the appropriate political manner. If incentives for the SFE can be produced to allocate rather than timber-mine high quality natural forest, then the entire process can begin appropriately. Allocating good forest to local people could mean less incentive to convert that forest to plantation and could also reduce non-allocated forest exploitation as long as silvicultural methods are implemented in the allocated natural forest to increase the productivity of desirable products.

References

Gibson, C.C., Andersson, K., Ostrom, E. and Shivakumar, S. (2005). *The Samaritan's Dilemma: The Political Economy of Development Aid*. Oxford: Oxford University Press.

Gibson, C.C., Ostrom, E. and McKean, M.A. (2000). 'Forest, People and Governance: Some Initial Theoretical Lessons'. In C.C. Gibson, M.A. McKean, and E. Ostrom

(Eds), *People and Forests: Communities, Institutions and Governance* (pp. 227–242). Cambridge, MA: The MIT Press.

Ho Hy. (2005). 'Policy Structure and Challenges in Land and Forest Allocation in Thua Thien Hue Province'. Paper presented at the conference on Participatory Forest Conservation in Central Vietnam: Implementing and Monitoring Strategies, January 9–11, 2006. Hue City: Hue University of Agriculture and Forestry.

Nagendra, H. (2002). 'Tenure and Forest Conditions: Community Forestry in the Nepal Terai'. *Environmental Conservation, 29*(4), 530–539.

Nam Dong District Report. (2004). *Report on Preliminary Results of Land Use Planning and Forest Land Allocation (LUP-FLA) in Nam Dong District* (in Vietnamese). Vietnam: Office of People's Committee of Nam Dong District.

Ogle, A.J., Lung, N.N. and Ty, H.X. (2004). *External Evaluation of the First Phase of the Project 'Strengthening Forest Management Capacity in Thua Thien Hue Province'*. Final Report: June 2004. Hanoi, Vietnam: Netherlands Development Organization (SNV).

Ostrom, E., Gardner, R. and Walker J.M. (1994). *Rules, Games, and Common-Pool Resources*. Ann Arbor, MI: University of Michigan Press.

Sikor, T. and Apel, U. (1998). *The Possibilities for Community Forestry in Vietnam* (vol. 1). Working Paper Series. Asia Forest Network. Berkeley, CA.

Thang, T.N. (2004). 'Forest Use Patterns and Dependency of Ka Tu and Ta Oi communes of Nam Dong and A Luoi districts, Hue Province, Vietnam'. M.Sc. dissertation, Asian Institute of Technology, Bangkok.

Thiha, Webb, E.L. and Honda, K. (2007). 'Biophysical and Policy Drivers of Landscape Change in a Central Vietnamese District'. *Environmental Conservation 34*(2): 164–172.

Tiziano, G., Pettenella, D., Trieu, G.P. and Paoletti, M.G. (2000). 'Vietnamese Uplands: Environmental and Socio-economic Perspective of Forest Land Allocation and Deforestation Process'. *Environment, Development, and Sustainability, 2*(2), 119. ABI/INFORM Global.

Wetterwald, O., Zingerli, C. and Sorg, J.P. (2003). 'Non-timber Forest Products in Nam Dong District, Central Vietnam: Ecological and Economic Prospects'. *Schweiz. Z. Forstwes, 155*(2), 45–52.

Wollenberg, E., Edmunds, D. and Buck, L. (2000). *Anticipating Change: SCENARIO as a Tool for Adaptive Forest Management*. Bogor: Center for International Forestry Research (CIFOR).

11

FACILITATING DECENTRALIZED POLICIES FOR SUSTAINABLE GOVERNANCE AND MANAGEMENT OF FOREST RESOURCES IN ASIA

GANESH P. SHIVAKOTI and ELINOR OSTROM

As discussed earlier in Chapters 1 and 2, decentralization has frequently been recommended in the initial years of the 21st century to deal with the overuse of natural resource systems (Mukand and Rodrik, 2002; Ribot, 2002). This is a radical departure from early policy prescriptions. For decades, the presumption in many policy circles has been that the users of natural resources were shortsighted resource-grabbers who did not realize that unsustainable harvesting practices would lead to their own ruin (Ophuls, 1973; Vedeld, 1993). To counter this presumed failure of those using resources to seek out long-term solutions to overharvesting, governments pre-empted local community stewardship throughout Asia (Arnold and Campbell, 1986). Land was taken away from traditional or community ownership and declared to be owned by the national government.

Chapter 1 provides a brief history of the policy of centralization throughout Asia followed in very recent times by various decentralization policies. Unless decentralization policies are crafted in ways that take into account the ecological condition of a local forest, the economic pressures surrounding specific forest products, the local tradition in some locations for sustainable management and a host of other factors that affect performance, these new policy recommendations will turn out to be another series of 'quick fixes' and rapid failures (Bardhan and Mookherjee, 2000; Agrawal and Ribot, 1999). Pritchett and Woolcock (2003) bemoan the problem of trying to find solutions when 'the' problem is actually the blueprint solution recommended by donors and national governments for solving a problem.

The case studies in this volume provide an initial foundation for beginning to think about factors that help account for successes or failures of local systems of governance of forest resources. Many variables are considered by contemporary policy analysis to be responsible for policy successes or failures. Scholars identify variables such as the size of the group using a resource and its heterogeneity, dynamic leaders, the availability of adequate funds and the clear assignment of responsibilities as among the factors that may make a difference between a success and a failure (Poteete and Ostrom, 2004; Burger *et al.*, 2001). All of these variables tend to be important. The problem that we face in analyzing successes and failures and proposing new policies is how to link the challenges that face a particular social-ecological system (including both the resource as well as the humans facing incentives to use the resource) that accounts for results. In our effort to gain some real lessons from the excellent case studies, we have tried to develop a framework for comparing experiences that is more than a simple two or three variable analysis. We will first discuss the basic elements of this framework and then apply it to the case studies as our effort to explain both the successful and unsuccessful outcomes.

CHALLENGES

In this effort, our first attempt is to address the challenges that face any particular social-ecological system. The first challenge is to understand the prior history of a forested area before a new policy reform is implemented. Forests that had been managed by local communities for multiple decades, if not centuries, that were then centralized in the 1960s or 1970s, may have been overharvested in the last part of the twentieth century due to a sense of loss of control by local populations. If a new policy reform comes along that turns the management of a degraded government-owned forest over to users, who had been the stewards of the forest and protected it before it was nationalized, that is a much more difficult problem than when the forest has been protected by the national government itself for a very long time and is in good condition.

The condition of the forest itself at the time of turnover to a co-managed or decentralized system makes a difference regardless of earlier history. Even if a local group had not previously had its initiative in managing a forest undermined by nationalization, a forested area that is substantially degraded is much more challenging for any government, private or community group to decide how to spend substantial time at planting, weeding, controlling access to and all the other time-consuming practices that are needed to turn a degraded forest into a productive forest.

In addition to the prior history and the condition of the forest at the time of turnover, the relationships of the size of the forest to the size of the user group and its heterogeneity are also important factors. A large forest to be co-managed by a small group or a small forest to be co-managed by a large group, are particularly difficult situations.

STRUCTURAL VARIABLES

At least four structural conditions have occurred in the cases discussed in this volume. Some of the cases have remained managed by a central government authority in current times and some have remained or evolved towards a local management system with no overlapping authority by a national government. More of the systems discussed in the case studies have been co-managed in some way or other involving local communities along with larger-scale government units, at times complemented by NGOs. The co-managed systems have at times evolved in a way that participants at multiple scales interact with one another in a constructive problem-solving manner. In these systems, little conflict has emerged between the units. Others have involved high levels of conflict over exactly which unit was supposed to do what and arguments about lack of commitment, resources, information and other relevant factors.

SUPPORT STRUCTURES

Surrounding any particular social-ecological system is a wide diversity of potential support structures that can make a huge difference in whether a resource system is used sustainably over time or allocated in ways that undermine the possibility of long-term use. In our analysis of the cases, we have tried to examine the kinds of social networks that may exist among members of a local community that link them to better information, external resources and reciprocal exchanges. A second important factor is whether all the rules of a particular type of local resource governance unit must be the same or whether there is recognition that so long as rules meet certain standards of openness, fairness and equity, it is better to allow pluralism of specific rules across resource sites. Further, the specific links to higher-level governments that may provide reliable information and conflict-resolution mechanisms are particularly important as is the effort to build social capital at local levels by encouraging cooperation, providing mechanisms for exchange of information and learning, etc.

RESULTS

Instead of focusing on a single set of results, it is more realistic to look at a variety of outcomes that have occurred in the cases described in this volume. Obviously, the condition of the forest is an important result. If everyone is happy and well fed, but they have destroyed the forest, one would not be inclined to consider this a successful outcome. It is also important to examine factors in addition to forest conditions. How have benefits been distributed? Is there a fundamental sense of equity in the allocation of responsibilities and benefits? In some cases, the local elites have been able to organize themselves effectively so that they capture most of the benefits. That kind of capture by elites can itself lead to substantial conflict. Have such conflicts broken out and have they been coped with locally or required external authoritative resolution?

Another factor has to do with how a social-ecological system copes with initial indicators of failure. Early in a process it is possible that massive overharvesting or free riding occurs. If such has happened, how has someone inside the system or outside the system generated corrective measures? Or, have the resource and the social system related to it continued on a downward decline? Finally, it is important to examine the evidence that the social practices as well as the forest conditions are likely to be sustainable over time. This is usually associated with some levels of effective monitoring so that participants know that others are following rules and are thus more willing to abide by the rules themselves. Effective monitoring enhances the likelihood that the entire system can improve over time (Gibson *et al.*, 2005; Ostrom and Nagendra, 2006).

A COMPARATIVE SYNTHESIS OF
POLICY PERFORMANCES OF FIELD CASES

The policy challenges of Asian forest governance under changing contexts are among the most important challenges of contemporary times. Among these challenges are devising policies that work related to the roles of national governments and local communities while involving multiple stakeholders such as local leaders, scientists and academics, responsible forest managers and international NGOs. Simple policy prescriptions advocating uniform decentralization policies without an understanding of the diversity and richness of local self-governance mechanisms and drawing on these experiences through locally adopted decentralization policies create another blueprint—that does work in some settings but definitely not in all (Korten, 1980). Therefore, we present a synthesis of our analysis of challenges, structural variables, support structure and results of cases from Bhutan, India, Indonesia, Nepal, Thailand and Vietnam as presented in Chapters 3 through 10 in this volume using the framework we just presented.

A tabular analysis of the challenges that were faced in these cases is presented in Table 11.1. Several forest systems have experienced changes in the management regime from state-controlled systems to the co-management systems or to community-managed forest systems either very recently or within the last two decades. Therefore, the prior history of these forest systems in the South and Southeast Asian countries varies substantially. Some have been the result of 'overnight decisions' by the state to turn over the forest to locals and others have involved long-term community management. Some of the systems recently turned over to communities were substantially degraded prior to this new policy direction. Nepal's history of nationalizing all forested land during the 1950s and then handing these forests back to communities after considerable deforestation during the last two decades is a classic example of this type of U-turn policy change. The cases from Bhutan (Chapter 3), India (Chapter 4) and Thailand (Chapter 9) point to a

TABLE 11.1
Challenges of Asian Forest Systems

Country	Cases (Management Type)	Prior History	Size of Forest	Size of User Group	Heterogeneity of User Group	Condition of Forest
Bhutan						
	Community-managed (sokshing)	Long-term	Small	Small	Homogeneous	Very good
	Government-managed (non-sokshing)	Long-term	Large	Large	Heterogeneous	Degraded nearby community Very good interior
India						
	Self-initiated	Relatively recent	Large	Small	Mixed	Very good and protected
	System introduced by forest department	Very recent	Large	Medium	Homogeneous	Good
	NGO promoted	Very recent	Large	Small	Homogeneous	Degraded
Indonesia						
	Conservation forest	Long-term	Large	Large	Heterogeneous	Good
	Protection forest	Medium-term	Large	Large	Heterogeneous	Degraded
	Adat forest	Long-term	Small	Small	Homogeneous	Good

(*Table 11.1 continued*)

(Table 11.1 continued)

Country	Cases (Management Type)	Prior History	Size of Forest	Size of User Group	Heterogeneity of User Group	Condition of Forest
Nepal						
	Flat area (*Terai*)					
	Community forestry	Medium-term	Medium	Small	Relatively homogeneous	Degraded
	Buffer zone	Recent	Medium	Large	Heterogeneous	Degraded but improving
	Middle hills					
	Community forestry	Medium-term	Medium	Medium	Heterogeneous	Very good
	Semi-government	Recent	Small	Medium	Heterogeneous	Excellent
	Leasehold forestry	Recent	Small	Small	Homogeneous	Degraded
	Government	Long-term	Large	Large	Heterogeneous	Degraded
Thailand						
	Conservation forest	Medium-term	Medium	Medium	Homogeneous	Good
	Utilization forest	Medium-term	Large	Medium	Homogeneous	Very good
Vietnam						
	State forest	Medium-term	Medium	Large	Heterogeneous	Degraded to very good
	Allocated forest land (plantations)	Recent	Small	Small	Heterogeneous	Barren and degraded but improving
	Allocated natural forest	Recent	Small	Small	Homogeneous	Degraded to moderate

different challenge. In these countries the bureaucratic grip of the state continued throughout the past half-century, albeit allowing for some policy experiments of joint management and co-management. Indonesia (Chapter 5) and Vietnam (Chapter 10), on the other hand, have practiced different forms of decentralization policies through an effort to integrate forest systems governance through traditional indigenous institutional arrangements for overall village governance and through effective forest allocation mechanisms to the individual community members (and more recently to the communities on an experimental basis).

Therefore, based on the prior experiences, the adoption of new management regimes is a recent trend in forest governance. Variations in the management mechanisms are based on local challenges such as size of forest and user groups. The heterogeneity within a group also influences the condition of the forest. Our analysis (see Table 11.1) shows that smaller size of forests and smaller groups of forest users are no guarantee that a forest will be managed effectively since in some cases small forest size and user groups have been able to maintain excellent conditions of their forests while others face degraded conditions. Therefore, the challenges in managing forests are not strongly affected by these variables. Rather they depend upon governance mechanisms and facilitating policies including the external recognition of internal self-governance mechanisms.

This brings us to the issue of the structural arrangements for forest management (see Table 11.2). Case studies presented in this volume represent a wide range of management types. Centrally-managed systems exist in Bhutan, India, Indonesia and Vietnam, while primarily locally-managed systems exist in all of the remaining countries studied in this volume. Co-managed systems exist with varied level of conflicts in all the countries studied in South and Southeast Asia. Our analysis highlights one important issue for policy consideration, which is related to models of co-management. Systems that are co-managed with low conflict within and among the systems have more autonomy and flexible rules for the management of the systems than co-managed systems with high conflict levels. Many of these conflicts are attributable to strong control from the state, lack of specificity and permanence of property rights as well as unspecified benefits-sharing mechanisms and compliance with the rules (Table 11.2).

The analysis of cases on support structure variables shows a wide variation in network mechanisms, but these networks are more effective in community-managed and co-managed systems with low

TABLE 11.2
Structural Variables Affecting Intensity of Forest Management in Asia

Country	Cases (Management Type)	Centrally Managed	Co-managed with High Conflict	Co-managed with Low Conflict	Locally Managed
Bhutan					
	Community-managed (sokshing)				H
	Government-managed (non-sokshing)	M	L		
India					
	Self-initiated				H
	System introduced by forest department	H	L		
	NGO promoted			L	
Indonesia					
	Conservation forest	H			
	Protection forest	L		M	
	Adat forest				H
Nepal					
	Flat area (Terai)				
	Community forestry			L	H
	Buffer zone			H	L
	Middle hills				
	Community forestry			L	H
	Semi-government			H	L
	Leasehold forestry		M		
	Government	M			
Thailand					
	Joint-managed conservation forest			M	
	Community-managed utilization forest			L	H
Vietnam					
	State forest	H	H	H	
	Allocated forest land (plantations)			H	H
	Allocated natural forest		L	L	

Notes: H: High management intensity, M: Medium management intensity, L: Low management intensity.

conflicts (Table 11.3). The presence of legal plurality with flexibility is more pronounced in the case of community-managed and co-managed forests than state-controlled and managed systems. Similarly, social networks are weak in state-controlled systems. This invites frequent conflict among users within a system and also among the users of different forest systems. This issue is complicated further with the multiple characteristics of forest products and the overlap of diverse community needs. This also relates to provision and availability of multiplicity of rules. Our synthesis of cases shows that systems managed by community and co-managed systems with low conflict have more flexible rules, with several sources and availability of mechanisms for exchange of information. Our case analysis also shows variation in availability of information that is linked with the governance mechanism (Table 11.3). The self-governing and co-managed systems have effective links with the higher level of government either through a federation of users and their representatives or through the formal linkage established with several stakeholders. Similarly, we found higher levels of provision for building social capital in the community-managed systems than in cases of government-controlled systems. Conflict-resolutions mechanisms in cases of community-managed systems tend to be simple and based on local culture and norms with built-in flexibility. The conflict-resolution mechanisms are more rigid in cases of government or externally assisted and managed systems.

Our examination of a multiple set of results to analyze performance of forest systems reconfirms the need for a polycentric local governance mechanism for effective management of forest resources. Overall, systems that have performed better, however, have better forest conditions with effective monitoring mechanisms in place, equitable distribution of benefits, less occurrences of elite capture and presence of multiple arenas for conflict management with multiple evidences of sustainability over time (Table 11.4). We also find degraded forests present in the community-managed systems. However, as in the case of leasehold forestry in Nepal (see Chapter 7), this is frequently the outcome of national governments handing over already degraded forests to local communities. Thus, the degraded condition of the forest is not the result of community management. This has a direct relationship with the recovery from initial failure. Systems with resilient characteristics

TABLE 11.3

Support Structures for Sustainable Forest Governance in Asia

Country	Cases (Management Type)	Networks	Legal Plurality	Reliable Information	Effective Link to Higher Level Governance	Provisions for Building Social Capital	Conflict-Resolution Mechanisms
Bhutan							
	Community-managed (sokshing)	Excellent	Present	Available among users	Not effective	Yes at high level	Simple, indigenous and flexible
	Government-managed (non-sokshing)	None	Absent	Not available	Not structured	None	Available, rigid and exogenous
India							
	Self-initiated	Good	Available, less flexible	Available among users	Not developed	Yes at high level	Simple, indigenous and flexible
	System introduced by forest department	Medium	Available, less flexible	Available but scarce	Better	Yes at low level	Standard, Joint Forest Management structured
	NGO promoted	Excellent	Available	Available and transparent	Excellent	Yes at medium level	Available but ambiguous
Indonesia							
	Conservation forest	Good	Weak	Available	Effective	No	Available
	Protection forest	Medium	Present	Less reliable	Effective	Yes at moderate level	Less available
	Adat forest	None	Present	Less reliable	Less effective	Available	Available

Country / Forest type							
Nepal							
	Flat area (*Terai*)						
		Community forestry	Very good	Available	Available among users	Yes, high through federation	Yes at high level	Available, flexible
	Buffer zone		Medium	Available, less flexible	Less reliable	Less effective	No	Less available and rigid
	Middle hills							
		Community forestry	Excellent	Available	Available	Yes, high	Yes	Available, flexible
	Semi-government		Excellent	Available	Available	Yes	Yes, low	Available, rigid
	Leasehold forestry		Medium	Not available	Available but difficult	Rarely	Available	Rigid
	Government		Medium	Weak	Absent	Less available	No	Available, rigid
Thailand	Conservation forest		Medium	Present, less	Available through project office	Less effective	Yes at moderate level	Available, rigid
	Utilization forest		Good	Present, high	Available	More effective	Yes at higher level	Available and flexible
Vietnam	State forest		None	Present, low	Less reliable	Less effective	Yes, moderate	Complicated, rigid
	Allocated forest land (plantations)		Very good	Present, high	Available	Not structured	Yes	Self-resolution
	Allocated natural forest		Good	Present, high	Available	Not structured	Yes	Self-resolution

TABLE 11.4

Variations in Asian Forest Management: Variations in Forests Conditions, Rules in Use and Performances

Country	Cases (Management Type)	Monitoring	Forest Condition	Equity	Elite Capture	Conflict Management	Recover from Initial Failure	Sustainability Evidence
Bhutan								
	Community-managed (sokshing)	Yes	Good	More equitable	Low	Easily solved	Recovered	Yes, abundant
	Government-managed (non-sokshing)	Yes but minimum	Fair bordering sokshing, good in interior	State control	Some	Difficult	Good	Yes but low
India								
	Self-initiated	Highly effective	Degraded but regenerating	High	Less	Excellent	Good	Available
	System introduced by forest department	Least effective	Degraded	Low	High	Non-existent	Degraded	Not available
	NGO promoted	Moderately effective	Good	High	Some	Medium	Good	Available
Indonesia								
	Conservation forest	High	Very good	Low	Low	Difficult	Good	High
	Protection forest	Yes but low	Degraded	Low	Low	Difficult	Degraded	Medium
	Adat forest	Low	Good	High	Low	Easily solved	Good	High

Nepal							
Flat area (Terai)							
Community forestry	High	Good	High	Some	Easily solved	Not recovered	Available but degraded
Buffer zone	High	Some degraded	Low	More	Difficult	Recovered	Available at higher level
Middle hills							
Community forestry	High	Good	High	Less	Easily solved	Good	Yes, at medium
Semi-government	High	Very good	Medium	More	Solved with difficulty	Good	Yes, at higher level
Leasehold forestry	High	Degraded	High	Less	Difficult to solve	Improving	Less degraded
Government	Minimum	Degraded	Open access	Less	Difficult to solve	Degraded	Yes at medium level
Thailand							
Conservation forest	Yes but low	Good	Low	Some	Difficult	Good	Medium
Utilization forest	Yes at higher level	Very good	High	Less	Easily solved	Very good	Higher
Vietnam							
State forest	Not effective	Degraded	Low	High	Somewhat difficult	No, difficult	Low and decreasing
Allocated forest land (plantations)	Effective	Good	High	Less	Easy	Easy	Abundant
Allocated natural forest	Effective	Some degraded	High	Some	Easy	Difficult	Sustainable

have recovered in a relatively short span of time as contrasted with those systems having non-resilient characteristics. We also find that the forest conditions are directly related to the level of monitoring. Systems that are managed by the central government and have effective monitoring mechanisms also have better forest conditions. The conservation forests managed through several effective monitoring mechanisms in many South and Southeast Asian countries have better forest conditions.

FACILITATING POLICIES FOR SUSTAINABLE FOREST GOVERNANCE

In order to facilitate policies for sustainable forest governance and management, several policy alternatives emerge based on the analysis of different forest systems presented in this volume. Let us summarize some of these findings.

We have observed that community governance and management of forests are more effective when these systems have legal standing and are recognized by a central authority. For this, the promotion of polycentric governance and provision for a federation of users' associations and their legal standing and recognition by authority are equally important. We hope this begins to build a firmer foundation for future policies based on these realities revealed in the case study chapters.

In Chapter 2 we raised the issue of policies addressing local flexibility and empowerment issues related to elite capture and the link between formal and informal rules and understanding user behaviors in order to effectively implement decentralization. Drafting and implementing a blueprint decentralization policy based on the presumption that one policy fits all forests is unlikely to be successful. Decentralization policies must be flexible to accommodate local-level diversity in maintenance and harvesting rules. Both exogenous and endogenous factors need to be considered. While the elite capture issue may be related to endogenous factors, it is also dependent upon the structure of the property rights supported by the government. Similarly, the issue of international assistance from such organizations as IFAD/FAO and the UN policies such as CDM/GEF about the livelihood strategies linked to the condition of the natural resources should be revisited, relating these interventions to community forestry management (see also Gibson *et al.*, 2005). We can draw specific lessons from cases from India (Chapter 4), Nepal (Chapters 7 and 8) and Thailand (Chapter 9).

The issue of decentralization is one of the important policy concerns, but again decentralization should mean self-governance, not centralized decentralization. If we support self-governance of community forests, there should be a forum at the local level that should then be federated to increase the bargaining power with the central government. There are also key issues to be resolved between central and local authorities, including financial autonomy (the revenue generated as fees should be retained at the local level) and organizational autonomy (to be able to challenge the inappropriate decisions by the government decrees that are not conducive to the local-level management of forest resources). Again, we can draw several examples from the cases presented in this volume.

The emergence of co-production, co-management, polycentric and interactive policy experiments during the recent past in community forest management have produced mixed results. We have evidences of these self-governance and co-management approaches well documented in the volume, again from almost all of the cases.

The existence and use of social capital at the local level has both dark and bright sides. We have several examples of how to avoid policies promoting elite capture and related local-level feudal structures. In these instances, social capital has been instrumental in maintaining sustainability, financial autonomy, maintenance of biodiversity and helping global agendas such as climate change reduction of global warming. Indigenous knowledge systems have been incorporated and developed with a local-level partnership in developing flexible community forestry policies. We have several such examples from India (Chapter 4), Indonesia (Chapter 5), Nepal (Chapter 8) and Thailand (Chapter 9).

The evolution of institutions for managing community forestry has been facilitated or constrained by several facets of policy intervention and governance mechanisms of the central government. The examples from Nepal (see Chapter 6 for example), Bhutan, India and Thailand show at least three different types of governance mechanisms developed, as identified earlier in this chapter. The lessons learnt from what worked and what did not, with respect to reforming future policies, are important findings from this volume. There is a valid basis in redefining the role of central governmental authorities in community forest governance and management. These include the issue of property rights specification, relationship between conservation and utilization, the role of central government in protecting the forests from elite capture, redefining the role of market and functionaries in private investment and development of forest plantations and product harvest. The challenge is how to make the central government support the policy for promotion of innovation and entrepreneurship. The policy context explanation of anomalies identified by remote sensing and GIS techniques, using training samples in order to understand the policy puzzles, are some of the interdisciplinary efforts for disentangling a complex web as suggested from Nepal's buffer area management (see Chapter 8 for details).

Yet another issue is the explanation of land-use and land-cover changes over time, which are dependent not only on forest resources conservation and utilization but also on the interaction of forest with water and farming practices as mediated by the institutions at the local level and policies at a higher level. We have several examples of prior experiences of local knowledge systems in managing these complex relationships of resource management, and this expertise has evolved over time. One of the arguments for why Nepal's community forestry has been so successful, as compared to other countries, relates to the prior experiences of community leaders in the context of managing farmers' self-governing irrigation systems. Therefore, when thinking about policy reforms at local levels, the interdependencies and prior experiences of local peoples across sectors should be carefully considered. This brings to the fore the issue of documenting farmer-to-farmer training models and learning from the past successes in sustainable management of resources, including forests.

An important issue of policy support is the civil society's role in the development and sustenance of community forestry, drawing on the lessons learnt from several case studies in this volume. The efforts of several federated arrangements of artisanship in maintaining social capital are noteworthy. However, just trying to impose a federation on a group of resource users can become another 'cure all' and should definitely be avoided as a quick-fix policy prescription. We can draw on the lessons learnt from Nepal's community-managed forestry development strategies in trying to protect the interest of users, condition of the forest, and negotiating with the government in drafting separate community forestry management plans and policies for hills and *terai* (flat lands). This is a good example that illustrates the importance of the context, use pattern and the nature of the use of the resource itself. Another important outcome of this federated representation arrangement at the national level has been the development of the bargaining capacity of the users not only with the national-level government, but also with the representatives from bilateral and multilateral donor agencies.

Another important policy issue is the recognition of formal local rights both for use and management of forestry resources by providing legal pluralisms. This policy provision will drastically reduce conflict at several levels. Recognizing multiple rights and responsibilities will not only empower a local community but will also encourage the basic tenets of establishing/modifying rules, roles and modes of resource use and management, that in turn will minimize conflicts.

Thus, the overall lesson of the cases presented in this volume is that there is no single prescription or attribute of a resource or user group that dominates all other factors associated with results of forest governance. In the cases where considerable creativity was enabled to craft local rules considered legitimate by forest users and backed by government officials, conflict levels were lower and good signs of eventual (if not already existing) forest protection were in evidence. There is no easy solution to the complex problem of managing forest resources with diverse histories and ecological structures. What is encouraging is the creativity that has been illustrated in many of the specific cases in this volume.

REFERENCES

Agrawal, A. and Ribot, J.C. (1999). 'Accountability in Decentralization: A Framework with South Asian and African Cases'. *Journal of Developing Areas*, 33(4), 473–502.

Arnold, J.E.M. and Campbell, J.G. (1986). 'Collective Management of Hill Forests in Nepal'. In *Proceedings of the Conference on Common Property Resource Management* (pp. 425–454). National Research Council, Washington, DC: National Academy Press.

Bardhan, P.K. and Mookherjee, D. (2000). 'Capture and Governance at Local and National Levels'. *American Economic Review*, 90(2), 135–139.

Burger, J., Ostrom, E., Norgaard, R., Policansky, D. and Goldstein B. (2001). *Protecting the Commons: A Framework for Resource Management in the Americas.* Washington, DC: Island Press.

Gibson, C., Williams, John T. and Ostrom, E. (2005). 'Local Enforcement and Better Forests'. *World Development*, 33(2), 273–284.

Korten, D.C. (1980). 'Community Organization and Rural Development: A Learning Process Approach'. *Public Administration Review*, 40(5) (September/October), 480–511.

Mukand, S. and Rodrik, D. (2002). *In Search of the Holy Grail: Policy Convergence, Experimentation, and Economic Performance.* Cambridge, MA: National Bureau of Economic Research.

Ophuls, W. (1973). 'Leviathan or Oblivion'. In H.E. Daly (ed.), *Toward a Steady State Economy* (pp. 215–230). San Francisco, CA: Freeman.

Ostrom, E. and Nagendra H. (2006). 'Insights on Linking Forests, Trees, and People from the Air, on the Ground, and in the Laboratory'. *PNAS*, 103(51), 19224–19231.

Poteete, A. and Ostrom, E. (2004). 'Heterogeneity, Group Size and Collective Action: The Role of Institutions in Forest Management'. *Development and Change*, 35(3), 435–461.

Pritchett, L. and Woolcock, M. (2003). 'Solutions when the Solution is the Problem: Arraying the Disarray in Development'. *World Development*, 32(2), 191–212.

Ribot, J.C. (2002). 'Democratic Decentralization of Natural Resources, Institutionalizing Popular Participation'. Proceedings of the World Resources Institute Conference on Decentralization and Environment, held at Bellagio, Italy, February 2002. Washington, DC: World Resources Institute.

Vedeld, T. (1993). 'The State and the Commons in the Sahel'. In Henrik Secher Marcussen (ed.), *Institutional Issues in Natural Resources Management* (pp. 121–156). Roskilde, Denmark: International Development Studies.

ABOUT THE EDITORS AND CONTRIBUTORS

THE EDITORS

Ganesh P. Shivakoti is serving as Professor, Agricultural and Natural Resource Economics at the Asian Institute of Technology, and concurrently Non-resident Scholar, Workshop in Political Theory and Policy Analysis, Indiana University. He has published more than 50 articles in international journals and has edited several volumes. His recent publications include two co-edited books, *Improving Irrigation Governance and Management in Nepal* (2002) and *Asian Irrigation in Transition: Responding to Challenges* (2005). Professor Shivakoti's professional interests include farming system economics, common property resources, institutions and policies related to forestry, land and water, and population and environment relationships.
E-mail: ganesh@ait.ac.th

Edward L. Webb is an Associate Professor, Natural Resources Management at the Asian Institute of Technology, Thailand. He has been a recipient of two MacArthur Foundation grants for research and conservation activities in central Vietnam and has published extensively on the ecology and management of tropical and Himalayan forests. His current research interests include the vegetation ecology of tropical and subtropical forests, the impacts of community-based management activities on forested ecosystems, and conservation of forests by rural communities.
E-mail: ewebb@ait.ac.th

THE CONTRIBUTORS

Arun Agrawal teaches at the School of Natural Resources and Environment at the University of Michigan, Ann Arbor. He has published a number of books and articles on indigenous knowledge, community-based conservation, common property, population and resources, and environmental identities. His recent interests

include the decentralization of environmental policy, comparative analysis of common property institutions, and the relationship between poverty alleviation and biodiversity conservation. He is working on a book on 'Environmental Politics and Institutional Choices in the Developing World, 1980–2005'.
E-mail: arunagra@umich.edu

Lam Dorji is the Executive Director of the Royal Society for Protection of Nature, a pioneer national conservation NGO under the patronage of His Majesty Jigme Khesar Namgyel Wangchuk, the fifth King of Bhutan. He obtained his Doctorate degree from the Asian Institute of Technology, where he also served as Visiting Faculty. His research interests include policy and institutional analysis, property rights, user rationalities in the context of people-resource interactions and environmental conservation, and finding the best possible framework for community-based integrated conservation and development programs as a practical tool for implementing the *Middle Path* or sustainable development policy of Bhutan.
E-mail: ldorji@rspnbhutan.org; ldorji@hotmail.com

Ngo Tri Dung is a lecturer at Faculty of Forestry, Hue University of Agriculture and Forestry, Vietnam. He completed his M.Sc in Natural Resource Management from the Asian Institute of Technology, Thailand. At present, he is working on his Doctorate in Natural Resources Management. His research has largely focused on local knowledge for community-based forest management, potential indicators for forest monitoring after allocation and community forestry in central Vietnam.
E-mail: dzungtringo@gmail.com

Ambika P. Gautam is independently specializing in Natural Resource Management and is based in Kathmandu. He holds a Doctorate in Natural Resource Management from the Asian Institute of Technology, Thailand. He has 20 years experience in program development, implementation, graduate teaching, and research related to different dimensions of Natural Resource Management in South and Southeast Asia. His research findings have been published in several international journals and conference proceedings. His current work focuses on forest–people inter-actions and their outcomes, community-based and indigenous forest management systems, and human dimensions of changes in a biophysical environment.

E-mail: gautam.ambika@gmail.com

Rucha Ghate is Director (Projects), SHODH, the Institute for Re-search and Development Nagpur; and Director, Collaborative Research Center of International Forestry Resources and Insti-tutions (IFRI) network. Her Doctoral thesis was on *Forest Policy and Tribal Development*. She completed her Post-Doctorate at the Workshop on Political Theory and Policy Analysis, Indiana University. She is a Fellow of the South Asian Network for Devel-opment and Environmental Economics (SANDEE). Her research interests are rural development and institutional aspects of com-mon property resources.

E-mail: ruchaghate@gmail.com

Mukunda Karmacharya, Co-Director of the Nepal Forest Re-sources and Institutions, has been associated with the IFRI Research Program since 1994 as a Researcher. He has served for more than 25 years in the Department of Agricultural Marketing Services and the Department of Agricultural Development. He has expertise in farming systems, agricultural marketing and socio-economic research as well as resource governance and institutional analysis. He graduated in Economics from Tribhuvan University, Nepal.

E-mail: nepal@ifri.wlink.com.np

Birendra Karna is Doctoral student of Natural Resources Man-agement at the Asian Institute of Technology. He has served as Research Program Co-director at the Nepal Forest Resources and Institutions (NFRI) until 2005. He is interested in human dimen-sions of environmental change, especially the relationship between local communities and their forests, as well as institutional design and collective action for the governance and management of forest resources.

E-mail: birendra_karna@hotmail.com

Nitaya Kijtewachakul is serving at Walai Rukhavej Botanical Research Institute (WRBRI), Mahasarakham University, Thailand. She earned her Doctoral degree from the Asian Institute of Technology. Her research interests include community governance of forest resources.
E-mail: nitkl@yahoo.com

Deepshikha Mehra is Senior Research Associate at SHODH, the Institute for Research and Development, Nagpur, and is working on her Doctorate from Nagpur University. Having been actively involved in a number of research assignments at SHODH for the past five years, her research interests are collective action, protected areas and relocation issues.
E-mail: deepshikha_mehra@hotmail.com

Harini Nagendra is a Branco Weiss Fellow at ETH, Zurich; Asia Research Coordinator at the Center for the Study of Institutions, Population, and Environmental Change at Indiana University; and Adjunct Fellow at the Ashoka Trust for Research in Ecology and the Environment, India. She holds a Doctoral degree in Ecology from the Indian Institute of Science. She has used a combination of satellite images, biodiversity studies and social interviews to study forest change in different biophysical, social and institutional environments across South Asia. Her research work has been recognized by the Indian National Science Academy, the Indian Academy of Sciences and the Global Change System for Analysis, Research and Training (START).
E-mail: nagendra@indiana.edu

Elinor Ostrom is Arthur F. Bentley Professor of Political Science; Co-Director of the Workshop in Political Theory and Policy Analysis, Indiana University; and Founding Director, Center for the Study of Institutional Diversity, Arizona State University. She was elected to the National Academy of Sciences in 2001. She is a member of the American Academy of Arts and Sciences; and is a recipient of the Frank E. Seidman Prize in Political Economy and the Johan Skytte Prize in Political Science. Her books include *Governing the Commons; Rules, Games, and Common-Pool Resources* (with Roy Gardner and James Walker); *Local Commons and Global*

Interdependence (with Robert Keohane); *The Commons in the New Millennium* (with Nives Dolsak) and *Understanding Institutional Diversity*.
E-mail: ostrom@indiana.edu

Yonariza is lecturer at the Department of Agricultural Socio Economic, Andalas University in Padang, Indonesia. He is also a Research Associate at the Center for Irrigation, Land and Water Resources and Development Study of Andalas University. His research interests include property rights issues of natural resources, especially land and forest. Along with colleagues from the Philippines and Thailand, he has conducted research on Southeast Asian land tenure in transition. He holds a Ph.D. in Natural Resources Management from the Asian Institute of Technology. His dissertation research focused on forest governance, decentralization and protected area management in West Sumatra, Indonesia.
E-mail: yonariza@hotmail.com

INDEX